Roger Paynter
July 3, 2020

The Collected Sermons of
David Bartlett

The Collected Sermons of

David Bartlett

David Bartlett

WESTMINSTER
JOHN KNOX PRESS
LOUISVILLE · KENTUCKY

© 2020 Estate of David L. Bartlett
Foreword © Westminster John Knox Press

First edition
Published by Westminster John Knox Press
Louisville, Kentucky

20 21 22 23 24 25 26 27 28 29—10 9 8 7 6 5 4 3 2 1

Book design by Sharon Adams
Cover design by Rebecca Kueber
Cover photo courtesy of Yale Divinity School

Library of Congress Cataloging-in-Publication Data

Names: Bartlett, David Lyon, 1941-2017, author.
Title: The collected sermons of David Bartlett / David L. Bartlett.
Other titles: Sermons. Selections
Description: First edition. | Louisville, Kentucky : Westminster John Knox Press, 2020. | Includes index. | Summary: "This collection of fifty-two sermons shows beloved New Testament scholar David Bartlett at his best. Bartlett, who died in 2017, spent his career teaching and mentoring preachers at The University of Chicago Divinity School, Yale Divinity School, Union Presbyterian Seminary, and Columbia Theological Seminary, as well as serving as a pastor in American Baptist churches. Thus, he has generations of friends and former students who knew him for his quick wit, passion for justice, and deep knowledge of the Bible. Those traits show through in these sermons. As Nora Tisdale says in the foreword: "All of the sermons in this volume give witness to David's passion for preaching that is solidly grounded in the biblical text. Most of them actually begin, as Karl Barth urged preachers to begin, with the biblical text. If they don't begin there, they always get there fairly quickly. And David's interpretations of texts often surprise the reader with their freshness and clarity." In addition to individual sermons, several multiweek sermon series, including a series on Who Is Jesus? and Great Words of the Faith, are included"— Provided by publisher.
Identifiers: LCCN 2019050506 (print) | LCCN 2019050507 (ebook) | ISBN 9780664235017 | ISBN 9781611649741 (ebook)
Subjects: LCSH: Sermons, American.
Classification: LCC BV4253 .B365 2020 (print) | LCC BV4253 (ebook) | DDC 252—dc23
LC record available at https://lccn.loc.gov/2019050506
LC ebook record available at https://lccn.loc.gov/2019050507

Most Westminster John Knox Press books are available at special quantity discounts when purchased in bulk by corporations, organizations, and special-interest groups. For more information, please e-mail SpecialSales@wjkbooks.com..

Contents

Acknowledgments

The Bartlett family wants to first thank David Dobson and the WJK Press staff for their continuing interest in publishing the sermons of David Bartlett following his death. He would be both humbled and very pleased.

We also want to thank the congregations that called David to be their pastor and the students and faculties at the schools where he taught that allowed him to teach and preach the "Good News." These include University Baptist, Minneapolis; Hyde Park Union, Chicago; and Lakeshore Avenue Baptist Church, Oakland; along with American Baptist Seminary of the West and Graduate Theological Union, Berkeley, California; the Divinity School of the University of Chicago; Union Theological Seminary, Richmond, Virginia; Yale Divinity School, New Haven, Connecticut; and Columbia Theological Seminary, Decatur, Georgia.

We also want to thank The Congregational Church of New Canaan, New Canaan, Connecticut, the congregation, pastor, and staff for inviting and making it possible for David to preach and teach over many, many years.

A thank you to Yorkminster Baptist Church in Toronto, Canada, for opening up their pulpit every other year for three Sundays for at least fifteen years.

A thank you to Holden Beach Chapel, Holden Beach, North Carolina, for inviting David to preach every summer and for being our church away from home.

A thank you to Trinity Presbyterian Church, Atlanta, Georgia, for asking David to serve as Theologian in Residence where he loved to preach and teach.

As David said, on the last day of teaching at Columbia Theological Seminary, "Finally, it's all THANKS." Amen.

Foreword

I first came to know David Bartlett when the two of us were called at the same time to teach preaching and worship at Union Theological Seminary in Virginia (now Union Presbyterian Seminary). The year was 1987. I had just completed my PhD course work at Princeton Theological Seminary, and had not even begun writing my doctoral dissertation. David Bartlett was a seasoned Biblical scholar with a PhD in New Testament from Yale University, several published books, and fifteen years of pastoring churches while serving as adjunct seminary faculty under his belt.

What do I remember about David Bartlett from those early years of teaching and working together?

I remember that David was an enjoyable and respectful colleague with a quick wit and a delightfully self-deprecating sense of humor. He took what we were doing seriously, but he never took himself too seriously. When designing classes together, David was always willing to listen to my point of view, to compromise if need be, and to share equally in classroom teaching time. On occasion—often at his suggestion—we took our theological differences into the classroom with us and allowed the students to see how two professors who both claimed the Reformed theological tradition as our heritage (he as an American Baptist and I as a Presbyterian) might interpret it differently. One classic example was that when we taught students about baptismal theology during the worship segment of the course, I would present the classic Calvinist case for infant baptism and David would counter with the Barthian case for believers baptism. We would then engage the students in conversation regarding where they found themselves on the theological spectrum.

I remember that David strongly believed in biblical preaching—not in a fundamentalist way, but in a way that honored contemporary biblical scholarship and was rooted in solid and thorough exegesis of the biblical text. Union Seminary in Virginia had a strong biblical department with the journal *Interpretation* published there. David did a great job of bridging the worlds between biblical studies and preaching. The expectation in preaching classes was that students would bring the solid exegetical skills learned in biblical classes to their work, and, in a very real sense, bring them to fruition through the interpretive work of preaching. The goal was not to take people back to Bible land and have them dwell there; the goal was to interpret present contexts in light of the Bible, and to have the exegetical study of texts undergirding and supporting the sermon like the scaffolding of a solid building.

David not only taught with the keen mind of a seasoned scholar; he also taught with the large heart of a compassionate pastor. By the time he reached Union Seminary, David had served as senior minister in three different congregations: University Baptist Church in Minneapolis (1973–1975), Hyde Park Union Church in Chicago (1976–1979), and Lakeshore Baptist Church in Oakland, California (1981–1987). During each of his pastorates he also taught full or part-time at local seminaries: United Theological Seminary of the Twin Cities, the Divinity School of the University of Chicago, and the Pacific School of Religion in Berkeley. David intentionally chose to live out his own vocational life with one foot solidly planted in the parish and another foot planted in academia. It was an unusual pattern for scholars of his ilk, but it was also a pattern David followed for his entire career. For him pastoring and teaching were two parts of the same vocation: using his scholarship in service of the church and its ministry. His students were the prime beneficiaries of his dual ministry career. From David they not only learned how to hone their skills in biblical exegesis; from him they also learned how to be sensitive to the varied needs and life situations of the congregants who would gather before them on Sunday mornings. They learned not only how to listen to texts with their heads; they also learned how to interpret them with their hearts—and with a heart for God's whole broken world.

What also struck me about David Bartlett during those years of teaching together was his passion for justice and equality. David firmly believed that the gospel of Christ had a prophetic edge to it, and he believed that our teaching, our preaching, and our living should reflect that reality. Frequently, the sermons he preached in our chapel encouraged us all to live more just lives and advocate more just causes as people of God. David also had a passion for racial justice and unity. In Richmond at the time, there were three theological institutions that made up the Richmond Theological Consortium: Union Theological Seminary in Virginia, the Presbyterian School of Christian Education, and the School of Theology of Virginia Union University—a historically African American institution. Early during his tenure at Union, David approached one of the preaching faculty at Virginia Union, and the two offered a course together entitled "Preaching Black and White." It was the first such course to be offered in this city that had once been the capital of the Confederacy and was equally comprised of African American and Anglo American students.

Finally (and on a lighter note), I remember David as a man who did not waste words. He would often respond to my lengthy work-related emails with a very few well-chosen words that expressed his point of view without elaboration. For many years after our time together at Union, I was included in the Bartlett family's Christmas letter list, and that pattern continued. My husband and I used to joke that if David added more than three or four words of greeting at the end of the letter he was being downright loquacious!

In many ways, the traits I experienced in David Bartlett as a colleague and human being are also the traits evidenced in his wonderful sermons in this volume.

The very first sermon in this volume, "Having Nothing, Possessing Everything," preached at a seminary commencement, gives witness to the theological heart of the humility that David expressed and espoused in his life. With the apostle Paul, David truly believed that we pastors and preachers and teachers have been given the gift of God's grace, and that is all we need to sustain us in ministry. Not credentials. Not power or influence. Just grace. That is what we are called to offer others in the name of Christ. And that is all we need.

All of the sermons in this volume give witness to David's passion for preaching that is solidly grounded in the biblical text. Most of them actually begin, as Karl Barth urged preachers to begin, with the biblical text. If they don't begin there, they always get there fairly quickly. And David's interpretations of texts often surprise the reader with their freshness and clarity. For instance, in a sermon he preaches on the parable of the Prodigal Son in Luke 15, David readily acknowledges that he used to preach this parable in the classic way, focusing on the younger son and the father's radical welcome of him. However, it was the comment of a parishioner about his own sympathies with the older brother that caused David to look at the parable anew, and to focus on the fact that there are actually *two returns* (the title of the sermon) in this story: the return of the younger son to the father, and the return of the older son to the recognition that this prodigal is indeed his brother. "Jesus," says Bartlett, "is the one who brings us to our brothers or our sisters when we stand outside the party in some old conviction of our own specialness" (p. 136).

The heart of David as a pastor also shines through in these sermons. When preaching at an Atlanta retirement home ("Whether We Live or Whether We Die"), he addresses the existential reality of death and the comfort that comes in facing it, and he reminds us that Christ is the Lord of the dead and the living. On the Sunday following the shooting at Emmanuel AME Church in Charleston, South Carolina, in which nine African American people of faith lost their lives to a white supremist gunman, David sets aside the sermon he had planned to preach and instead addresses the question of the role of God in the face of such suffering. After acknowledging that he has no answers as to "why," he asserts: "Look out when theologians tell you they can explain exactly why Jesus had to suffer so that we might come closer to God. But listen to the old old story and trust the old old assurance: that awful time of his death was also the gracious time when God got just as near to us as breathing; hurt with our very hurts, wounded with our very pain. The most unacceptable time is the time in which God accepted us most deeply ("The Acceptable Time," p. 129).

In like manner these sermons give witness to David's deep passion for social justice and racial reconciliation. In his sermon "What Child Is This?" he powerfully reminds us of Jesus' special care for children and calls us as Christians to exhibit that same compassion and care. In "The Things That Make for Peace," preached in Berkeley in 1971, he challenges a nation enmeshed in the Vietnam War to learn again to see the enemy as our siblings. In that same sermon he confronts the nationalism so prevalent at the time with these words: "to think that one's loyalty is first of all to country is not good Christian doctrine; it is simple blasphemy. We have only one king and that is Jesus Christ; when we must choose between supporting our government and supporting his kingdom, we have no real choice" (p. 72).

Finally, David's sermons are marked by their economy of well-chosen words. They are eloquent. But they are also lean. There is nothing about them that is fluffy or showy or padded. Rather, they point us time and time again to the God revealed in Jesus Christ, calling us to take on the mantle of discipleship and to live it more faithfully in the world.

My early years teaching with David Bartlett proved to be much too short. In 1990 he left Union Seminary to go to Yale Divinity School, where he had earned both his MDiv and PhD degrees. He taught there for fifteen years as the Lantz Professor of Preaching and also served as Dean of Academic Affairs. He officially "retired" from Yale in 2005, but not for long! Columbia Theological Seminary in Decatur, Georgia, called him to become Distinguished Professor of New Testament, and he served there for another ten years. His pattern of ministering to local congregations while teaching in seminaries continued as he served as theologian in residence at Trinity Presbyterian Church in Atlanta and also preached regularly at The New Canaan Congregational Church in Connecticut. (Included in this volume are sermons and sermon series preached in both venues.)

I would be remiss if I did not mention that David was also a prolific writer and editor of twenty books that brought his scholarly love of biblical studies, preaching, and the church together. Perhaps his greatest labor of love was the twelve-volume Feasting on the Word commentary series that he and Barbara Brown Taylor co-edited. It has become the gold standard for lectionary-based commentaries written for preachers, and nearly every pastor of my acquaintance consults it regularly.

I am happy to report that there was a lovely "coming full circle" in my life as a colleague of David Bartlett's—and it happened just before his untimely death in 2017. Over a quarter century after we taught together at Union Seminary in Virginia, David and his beloved wife, Carol, retired to New Haven, Connecticut. I was then teaching preaching on the faculty of Yale Divinity School, where I had delighted in having their son Jonah as one of my students. David taught occasional courses in Bible after retirement. We shared offices side-by-side on the same hallway, and I loved hearing his booming voice and laugh coming down the hallway. I was present in Marquand Chapel when he preached what no one knew at the time would be his last sermon. It is the last sermon in this volume, and it is vintage David Bartlett for all the reasons I have already noted above.

In his tribute to David Bartlett at the time of his death in 2017, Dean Gregory Sterling of Yale Divinity School wrote these words: "David was far more than a scholar and a minister; he was a model Christian, a first-rate human being." Perhaps more than anything it is those traits that shine forth in this collection of sermons—that they were penned not only by an outstanding scholar and minister, but by a model Christian, and a first-rate human being. I am more grateful than I can say to the Bartlett family for compiling these sermons for us, so that generations to come can be uplifted, challenged, and encouraged in their own journeys of faith by David Bartlett. And to David I say, "Well done, good and faithful servant. Well done."

Leonora Tubbs Tisdale
Clement-Muehl Professor Emeritus of Divinity
Yale Divinity School

1

Having Nothing, Possessing Everything

2 CORINTHIANS 6:1–11

This sermon was preached at Colgate Rochester Crozer Divinity School, in Rochester, New York, at its Commencement Ceremony on May 6, 1978. The University and Divinity School mentioned in this sermon is the University of Chicago and its Divinity School where David was teaching New Testament and serving as minister at the Hyde Park Union Church.

Second Corinthians shows Paul at his Pauline worst—angry, egotistical, defensive, desperately threatened. All the things we learned in classes on pastoral care we were never supposed to be. Here he is caught in that most exasperating bind. Opposition has arisen behind his back in a church he loves. Sly strangers question his credentials, his devotion. The church people, all too gullible, begin to waver. Whom can they believe? Out it comes—all the hurt and anger, all the weakness and the boasting, all the vulnerability of the beleaguered apostle—and all the grace, which time after time shines through his vulnerability.

> We are treated as deceivers, yet we are true. We are treated as unknown, though we are known through and through. We are treated as though we have nothing, yet we possess everything. Having nothing; possessing everything.
>
> (6:8–11, author trans.)

Paul admits it. As far as they go his opponents are right. He has nothing—no credentials, no wisdom, no power, no personal attractiveness. But

1

his opponents are also wrong. He possesses everything, everything that matters—every gift of faith, hope and love, every amazing grace. Having nothing;
possessing everything—that is the punch line in Paul's defense of his ministry.

Here's how he spells that out. Here's how we spell that out for us. Having
nothing; possessing everything. We are poor but we make many rich. Here is
what this might mean for us.

We have no credentials but we possess the word of grace. That is so hard
for us. We would so much rather find some way to commend ourselves. Like
our desperate wish to be thought of as "professionals." If that means we want
to be more careful and more skilled in what we do, that is a fitting wish. But
too often we want to be professionals because we want to claim that our credentials are every bit as good as those of the other professionals—physicians
and lawyers. Enjoy this wish as long as you can. Call yourself a professional.
Talk about the privileges of the profession. Then in ten years check with
your peers who are doctors or lawyers. Compare their salaries to yours. See
who society thinks are the real professionals. Having nothing, yet possessing
everything. We have no credentials worth talking about, but we possess the
one word always worth saying: we possess the word of grace.

There is a moving moment in Frederick Buechner's novel *The Final Beast*.
A woman named Rooney has been involved in a brief, unhappy adulterous
relationship. Her minister, Roy Nicolet, has tried to help her with all the pastoral skills he has—all those theological insights and humane hints he picked
up at seminary. And it just won't do. So he goes for advice to an older woman
in his congregation, and this is what she says:

> "Give Rooney what she really wants, Nicolet."
> "Give her what, for Christ's sake?"
> "She doesn't know God forgives her. That's the only power you have,
> to tell her that. . . . Tell her he forgives her for being lonely and
> bored. For not being full of joy with a houseful of children. Because
> whether she knows it or not, that's what she wants more than any-
> thing else, what all of us want. What on earth do you think you were
> ordained for?"[1]

Having nothing, but possessing everything. Having no credentials, but
entrusted with the word of grace. "She doesn't know God forgives her and
that's the only power you have, to tell her that."

Having nothing but possessing everything. Paul spells it out: "We are
treated as deceivers but are true." We apply that word, too.

We have little intellectual appeal, but we possess the foolishness of grace.
We have little intellectual appeal. How I wish that weren't true. I teach at

---

1. Frederick Buechner, *The Final Beast* (San Francisco: Harper & Row, 1965), 115.

an originally Baptist university. The first presidents of the University were teachers of biblical studies. The Divinity School, where I teach, sits at the center of the main quadrangle and we tell divinity students that we sit at the center of the University. But it isn't necessarily so. The folks do not flock to our doors, or if they do it is because we have an inexpensive coffee shop in the basement. We keep teaching dialogical courses—theology and literature, theology and psychology, theology and the physical sciences. But I notice that the courses are full only of theological students—literati, psychologists and physicists alike almost never come. It feels as though we have nothing, so why do we keep at it?

Why do we keep trying to think through the ways in which we can reason out the implications of our faith? We do it because we possess everything. We do it because we possess the foolishness of grace. We continue to teach and study in seminaries and universities since we believe that we seek God because God first sought us. We continue to speak, even when no one much listens, because we believe that behind the hypotheses and the probabilities that our colleagues tally there is merciful love moving the universe. We continue to write, though no one much reads what we write, because we believe that within the history our colleagues scan, personal love took shape in the man Jesus. We continue with the odd task of the intellectual love of God because we possess everything, or at least because we continue to hope for everything.

Augustine has said it for us: "Thou hast made us for Thyself, O God, and our hearts are restless till they find their rest in Thee."[2]

Having nothing, possessing everything. Paul spells it out. We are treated as unknown, though we are known through and through.

We apply it: We have no political power, but we possess the weakness of grace. Having nothing; having no political power. How we long for political power. When I was a student in seminary, we got hold of a little bit. We had enough political power to close a university for a few days; enough to shake a President of the United States, at least a bit. But not enough power to get tenure for our favorite professor. Some things cannot be shaken.

We loved power. That's where our salvation would be. We'd use our power for good of course, but it was power all the same. Then there was trouble. We didn't keep our power. It lasted for a little while and perhaps we accomplished a little bit. But by the end power turned sour in our mouths because we always had to use power against someone. And that someone so easily became the enemy. And before we knew it, we had learned the power of hate.

Having nothing, but possessing everything. Instead of striving for the cor-rupting satisfactions of power, we live out the weakness of grace.

---

2. Saint Augustine, *Confessions of Saint Augustine* (New York: Penguin, 1961), 1.

It is hard to know what that will look like. There will be no less zeal for justice, I hope, but a deeper realization that all of us are victims. There will be no less concern for action, I hope, but the humble remembering that our best actions are only poor parables of the Kingdom that God is bringing and will bring.

Will Campbell is a white, Baptist, southern preacher. The moment of truth came for him early in the civil rights movement. A northerner who had come to help in the cause of civil rights had been murdered. Will Campbell hated the murderer, Thomas Coleman. Then in a bitter night Campbell discovered that the one thing he possessed was not his political savvy or his moral indignation. What he possessed was the weakness of grace.

"I was laughing at myself," he writes, "at twenty years of a ministry which had become, without my realizing it, a ministry of white liberal sophistication, and an attempted negation of Jesus, a ministry of human engineering, of riding the coattails of Caesar, of playing in his ball park by his rules and with his ball. A theology of law and order. I had neglected to minister to my people, the Thomas Colemans, who are also loved by God. And if loved, forgiven. And if forgiven, reconciled."[3]

The weakness of grace does not get us off the hook of social concern. It increases the scope and the depth of that concern. "Loved, and if loved, forgiven; and if forgiven, reconciled." The shape of that concern is radical indeed. Having nothing and possessing everything.

Having nothing, and possessing everything. Paul spells it out: "We are treated as dying, but look! We live."

We spell it out. We don't even have ourselves, but we possess the vulnerability of grace. Now that is the hardest of all. We can let everything else go—the credentials, the intellectual prestige, the political power. But ourselves? Surely that is what we bring. Surely that is what this seminary education is about. Who am I, theologically, personally? What does it mean to sort ourselves out, to know ourselves, to be ourselves? But here, most painfully of all, we discover that we have nothing. Any minister can tell you; any person can tell you.

It was Good Friday. I was sitting at dinner when the phone rang. It was the university down the road from our church. There had been an accident on a student trip to Jamaica. A young man in our church had drowned. His first trip away from home. An only son. My colleague and I went to tell his parents the news.

3. Will D. Campbell, *Brother to a Dragonfly, Twenty-Fifth Anniversary Edition* (New York: Continuum, 2000), 222.

I searched through my seminary education and my experience and my soul and discovered that I had nothing to bring. I didn't even have myself. All this work we do in seminary, getting hold of ourselves. We have sharing sessions and encounter groups; late night discussions; CPE. At the end of it there are fewer surprises about who we are. We are more together, more open, more honest.

Then the crises come, and we rush in more together, more open, more honest. We try to hand ourselves to the desperate needs of the other and not even ourselves will do. Listen, it's not what we own, it's who owns us. It's not who we are, it's whose we are. Nothing can save but grace, not credentials, not wisdom, not power, and God knows, not ourselves.

A student of mine in his first parish wrote, after one of those days when everything went systematically wrong: "To some God has given the gift of apostleship, to some preaching, to some teaching, to some prophecy. And to some God has given a terrible vulnerability."

That's it, I think. That's as close as we can come. The vulnerability of grace. The vulnerability that knows that we have nothing to bring to the awesome pain and the awesome joy of those we serve. The vulnerability that knows God brings us into that awesome pain and that awesome joy. The vulnerability that knows that therefore we possess everything. We possess grace; we possess a word called the gospel; we possess—we are possessed by—Christ, in whom that grace came.

That is all we have. That is all we need. That is, God knows, more than we have ever deserved or dared to ask. We are treated as deceivers, yet we are true. We are treated as unknown, though we are known through and through. We are treated as dying, but look! We live. We are treated as though we are poor, but we make many rich. We are treated as though we have nothing. But we possess everything.

To God the Father, Son, and Holy Spirit be thanks and praise.
Amen.

2

Going Before

MARK 16:1–8

The surprising ending of Mark's Gospel always fascinated David, and he took advantage of Year B of the Revised Common Lectionary to revisit the text. This is for the congregation of Lakeshore Avenue Baptist Church in Oakland, California, where David was pastor from 1981–1987, and it was preached on Easter 1982.

"And they went out and fled from the tomb; for trembling and astonishment had come upon them; and they said nothing to any one, for they were afraid" (Mark 16:8, RSV).

Period. The end of the story. The end of Mark's gospel. Fear. Astonishment. Silence.

Fear, astonishment, silence—because we are dealing with mystery. Not deep, dark mystery but deep, bright mystery. Mystery so bright that no one can look at it directly, but only from one side, at an angle.

The mystery of resurrection. No one can look at it directly. No New Testament writer tells us exactly how it happened; makes us look at it straight on. Each tells us something about what resurrection means—what it might mean still.

Mark is no exception. He makes two claims that help us celebrate this mystery.

The first claim is this. Christ will be with us. Note the future tense, will be with us. Not was with us. Not used to be with us, but will be with us. The women who came to the tomb on that first Easter wanted to put Jesus in the past tense. They assumed that he was where he belonged, so they came to embalm him. How were they to know the mystery that he belonged, not to their past, but to their future?

And we do it, too. We think that Christ belongs to some magic moment in our past and if only we could relive that moment, we'd have faith in him again. I knew a woman who moved with her husband from Newton Centre, Massachusetts, to Evanston, Illinois, in 1910. In 1960 she said, "I have lived in Evanston for fifty years, but I left my heart in Newton Centre."

Too often we have our hearts camped out in some imaginary Newton Centre, thinking that we need to return to that lost home if we are to know the blessing of our God.

There's the home of an early religious experience. If only I could believe with the simplicity of that time, before all these doubts crept in. Perhaps if I just sing the same old songs, return to the same old church camp, or insist on believing what I really no longer find it possible to believe.

Or there's the lost home of a past relationship, interrupted sadly by change or separation or most sadly, by death. "Then my heart was happy," we think. "Then God was real and near, but not now, not now."

Or there's the lost home of our youth, when life lay all ahead, and death was so far off it was unthinkable.

That's where Jesus is, we suspect, in that blessed past. Now if you'll excuse me, I'll just go to the tomb, anoint the body, and hope somehow to find him again.

Except that there is this odd message: "He is not here. He is risen. He is going before you." Before you . . . ahead of you. Not back there in your early and simple religious experience, but in the deeper faith which knows that faith and doubt are all part of a longing deep enough to hold you for the days and years ahead.

He is going before you. He is not confined to that lost relationship, however precious. He enables you to find new relationships, new possibilities for your life.

He is going before you even into that future that lies on the other side of the valley of the shadow of death—so that whatever else we may know or fail to know about that world to which we go, we know that it will be his world, still.

He is not here. He is risen. He is going before you. This is the Resurrection promise: Christ will be with you.

I have a friend whose wife died this year past from liver cancer. A gentle lady, far too young, to whom that ravishing disease arrived in all her goodness and gentleness. Theirs was one of those marriages where publicly he was the pillar of strength and privately we knew that she was the strong one, the sustainer, and now she is gone, much too soon.

My friend writes a great deal. He publishes his thoughts and his grief and his hopes and thereby he helps the rest of us. For Good Friday he wrote that he had found some words that helped him most of all. "The deepest truth I have discovered is that if one accepts the loss, if one gives up clinging to what is irretrievably gone; then the nothing which is left is not barren but enormously fruitful."[1]

Then my friend says:

> Accepting the loss, giving up clinging, are arts and sciences for which no one can prepare yet which one has no choice but to learn. One gives up clinging to time lost, events past, persons irretrievably beyond grasp . . . then what is left is not barren but enormously fruitful.

Christ is not there, not in that tomb, not in the past of our longing or our imagining. He is going before us, into the future, there we will see him. Christ will be with us.

And then Mark's second affirmation. Not only that Christ will be with us, but looking at the mystery of Resurrection, Mark can also say Christ will still be wounded.

Our translations don't catch Mark's nuance very well. When he records the announcement of the young man at the empty tomb, he writes something like this: "You seek Jesus of Nazareth. The crucified one is also risen. He is going before you."

The crucified one is risen—still bearing his wounds. It could have been different: Jesus as a kind of Superman, a Captain Marvel of his time emerges from the tomb, brushing off the dust. "See, it was nothing. No real pain; no real wounds." Sometimes that's the Jesus we'd like to have, successful Jesus, the Resurrection proving that the crucifixion wasn't that important. "See, I'm just fine. You needn't have worried."

But that is not Mark's story. The one who rises is still wounded. A real suffering and a real death followed by a real resurrection. Otherwise how could he be our Lord? We, who do suffer, do die; do bear our own more modest wounds.

We could cheer Superman or Captain Marvel, munching our popcorn and then go home. But do they comfort us? Not in the least. Does their invulnerability point us toward Easter? It does not.

---

1. Robert N. Bellah, *Beyond Belief: Essays on Religion in a Post-Traditionalist World* (Berkeley, CA: University of California Press, 1991), xx–xxi.

The only "Hallelujahs" we can sing are for the King of Kings and Lord of Lords who lifts his hands in triumph, and look! The wounds are there.

The one who leads us out of the past into the future doesn't lead us into a fake future where everything is lovely, and we only imagined that he was hurt. Jesus Christ leads us into the real future, full of uncertainty, pain, and hope because he himself bears uncertainty, pain, and hope.

He will be with us in a future of richer faith, not because he had no doubts but because he doubted on the cross that God cared for him at all. What doubt can we live with that he does not know? Therefore he will be with us in our growing faith and in our continuing doubt.

He will be with us in a future that includes loss and loneliness. He knew the wounds of desertion and of betrayal; he wept when Lazarus died, when Peter left him. What loneliness can we fear that he has not known? Therefore he will be with us as we move into new relationships, a little nervously, a little fearfully, a little riskily. He will be there.

He will be with us as each of us faces the inevitable moment of our future, the moment of our death. He knew that moment, too, not gladly but reluctantly. "I'm not ready yet" he said, and then he died. So in our dying and in the hope for what lies on the other side of death, he will be there.

He will be with us, but he will be wounded. He goes ahead of us into the future, but he does not con us into thinking that our future will be easy, soft, or free of pain. The future will not be easy, soft, or free of pain, but it will be his future. Crucified and risen, he leads us all the way.

Edward Albee is best known for his play *Who's Afraid of Virginia Woolf*, but he wrote an equally moving play called *A Delicate Balance*. In that play one middle-aged couple, Agnes and Tobias, have their lives interrupted by two of their friends, Edna and Harry. Edna and Harry find themselves one night simply terrified of the future, not for any discernible reason, but terrified all the same. So they come to visit Agnes and Tobias, and finally, to shield themselves from terror, they ask to stay.

Tobias and Agnes have their doubts about this arrangement, as you can imagine, but finally Tobias decides that he can understand Harry's fear of the future. He and Harry are not so different. So he decides that they should provide shelter for Harry, too.

Here is what Tobias says:

> [W]e've known each other all these years, and we love each other, don't we? . . . Doesn't friendship grow to that? To love? . . . We've cast our lot together, boy, we're friends, we've been through lots of thick OR thin together. So, bring your wife, and bring . . . your plague. You bring your terror and you come in here and you live with

us! You bring your plague! You bring your terror and you come in
here . . . and you stay with us! You bring your plague! You stay with
us! By God . . . you stay![2]

So when we face the uncertain future with uncertain hope, the wounded,
risen Lord can say, "Listen, I've known you all these years and loved you, too,
whatever thick or thin you have been through I've been through that too. You
bring your terror and you come along and follow me. You bring your fear.
You stay with me. By God you stay."
     Amen.

2. Edward Albee, *A Delicate Balance* (New York: Samuel French, 1996), 87–88.

3

Enough Faith

HABAKKUK 1:1–4, 2:1–4
LUKE 17:1–10

This sermon was preached at Battell Chapel, Yale University, October 8, 1995. The reference to the judicial case is to the acquittal that week of O. J. Simpson, who had been accused of a double murder. After his college career, Stanley Sanders went to Yale Law School at the same time David went to the Divinity School. He was later an unsuccessful candidate for mayor of Los Angeles. The Lakeshore neighborhood is home to the Lakeshore Avenue Baptist Church, where David served as senior minister for seven years in the early 1980s.

I.

In the church of my youth, in Los Angeles, one of the pillars of faith was a woman named Mrs. Bibby. In addition to having a firm belief in the literal meaning of every word of scripture, Mrs. Bibby had an unshakable belief in the power of prayer. Even in those days, Los Angeles was a crowded city, long on cars and short on parking. Never daunted, Mrs. Bibby was famous for driving directly where she wanted to go and praying for a parking place. Miraculously, time after time a Buick or Packard eased out of a comfortably large space just in front of her. Traffic parted and Mrs. Bibby pulled her DeSoto in.

At first glance it looks as though Jesus' words to the disciples in Luke's gospel were made just for the Mrs. Bibbys of this world. "If you have a mustard seed's worth of faith, you can say to the mulberry tree that blocks your ocean

11

view, 'jump up, and be planted in the sea.' And the tree will obey" (Luke 17:6, au. trans.).

"Say to the Buick, 'move' and it will move, to the Packard 'out of my way.'" And behold a parking place.

However, the context of the apostles' odd request makes it clear that something more is at stake here than a displaced tree or easy parking. Jesus has just warned the disciples about the difficulty of the faithful life. If you cause other folk to go astray, you might better have a millstone tied around your neck and be cast into the sea. If someone sins against you seven times in the same day, and seven times repents, seven times you must forgive.

It's hard to spend your life trying to keep from tripping up other people. It's even harder to forgive and forgive and forgive. It's a tough business to live a life where people are called to care for other people and where the most important business of every day is the business of forgiveness.

No wonder the disciples listen to the difficult demands of the gospel and say: "[Lord], increase our faith!" (v. 5). They've got it halfway right. On our own it's hard for people like us to care for the least among us and to forgive again and again. It's as hard for us to do that as for a mulberry tree to uproot itself from the bank and grow afresh at the bottom of the sea. Left to ourselves, we're not great at caring, and we're not great at reconciling.

"Lord, increase our faith."

II.

Now Jesus' reply seems straightforward enough. "If you had faith the size of a mustard seed, you could say to this tree, 'Be uprooted and planted in the sea,' and it would obey you." But if we look more carefully at the syntax of the original story we see that Jesus is not saying, "You poor disciples, you haven't got what it takes. If only you had a mustard seed's worth of faith you could accomplish miracles."

What Jesus is saying is much more like this: "Since you have already got a mustard seed's worth of faith, you can accomplish miracles. Since you already have a mustard seed's worth of faith, you can take on the difficult tasks of discipleship. You can care for those who need your care, and you can forgive those who do you wrong. You can work reconciliation."

And here's why the Lord can tell the disciples that they have a mustard seed's worth of faith: because they ask for more faith. Here is the good news for today. Asking for faith is the beginning of faith. Wanting to trust is the beginning of trust. Seeking for God is the beginning of finding. Maybe it's not all the faith we want, but for now, for today, it's all we need: A mustard seed.

III.

Dorothy Day is one of my heroes. She early developed a passion for caring for those in need and for working reconciliation among people. For a long time she hoped that Marxist ideology and strenuous work would give her all that she needed to serve the common good.

But it also happened that as she sought a better world, she gave birth to a daughter, Tamara. As Dorothy thought about Tamara's future, she writes:

> I knew that I was going to have my child baptized . . . , cost what it may. I knew that I was not going to have her floundering through many years, as I had done, doubting and hesitating . . . undisciplined. . . . I felt it was the greatest thing I could do for my child. For myself I prayed the gift of faith, I was sure, but not sure.[1]

"For myself I prayed the gift of faith." Asking for faith is the beginning of faith: a mustard seed. Tamara was baptized and then, almost to keep her company, Dorothy was baptized too.

At first the worship, the sacraments, the catechism were only obligations, until through prayer and practice and patience they became not only obligation but joy.

Then through reading and study and friendships Dorothy found a light to inspire her love of community and her dream of reconciliation. With others she founded the Catholic Worker movement where for decades now faithful people have done what Jesus told the apostles to do: care for those who struggle; reconcile those who need reconciliation.

Asking for faith is the beginning of faith. "Lord, increase our faith," said the apostles.

"Start with what you have," he said, "For now, a mustard seed will do."

IV.

The apostles beg Jesus for faith. The prophet Habakkuk begs God for justice.

> O Lord, how long shall I cry for help and you will not listen? Or cry to you 'Violence!' and you will not save? Why do you make me see wrongdoing and look at trouble? . . . The law becomes slack, and justice never prevails.
>
> (Hab. 1:2–4)

---

1. Dorothy Day, *From Union Square to Rome* (Maryknoll, NY: Orbis Books, 2006), 131.

Hard times in Judah. Pressure from without. Terrible divisions among the people. Cries for justice that apparently go unheard.

What these last few days have made us think about is not so much the complications of the judicial system or the ambiguities of one particular case. What we have had to think about is how divided our nation still can be. How differently people of good will experience what it is to be an American.

Recalling Mrs. Bibby driving around the streets of Los Angeles, I recalled Stan Sanders, too. Stan and I were both active in student government in L.A. in the fifties, he at one high school and I at another. But there were conferences for student politicians, and we got to know each other fairly well, visited each other's homes, went to church together once or twice. I would have said that life was treating us both fairly well.

Then we went our separate ways to college. In the terrible wake of deprivation and injustice, riots broke out in Watts—anger, destruction, distress. I picked up *Life* magazine to see the pictures, and the opening article was an interview with Stan Sanders. I had never dreamed what it felt like for him, growing up in the city we shared. Powers that seemed to me benign and even benevolent had proved to him oppressive. Issues I missed hit him every day. I thought we were fairly good friends, and I didn't even know that the neighborhood he lived in was called Watts.

Like any number of other Los Angeles young people, I oozed good will and missed the point. There are divides that are very hard to bridge and histories that separate more than they unite. Justice is slack, not just this week but week after week after week. Habakkuk had it right: "O Lord, how long shall I cry for help and you will not listen?"

V.

But then the Lord does listen, does respond.

> There is still a vision for the appointed time. . . . If it seems to tarry, wait for it; it will surely come, it will not delay. Look at the proud! Their spirit is not right in them, but the righteous live by their faith.
> (2:3–4)

"Look at the proud. Their spirit is not right in them." We had been proud enough: Proud of our comfort, our accomplishments, our security. Proud of our tolerance. Sure that with just a little good will we can undo centuries of injustice. Just invite Stan Sanders to a party, and by God, we will have overcome.

But the righteous live by faith: By the hope that God works every day to break down barriers, to broaden perspectives, to punish oppression, and to work righteousness.

What God's vision demands of us is the most difficult combination of patience and action. To stand strong like Habakkuk, at our watch post, but to stand in hope and faith, because, God help us, we need God's help.

Jesus tells the disciples: "Asking for faith is the beginning of faith."

God tells Habakkuk: "Hoping for justice is the beginning of justice."

Keep hoping. Keep working. The righteous will live by faith.

VI.

Another California city: Oakland. A few years before Stan Sanders and I were growing up in Los Angeles, just after the Second World War, African Americans who had grown up in Oakland and served in the war were returning. African Americans who had been stationed in the Bay Area were choosing to live there after the war. Because of the GI Bill many had been able to afford college educations, and the economy was doing well and a number of African American families began to buy houses in the Lakeshore area, which until then had been almost exclusively a white neighborhood.

For Sale signs started going up. So the pastor of the neighborhood church and the principal of the neighborhood elementary school went calling on the neighbors every night. They welcomed the new neighbors. They urged the long-time neighbors to stay. It wasn't a perfect solution, but forty years later the neighborhood is among the most integrated neighborhoods in the most integrated city in the United States and the church's membership is about 45 percent African American and 45 percent Euro-American and 10 percent Asian American or Hispanic American.

Because a couple of people hoped and worked. Righteous people, who lived by faith.

VII.

One of the ancient rabbis told this story about the crossing of the Red Sea. God had promised Moses that God would part the sea so that the Israelites could escape from Pharaoh. But when the children of Israel got to the shore, the Egyptian chariots chasing close behind them, there was the sea, deep, unmoving, and very wet.

Until by faith, the first Israelite took the first step into the sea—then the waters parted and Israel's people walked toward freedom.

One step, like a mustard seed. Like a prayer for faith. Like a hope for justice.

Keep working.

Keep hoping.

The righteous live by faith.

Amen.

4

A Sermon for Good Friday

JOHN 19

This sermon was preached on April 10, 1997, at Battell Chapel on the campus of Yale University. At that time the chapel was affiliated with the United Church of Christ. That is no longer true.

I.

Notice that in John's Gospel Good Friday is not a tragedy, it's a triumph. In Mark's and Matthew's Gospels Jesus cries the awful cry of abandonment: "My God, my God, why have you forsaken me?" In John's Gospel Jesus cries the cry of victory: "It is finished," which means: "I did it."

Even the small details play the note of victory. In the other Gospels the tired Jesus has Simon of Cyrene carry the cross up the hill. In John's Gospel the determined Jesus carries it all by himself. In going to Calvary he does not waver in Gethsemane but does just exactly what he wants to do exactly when he intends to do it. "It is finished."

J. Louis Martyn, who lives just down the road, has written a good deal about John's Gospel and helps us to understand why this journey from Bethlehem to Calvary is presented without the slightest hint of Jesus doubting or hesitating. When John's Gospel was written there was a struggle going on in the synagogues of John's community. For years Jews who believed that Jesus was God's son and Jews who doubted it had worshiped side by side. They worshiped the same God, after all, and there were all those years of shared stories and shared aunts and uncles. Then there was some kind of crisis, and the leaders of the synagogue decided that followers of Jesus were not good Jews after all, so they excommunicated Christians who were openly Christian—kicked them out of the synagogue.

This helps explain why some of the language about Jewish people in John's Gospel is so intemperate. It was a family feud between one group of Jews and another, and you know how it goes with family feuds—the rhetoric escalates and charity goes by the boards.

The synagogue crisis also helps explain why John tells the story of the crucifixion the way he does. Jesus is a sign of all the good that God promises to those who have the courage to confess Jesus and follow him. Jesus is also a sign of what courage looks like. You may have to give up everything you've cherished to be a Christian (just as Jesus had to lay down his very life). But the wonder is this: when you are willing to give up everything you will also gain everything—purpose, hope, comfort, and confidence—life that is really life.

Look at Jesus. He lost it all; he found it all. The cross, which looked like defeat, was really victory. "It is finished," he cries. "I won."

II.

Losing everything in order to find everything; dying to your old life, in order to find a new and better life. Jesus is the great example in John's Gospel, but when John brings us to the foot of the cross, we recall other examples, too.

There's Nicodemus. Nicodemus: a ruler of the synagogue; top of the heap; king of the hill. Nicodemus, the CEO of the most important firm in town; or Sterling Professor of Judaic; or partner in the biggest firm. Pastor of old First Church, Phi Beta Kappa and president of Rotary, all rolled into one. So Nicodemus, sneaking out to see Jesus at night because Jesus is the outsider, leader of the other party—sneaking out to see Jesus at night because there is some promise that Jesus offers, some prize that Nicodemus can hang up on his wall along with the diplomas and the honorary gavels and the pictures with the governor.

"What little thing can I add to my life in order to be part of your Kingdom?" he asks Jesus.

"You must be born again," Jesus says (John 3:7 CSB). Which is just a polite way of saying, "You've got to die." Give up all the powers and perks and start all over again, psychologically as naked as a newborn babe. You've got to die to it all. Pull out of the synagogue, which is your family and your power and your prestige and your self-esteem, and cast your lot with this dubious band of believers in this risky venture. Wander out of University Church to Zion Holiness Church or out of Yale to some community college or out of whatever place makes you most comfortable to take that challenge that has absolutely nothing going for it—except the call of God.

To tell the truth, we don't know if Nicodemus ever makes the hard choice. He shows up twice again in the story. Once he shows up in time to say something vaguely commendatory about Jesus. This is a strategy that gives Nicodemus the advantage of not actually having to believe Jesus, or to follow him. And at the end—just after the cry of triumph on the cross—Nicodemus comes forward with a hundred pounds of spices to embalm Jesus. He's come halfway out of the theological closet. The one who had come to Jesus by night now shows up in full daylight. But he still comes to embalm Jesus, in the fear or the hope that if Jesus stays dead, nothing more will be asked.

My God, Jesus had asked a lot of him. It is so hard, dying in order to live.

III.

Losing everything, in order to find everything: there is the Samaritan woman, too. If Nicodemus has to give up his distinction, she has to give up her distinctions. Jesus is walking through Samaria, foreign territory, enemy territory. A Samaritan woman comes to the well, and he asks her for a drink. She says the perfectly natural thing: "How is it that you, a Jewish man, ask for a drink from . . . a Samaritan woman?" (John 4:9 CSB). Perfectly natural to define ourselves against each other: man versus woman; Samaritan versus Jew.

Perfectly natural to take pride in being the insider: Jew, male. But maybe equally natural to take pride in being the outsider. "I know who I'm not. Not a Jew like you. Not an oppressive male, like you."

"Thank God we're not like the powerless," say the powerful—not like the helpless and marginalized. "Thank God we're not like the powerful," say the powerless—not like the arrogant and bigoted. Some of us proud to be victors; some of us proud to be victims.

Jesus marches right past the distinctions. "Give me a drink from the well," he says, "and I'll give you drink from God. Give me what I need, and I'll give you what you need." He doesn't just cross the line between insiders and outsiders, he abolishes it.

The Samaritan woman doesn't give up yet. We love our distinctions because we've nurtured them for so long. All right, skip gender and skip race, I'll tell you what makes us different from one another. "We worship on the mountain. You worship in Jerusalem" (v. 20, au. trans). The rock bottom, inescapable, inevitable distinctions of theology. One of us has got to be right, and one of us has got to be wrong. Proud of our orthodoxy or proud of our heresy; proud of our bishops or suspicious of bishops.

"Neither in Jerusalem nor on the mountain," says Jesus. Neither the creeds nor a rugged individualism. Neither bishops nor just folk. "The hour is coming and now is," he says, "when you will worship the Father in spirit and in truth" (vv. 21–24, au. trans). The Spirit, which knows no distinctions; the truth that does not choose sides. "You've got to die to all those splendid categories," says this odd Jesus, "in order to find your life in God."

Soon after, the woman leaves the story. But before she goes we see her hurrying among the Samaritans, urging them to come down and see this Jew. Forgetting her own distinctions and ignoring her own categories in order to introduce people to this amazing life.

In her own way, dying in order to give life.

IV.

We don't know what had happened to the Samaritan woman by the time Jesus came to the cross. We do know what had happened to his mother and to the disciple called beloved. We do know what had happened to those two people who we may guess loved him most powerfully and mourned him most deeply. There they stood at the foot of the cross, as we are apt to stand in our grief and our love. Totally focused on the loss; totally separate from one another.

"Is there any sorrow like unto my sorrow?" the mother asked herself, the disciple asked himself. Nurturing and cherishing what they had every right to nurture and cherish—their exclusive, overwhelming love for the one who was dying. Their absolute devotion to him.

And then he called them to die, too. To die to their total attention to him, to the singularity of their grief. "Woman," says Jesus; she looks up from her tears. He points to the disciple: "Here is your son." "Son," he says, and the disciple must look up, too. "Here is your mother" (John 19:26–27).

Demanding the hardest death of all, the death of what we have every right to: our individual devotion and our private grief. The awful losses that no one can take away and that no one can understand. The relationship to a beloved companion, or a beloved Savior, that is ours and ours alone. Demanding that we die to that, not give it up, but transform it, transfigure it into love for the person who stands beside us. The one whose grief is not our grief but is grief just the same: the one who needs our love.

"If you really love me," Jesus says to his mother, "love him too."

"If you really love me," Jesus says to his friend, "love her too."

My God, Jesus asks so much of us. It is so hard, dying in order to find life.

V.

"It is finished," cries Jesus. A cry of absolute victory. All is lost. All is found. "It is finished," cries Jesus, and for him, for now, it is.

But not for us.

Trying to discover what pride and power we must give up if we are to be born again into a brand new life. Trying to get beyond the little distinctions that give us our identity and our pride and our appalling divisions. Trying to get beyond the absolutely valid grief and loss that keeps us to ourselves, keeps us from noticing the other one, who grieves beside us.

His arms outstretched in victory and loss embrace the world. Even when he's crucified, especially when he's crucified, he will not let us go.

My God, he asks so much of us.

My God, he gives so much to us.

Amen.

5

Requirement and Reassurance

Ordination Sermon for Jonah Bartlett

MICAH 6:1–8
ROMANS 8:31–39

On November 8, 2009, our son Jonah was ordained at First Baptist Church, New Haven, Connecticut. David was asked to preach the sermon.

I.

Not long before he died, William Sloane Coffin, who served for many years as chaplain of Yale University, told this story about his student days at Yale.

When Coffin was a student at the Divinity School he met an undergraduate who had a strong concern for social justice, was articulate and didn't mind hard work. Coffin listened to the undergraduate's vocational puzzling and decided that the student ought to think seriously about ministry.

So he brought him up the hill to the Divinity School and took him to visit Professor H. Richard Niebuhr. Now Niebuhr contributed a great deal to Christian thought but perhaps his greatest contributions were these. He insisted that if we read history faithfully we could discover God revealed, not easily, but clearly in the life of the entire world. And he insisted that God alone was God, sovereign over all the universe, and that anything else—nation, family, scientific progress—was less than God and therefore not worthy of our worship.

So Coffin brought the young man to chat with Niebuhr, and Niebuhr talked about the church and its ministry and his own theological concerns, and at the end the young man said to Professor Niebuhr:

"Well, sir I want to thank you for sharing with me. Your thoughts on ministry are very interesting but I'm really more interested in the big picture."

Of course Coffin laughed when he told the story because Niebuhr was for many of us the finest painter of the big picture of his century, and Coffin himself by then had given fifty years to ministry, pretty much convinced that his calling had a great deal to do with the very biggest picture of all.

II.

Now we ordain Jonah Bartlett to Christian ministry, to the service of Niebuhr's and Coffin's big picture. To the service of the promise that all of us here, ordained and lay alike, seek to serve: the promise of God's reign and the mercy of Christ's gospel.

Jonah chose the texts for today's service. And they are big picture texts, both of them.

The prophet Micah sets forth the requirements, not just for Israel nor for the church but for all of humankind:

> He has told you, O mortal, what is good.
> And what does the LORD require of you
> but to do justice, and to love kindness,
> and to walk humbly with your God?
> (Mic. 6:8)

The apostle Paul sets forth God's promise for the whole creation:

> Who will separate us from the love of Christ? . . . For I am convinced that neither death, nor life, nor angels, nor rulers, nor things present, nor things to come, nor anything else in all creation, will be able to separate us from the love of God in Christ Jesus our Lord.
> (Rom. 8:35–39)

What a gift from the young preacher to the old one. Just what I needed. A text on the minister as prophet and a text on the minister as pastor. Wrap it up with a few words on how to figure out when to be pastoral and when to be prophetic and then on to the hymn.

I even knew which catchy little phrase I could use to tie the sermon together. It's that ancient definition of what a sermon is supposed to do: "Afflict the comfortable and comfort the afflicted."

All I needed was the correct citation of this bit of homiletical wisdom— so to Google I did go, only to discover that the author of this gem was not a theologian but the early twentieth century journalist and humorist Finley Peter Dunne. And the clever definition about comfort and affliction was not about a sermon at all, but about a newspaper.

And then I realized the difference between the journalist's task and the pastor's task. The journalist always serves the news. The pastor always serves the Good News.

So even though Micah seems to be about requirements and Paul seems to be about reassurance—both Micah and Paul are singing redemption songs. Both of them write to remind us that requirements are reassuring and that reassurance carries its own set of requirements.

III.

Of course Micah reminds us that God has requirements. How can we not know that in Connecticut, which has the wealthiest town per capita in the nation and where our capital city, Hartford, is the second poorest.

There is no escaping the power of the judgment brought a century ago by Walter Rauschenbusch, the great Baptist prophet of the Social Gospel, a kind of Micah for America:

> If we come to have a well-defined wealthy class and a permanently poor class, we shall also have rich churches and poor churches with a gulf fixed between them. . . . No amount of gush about rich and poor meeting together in the church, no amount even of real Christian sacrifice will be sufficient to overcome the silent social forces which will stratify people in the churches according to their wealth.[1]

What does the LORD require of us? Justice: not just niceness and not only charity, but justice.

But with all the judgment in Micah there is good news, too. It is good news that God still trusts us enough to make requirements of us. The whole section of Micah begins with a great trial scene between God and God's people and by the time the trial is over we think, "Well if we were God we'd just pronounce the guilty verdict and afflict these comfortable people for eternity."

Not in Micah. When God has been as exasperated as God has every right to be, the final word is a requirement, which is of course, also a promise. Here's what you can do, God says.

---

1. Walter Rauschenbusch, "The Stake of the Church in the Social Movement," in *American Journal of Sociology* 3, no. 1 (1897): 22, http://www.jstor.org/stable/2761702.

You can do justice. Not perfectly of course because only God is perfectly just, but you can do justice. You are not trapped in the infinite circle of obsessive self-satisfaction.

You can love kindness. Not perfectly of course because only God is perfectly kind, but you can love kindness, you can be kind. You are not doomed to repeating those little fits of nastiness that sometimes warp your life.

And of course because only God is perfectly just and only God is perfectly kind, we can only walk humbly. But we can walk; we are not stuck; we can walk, and when we walk, we walk—here's the good news: We walk with our God. Redemption song.

IV.

Just as Micah reminds us that we live with requirements: Paul reminds us that we are enveloped in reassurance.

> What then are we to say about these things? If God is for us, who is against us? He who did not withhold his own Son, but gave him up for all of us, will he not with him give us everything else?
>
> (Rom. 8:31–32)

God will indeed in Jesus Christ give us everything else.

Including responsibility. Paul is very clear, when we live out of Christ's love we live out an entirely new way of relating to other people, too.

In Christ, says Paul, God's love will not let us go, and in Christ also God's love will not let us get away with it. In the letter to the Romans after Paul has talked for eleven chapters about how much God in Christ loves us, he begins the twelfth chapter saying: "Therefore!" "Do not be conformed to this world but be transformed by the renewing of your minds" (Rom. 12:1–2a).

Therefore love one another. Therefore love your enemies. Therefore rejoice with those who rejoice and weep with those who weep.

If we were not loved we could not be loving; but loved as we are—we can be nothing else.

When Gene Bartlett delivered the Beecher Lectures on preaching at the Divinity School he closed with one of his chapters: "Ending up in Debt."

What he claimed is what all of us who are clergy have discovered, what Jonah is beginning to discover. That even when we minister, we receive ministry. That the invitation to care is itself a most amazing kind of caring.

We are, all of us, in debt to our people. And we are all of us, pastors and people alike, in debt to our God. "What language can we borrow, to thank thee, dearest friend" the poet says to Christ.

And every day of every week, in the pulpit, in church classes, at the bedside, in the committee meeting, we are always borrowing language to thank our dearest friend, and to thank those other friends God has given to share our way.

Redemption songs.

V.

And finally a personal word (said he, as if every word had not been personal already).

One of the joys of knowing Jonah has been to watch his passions.

There was passion for the odd little action figures called Transformers. There was passion for professional wrestling. Then passion for the Oakland A's. Then passion for the Minnesota Vikings. This is not semi-passion; watching Jonah watch his team lose is enough to make strong men weep and strong women head for the other room.

Then the passion for music, first Joe Strummer and then the Pogues; and the passion for literature, John Updike and Raymond Carver.

Each of these passions amused and pleased those who loved you, but none surprised us.

But the latest passions are the deepest ones.

For Elizabeth.

For three very different churches: First Baptist Church of New Haven and Spring Glen Church and the Congregational Church of New Canaan.

And most sneakily, most surprisingly, this passion for the Gospel.

What language can we borrow?

Thanks and thanks and thanks.

Amen.

6

The Good Samaritan

LUKE 10:25–37

The Yorkminster Park Baptist Church is in Toronto, Ontario, Canada. For more than a decade David was invited every other summer to preach six sermons over a three-week period at the church. This sermon was preached on August 8, 2010.

I.

I doubt very much that familiarity breeds contempt, but as a preacher I know that sometimes familiarity breeds boredom. Now that we've heard the morning scripture, I am trying desperately to find some way to catch your attention before you drift off thinking: "Well, we've certainly heard this one before: Again, and again, and again."

The notion of the Good Samaritan has become so ingrained in our society that when Richard Price, one of the cleverest novelists of our time, wanted to write a novel about a man who sometimes got in trouble precisely because he was trying so hard to do good, Price could signal the whole theme of the novel by calling it *Samaritan*.

In the states we have a whole network of campgrounds for RVs and tents called the Good Sam camps, and the logo for the camps shows a smiling cartoon figure with a little halo only slightly askew above his head. Old. Trite. Clichéd.

So I turned with some trepidation to this morning's text, though of course I had chosen to preach on it in the first place. I wanted to see what's really there in the text but maybe not exactly what we always see when we see the text.

Let me start with a teaser to which we shall return: maybe a better title would be, not the Good Samaritan, but the brave Samaritan. We'll return to that toward the end.

But here are the three moves I see in the story; not the only three moves that are there, but three for this morning.

II.

First there's the move from contemplation to action. Notice that when the lawyer comes to Jesus he asks a kind of interesting theoretical question: "Who is my neighbor?"

And in an odd way Jesus doesn't really answer that question. He tells the story of the Samaritan and the man waylaid by thieves and then he says simply to the lawyer: "Go and do likewise" (John 10:37).

"Who is my neighbor?" turns into "Go be a neighbor."

Look, I know as well as you that sometimes the moral issues that we face as Christians are very complex. But sometimes we use intellectual complexity to avoid immediate responsibility.

Luke is very candid about this; he realizes that the lawyer's intellectual question is really a kind of stall, a defense mechanism: "Wishing to justify himself, he said to Jesus, "'And who is my neighbor?'" (v. 29 NASB).

We can translate it slightly differently: "Wishing to get off the hook, he asked, 'Who is my neighbor?'"

Some years ago during the Vietnam War my friend and teacher James Gustafson was lecturing his Divinity School class in Christian ethics on just war theory. On proportionality and cause and consequences and all the issues we sometimes think about.

And after the class one of his students—Gustafson tells this himself—one of his students came up to him and said: "Mr. Gustafson the issues are so visceral and you're so cerebral."

Every church I've served as pastor we've discussed the issue of how you help the people who come to the church asking for immediate financial help; or how you respond to the apparently hungry person who meets you on the street in downtown Oakland or downtown Toronto and says: "I need food."

I think the question of how to help can be pretty complicated; I think the question of whether to help can be pretty simple. Pretty visceral.

Jesus told another story where the punch line was pretty clear:

"I was hungry and you fed me, naked and you clothed me, sick and
in prison and you visited me." "Lord, when did we see you hungry or
naked or thirsty and minister to you?"
    "Here's what I tell you," Jesus said, "Whenever you do this to one
of the least of these, you do it to me."
                                        (Matt. 25:35–40, au. trans.)

When we see somebody wounded at the side of the road it's not a good
time to argue about the relative merits of the Canadian and the U.S. health
system. Help.
    Be a neighbor.

III.

But second, in contrast and almost in contradiction, we also notice in the
story the distinction between the simplicity of apathy and the complexity of
compassion.
    If you were in an English class and asked to diagram the sentences of this
story you'd notice an interesting feature. The action or inaction of the priests
and the Levites can be tossed off in one simple sentence each: "He passed by
on the other side." Wash your hands of responsibility; brush the dust off your
feet; move on.
    But the Samaritan . . . notice how complicated his life becomes. Diagram
the sentences of his activity and the diagram takes half a page. He sees; he pities; he pours wine and oil; he bandages; he puts the man on his own beast; he
takes him to an inn; he cares for him for a while; then he pays the innkeeper
to continue the care; then he arranges for a return visit so that he can pay the
innkeeper anything else that he may owe.
    We have a quick and easy evasion when we encounter the complicated
needs of others: "I don't want to get involved." I don't want to get waylaid,
slowed down, inconvenienced or stretched financially. The other side of the
road is a whole lot simpler.
    I think this has gotten even more obvious in an increasingly litigious soci-
ety. What if I mess up in my helpfulness and the poor victim at the side of the
road rises up, hires a lawyer and sues me? What if I turn out not to be a Good
Samaritan but to be a naive sucker?
    It's tough; it's complicated; it's risky.
    And there's one more way in which compassion is complicated while apa-
thy is easy.
    When Luke repeated Jesus' story of the Good Samaritan he told that story
for people who did not have much power in their society. The Romans were

in charge of the roads and the laws and the economy, and if the roads weren't in very good condition and the laws against highway robbery weren't being enforced, and even if the economy was so rotten that people were being driven to a life of petty crime—well that was the Romans' fault.

The little Christian community could just look on in amazement.

But now in the fairly pious United States and in the fairly secular Canada we who are believers have more power than Luke would ever have imagined.

Part of the complexity of compassion is that we can help the people in distress by trying to change the ways in which our society just distresses them more. Better safety; better health; more compassionate economies. All those are ways of being better neighbors.

No matter how complicated it gets, for faithful people passing by is really not an option.

Stop; help; heal. Who is the one who was neighbor to the man: The one who showed him mercy. Go and do likewise.

IV.

And then there's one more move that we need to notice. The move from stranger to neighbor.

The priest and the Levite weren't strangers in the same way as the Samaritan was. They shared a religious faith, an ethnicity, and a perspective on the world with the man lying in the ditch. If he weren't looking so needy they'd probably treat him with entire courtesy.

But the Samaritan—here's where you've heard the story so many times it's hard to get the punch—but think ardent Palestinians and fervent Israelis; think the most ardent separatist and the most convinced supporter of the union.

Think of the state of Arizona in the US where sadly a great many of my fellow citizens who have been there a few years and speak English have declared psychological war on others who are just arriving and speak Spanish.

There's a little irony in calling the hero of our story the "Good Samaritan." To be sure he is a good man who is also a Samaritan. But in our time, alas, sometimes a "Good Protestant" is worried about the Catholics, and a Good American thinks he or she is good especially because of how deeply others are denied.

In Jesus' day, a Good Samaritan had nothing to do with Jews, and a Good Jew had nothing to do with Samaritans. What we have here is not so much a Good Samaritan as a brave Samaritan. The stranger becomes a neighbor.

And think of it for just a minute from the perspective of the poor man in the ditch. "Help," he's been crying, but when help comes, there's the brave Samaritan; what's a good Jew to do?

Jesus is in the neighborhood business; Jesus is the leader of the world's most inclusive welcoming association; good Christians are not good Christians by being strangers to the rest of the world but by being neighbors, surprisingly, bravely, constantly.

A friend of mine is the pastor of a Baptist church in the state of Wyoming. In Wyoming Christians pride themselves on their individualism and their independence and their conservative attention to traditional values.

It happened that a woman in my friend's church developed kidney trouble and she had to be taken to dialysis once a day. The pastor asked in his church newsletter for people to help with her transportation, and he got a little help. And in other church newsletters, but people were busy.

Then one day the phone in the pastor's study rang. It was the minister of the Metropolitan Community Church—in our country the Metropolitan Community Church was founded to be a welcoming place for gay and lesbian people—and most of the membership would identify themselves as lesbian or gay.

"We heard about the woman in your church who needed transportation," said the other pastor. "We have found volunteers to drive her to the dialysis clinic every day."

The good Jew looked up from his ditch and saw a brave Samaritan. The good Baptist picked up his phone and found a brave stranger, now a stranger no more.

Seeking to justify himself, the lawyer said, well, now Jesus, who is my neighbor?

"Who do you think served as a neighbor to the man?" said Jesus.

"The one who showed mercy."

Go and do likewise.

Amen.

7

Welcome One Another

ROMANS 15:1–8

The Holden Beach Chapel is located in Holden Beach, North Carolina. It is a multidenominational chapel that serves both residents of the island and the surrounding communities and summer visitors. Every Sunday, year-round, a guest pastor or priest preaches and then is rewarded with a one-week stay on the beach. This makes on any Sunday morning a congregation that is diverse not only in terms of Protestant and Catholic, but also denominationally and theologically. This sermon was preached on July 24, 2011.

I.

Here is what Paul writes to the diverse and sometimes divided Christian congregations in Rome:

> May the God of steadfastness and encouragement grant you to live in harmony with one another, in accordance with Christ Jesus, so that together you may with one voice glorify the God and Father of our Lord Jesus Christ. Welcome one another, therefore, as Christ has welcomed you, for the glory of God the Father.
>
> (Rom. 15:5–7)

"Welcome one another." I will show you what such welcome looks like.

Sunday after Sunday at the worship of the Congregational Church of New Canaan, Connecticut—as in many churches—the congregation joins together

32

in a shared prayer of thanksgiving. In the third pew just to the left sits Janet Roberts. Janet just turned a hundred and one, does not see very well or hear very well. Like many of us who do not hear very well she sometimes speaks rather loudly; like many of us who do not see very well she usually reads rather slowly. So however slowly and deliberately the congregation says the words of the unison prayer Janet is always slower and more deliberate still.

Week after week communal prayer ends something like this:

Minister and almost all the people say: "Therefore with grateful hearts we come again into your presence, through Jesus Christ our Lord."

And then everyone sits absolutely still while Janet says alone and aloud: "Therefore with grateful hearts we come again into your presence through Jesus Christ our Lord."

Then everyone says: "Amen."

There's a word for that kindness, that courtesy, that love. The word is "welcome." Week after week that congregation makes Janet welcome.

When Paul writes his letter to the Romans he has heard that they are having a hard time welcoming each other in their churches. They are letting differences of opinion and differences of theology and differences of liturgy and differences of language get in the way of their unity.

They don't let people speak with one voice but at their own pace and in their own language. The Gentile Christians, who are in the majority, are always in danger of speaking and praying and singing loudly enough to drown the Jewish Christians out—they'll just roll right over their fellow Christians.

And the Jewish Christians are always in danger of getting sufficiently annoyed at the Gentile Christians that they'll take their prayer books and go to Simon's home and start their own little congregation—they'll just walk out on their fellow Christians.

II.

"Wait a minute!" says Paul. Remember how you got here. Remember who called you here. Not one of you is a member of God's family or of this church because you earned your membership. Not one of you bought your way into this church, or thought your way into this church, or bullied your way into this church.

All of you are here—all of us are here—because in Christ God has made us welcome. "Welcome one another . . . as Christ has welcomed you."

Some years ago, not long before he died, Fred Rogers, of the famous neighborhood, came to visit Yale University.

Mr. Rogers was to speak in the University chapel and well in advance of his speech faculty and graduate students took their children and headed to the chapel hoping for a good seat.

When they got there they discovered that every pew had long been filled with undergraduates. Undergraduates caught in a university loaded with pressure and rife with competition. Undergraduates, who woke every morning worrying about whether they had done well enough yesterday, or if they would do well enough today.

The chapel was full of undergraduates who for just a few minutes wanted to see the man who not that long ago had stood there in his cardigan sweater and his narrow tie and looked each of them in the eye and said: "I like you just the way you are."

God's welcome to us in Jesus Christ is like that. Not "I like everything about you" and not "There's nothing you could do better" but there's nothing you need to do to make me like you.

There's nothing you need to do to be welcome.

III.

One of the things we love about this chapel, those of you who worship here week after week and those of us who worship once or twice a year . . . one of the things we love about this chapel is the clear fact that all are welcome.

Look at the range of Christian denominations represented in the annual list of preachers. Double that, quadruple that and you will get an idea of the range of denominations represented in the pews.

Nobody asks here whether you are Episcopalian or Holiness Church; no one asks whether you were baptized as a child or as an adult or how much water was used—or even whether you were baptized at all.

Nobody knows whether you're Republican or Democrat or libertarian or annoyed independent. Nobody asks about your financial status or your political orientation or your sexual orientation or whether only men can serve communion.

On our most faithful Sundays we're not all one race or one nation and on every Sunday we're not one opinion.

Could this church be a parable of the churches many of us will return to when the summer is over? Could it be a sign of what God intends to do with Christ's people?

The Gospel of John tells us that when Jesus was crucified and they hung him on the cross they put up a sign that said, maybe mockingly, maybe sincerely, a sign that said: Here is the king.

And when they put up the sign they wrote it in Latin and in Hebrew and in Greek—in all the languages of the world in which they lived.

Not King for the Jews only or the Romans or the Greeks; King for all the world. Welcome.

What would it mean for our churches or our society if we took down all the signs that said: Members only; or whites only; or English-speaking only and put up the sign that said "welcome."

IV.

Listen, that's the great two-step of the Christian faith. Because we are forgiven, we forgive. Because we are treated justly, we seek justice. Because we are loved, we love and because we are welcomed, we welcome one another.

Mr. Rogers again. I said how for those Yale undergraduates he was a kind of picture of what God's welcome looks like. Another time when I watched Mr. Rogers he reminded me what our welcome can look like, too.

In Pittsburgh, his hometown, they held a memorial celebration for Mr. Rogers and they televised the celebration. There were clips from some of his most memorable shows.

The clip I will never forget was of Mr. Rogers talking to Jeff Erlanger, a severely disabled young boy who could get around only in a wheelchair.

For a while, Mr. Rogers asked Jeff about the wheelchair, and then about himself, and then about his disabilities. What was evident in every word was concern, attention, affection, welcome.

Then the two of them sang together: "It's you I like" and the episode ended.[1]

Now years later at the memorial celebration, after we had watched the clip from long ago, Jeff Erlanger wheeled himself onto the stage; he is now a grown man.

The host of the program tries to get a sense of how Mr. Rogers and his crew could plan and edit the moving sequence we had just seen. Surely it had taken cutting and editing and retakes and revising.

"Jeff," says the host, "that sequence played for nine minutes on the air. How long did it take to film it?"

"Nine minutes," Jeff says: "He just said it. He just did it."

Beloved in Christ: welcome one another as Christ has welcomed you to the glory of God the Father. Just say it; just do it. To the glory of God. Amen.

1. *Mr. Rogers' Neighborhood*, season 2, episode 3, February 18, 1981.

8

Love Is from God

I JOHN 4:7–21

SONG OF SOLOMON 8:6–7

This sermon was preached on the occasion of the marriage of Pam Driesell, the senior pastor of Trinity Presbyterian Church, and Joe Loveland. The wedding was performed during the morning worship service by David. At the time David was the Theologian in Residence at the church, in Atlanta, Georgia. The service took place in their sanctuary on May 6, 2012.

I.

As Pam and Joe and I were planning this service, I am happy to say that the Lectionary, the list of assigned texts for each Sunday, came through. The epistle text selected today is from the first Epistle of John and begins with a verse so powerful that we could not have done better.

> Beloved, let us love one another, because love is from God, and every-one who loves is born of God and loves God."
>
> (1 John 4:7)

Of course the elder named John, who wrote this epistle, isn't speaking directly about marriage. But he is speaking directly about love, about God's love for us and our love for one another, and I promise you that before long we'll say something about marriage too.

But we begin first with a word about God's love for us and a word about our love for each other.

II.

"Beloved, let us love one another, because love is from God."

Love is from God. Love is the very heart of what makes God, God. It is not just that God does lots of wonderful things and then adds on love as a kind of bonus.

Ours is not the God who creates, judges, redeems and then oh yes, I almost forgot, the God who loves.

The God we serve is the God who is above all the lover of this world and the lover of our souls. The God we worship is the God who creates out of love, and judges because of love, and redeems through love and one day will bring the whole creation to its glorious fulfillment which will look exactly like—love.

III.

And the God who is love also gives us love.

Gives us love! Love is never something we achieve; it is always something we receive.

In a few minutes we will be witnessing the vows of two very gifted people. They are gifted in lots of ways but most publicly one is a gifted pastor and the other a gifted attorney.

But the gift of love they share overshadows all that preacherly thoughtfulness and all that lawyerly wisdom. That gift transcends all our isolation and turns us into couples, companions, friends, families, and churches.

IV.

We need a quick aside, which isn't really an aside at all. For the elder John who wrote this epistle the main reason we know that God is love is that we know the love of God in Jesus Christ.

When Pam and Joe take their vows they're not just giving us an illustration of love, they are doing love; they are loving.

Christ on the cross, says the epistle, isn't just God showing love—a kind of divine PowerPoint presentation. Christ on the cross is God loving us, doing love. Christ on the cross is God's vow to us, and to the world.

"In this is love, not that we loved God but that God loved us, and sent his Son to be the atoning sacrifice for our sins" (v. 10).

The familiar hymn makes clear how hard it is to get that atoning gift quite clear. The poet prays to Jesus and says:

> What language shall I borrow
> To thank thee, dearest friend,
> For this thy dying sorrow,
> Thy pity without end?[1]

No language we can borrow can tell it all; but the best word is still the simplest word. God's name to us is love.

V.

The elder speaks not just about love from God but about our love for one another. Here's what John says: "Beloved, because God loves us so much, we can love one another" (v. 11, au. trans.)

Even when we want to love each other, what keeps us most from loving is the sense of our own un-loveliness. I'm not going to reach out to you if I suspect you'll turn away from me. Maybe I'm not worth it after all.

Except; except if I am loved so utterly by God I am encouraged—filled with courage—to love you, too. Because here's what love does: John says it perfectly. Love casts out fear.

Because we are entirely loved we no longer fear being lovers or spouses, parents or friends.

And here we all are this morning, we are here because we love Pam and Joe, but we are also here because we are a people loved by God called into one family, Trinity Presbyterian Church. As Trinity Church we are famously lovers of good music, famously lovers of splendid educational opportunities, famously lovers of fervent but dignified worship. But here's the best of all: we are growingly, graciously, giftedly being turned into finding more and richer ways to love each other, too.

"Beloved, because God loves us so much, we can love one another."

---

1. Attr. Bernard of Clairvaux, trans. James Alexander, "O Sacred Head, Now Wounded," *The Presbyterian Hymnal* (Louisville, KY: Westminster/John Knox Press, 1990), 98.

VI.

The word about love is not just a word about love, it is also a word about marriage. If we had only the New Testament letters we might think that Christian love was only about sisterly love and brotherly love and church suppers—and it is that but it is not only that.

In addition to the New Testament letter we've got Old Testament song. The beloved sings to her lover. The love that she sings of comes from God. It encompasses kindness and patience but also passion and romance:

> Set me as a seal upon your heart,
> as a seal upon your arm;
> for love is as strong as death,
> passion as fierce as the grave.
>   (Song 8:6)

That love is from God, too. Dear Pam and Joe, this love that you declare this morning is your gift to each other, and it is God's gift, too. It is as strong as death, says Song of Solomon, and even stronger says St. Paul.

"[F]aith and hope and love abide, and the greatest of these is love" (1 Cor. 13:13).

Cling to it; rejoice in it; protect it; defend it against your constant temptation to keep busy and against our constant refrain: "But we need you."

You need each other, too. These vows you are about to take are as sacred as the vows one swears at ordination and as binding as the vows one takes at court.

So help you God.

The poet Robert Browning imagines a scene where a shepherd is returning home to his lover. When the shepherd moves from the grazing field to home, he crosses over the ruins of an ancient city where years before all the trappings of power had reigned supreme. He walks by the crumbling remains of palaces and courthouses and even temples, too.

He imagines his wife waiting for him. And when he thinks of his marriage, without knowing it or naming it, he thinks of the gift of God. And so the shepherd contrasts what passes away with what abides.

> [The King] looked upon the city, every side,
>   Far and wide,
> All the mountains topped with temples, all the glades'
>   Colonnades,
> All the causeys, bridges, aqueducts,—and then
>   All the men!

When I do come, she will speak not, she will stand,
    Either hand
On my shoulder, give her eyes the first embrace
    Of my face,
Ere we rush, ere we extinguish sight and speech
    Each on each.

In one year they sent a million fighters forth
    South and North,
And they built their gods a brazen pillar high
    As the sky
Yet reserved a thousand chariots in full force—
    Gold, of course.
Oh heart! oh blood that freezes, blood that burns!
    Earth's returns
For whole centuries of folly, noise, and sin!
    Shut them in,
With their triumphs and their glories and the rest!
    Love is best.[2]

Amen.

2. Robert Browning, "Love among the Ruins," https://www.poetryfoundation
.org/poems/43763/love-among-the-ruins.

9

What Child Is This?

ISAIAH 11:1–9
MATTHEW 3:1–12

This sermon was preached during Advent, 2012, at Trinity Presbyterian Church in Atlanta. In response to the sermon the congregation established a "Least of These" task force, a group that seeks
better to understand and serve children in need in the Atlanta area.

I.

For many decades John William Bailey was Professor of New Testament at
Berkeley Baptist Divinity School in Berkeley, California. I never knew John
William, but I knew his widow, Louise, well. The rumor was that when John
William was alive Louise was perfectly happy to put him in his place, but after
he died his place improved considerably in her estimation. By the time I knew
her it was pretty clear that John William had never done anything wrong or
said anything even remotely forgettable.

Louise repeated one of John William's unforgettable thoughts every
Advent. "John William got so tired of the sweet little baby Jesus," Louise
said. "He just wanted to get all this sentimentality over with so that we could
get beyond the baby to the Teacher and Master who was so upright and
demanding."

Louise was John William's second wife, and they never had children; it
was reasonably clear that by the time John William was talking about the
undemanding little baby, his children from his first marriage had been grown
up for a long time.

II.

"Demanding?" Every parent, everybody who's spent time with a little baby in the manger or in the crib can show you demanding.

Demanding food; demanding attention; demanding a clean diaper. Demanding increased attention at the same time as we're wishing we could demand more sleep.

"What child is this, who, laid to rest, On Mary's lap is sleeping?"[1]

He is King of Kings, Lord of Lords, prince of peace, the Word made flesh. And he needs his parents and he needs his friends, and he needs food and he needs someone to change the swaddling clothes, and he is from day one entirely demanding.

If, as the ancient church has said, Jesus Christ is really God and really human then like every real human he was really needy. Demanding.

III.

Writing hundreds of years before Christ, Isaiah looks ahead to a child who will also be a king. "A little child will lead you," he says. He probably doesn't know that we will see that little child in the birth of Jesus, but he does know that when the right child comes he will be entirely demanding.

> A little child shall lead them. . . . With righteousness he will judge the poor and decide with equity for the meek of the earth. . . . Righteousness shall be the belt around his waist and faithfulness the belt around his loins.
>
> (Isa. 11:6b, 4–5)

John the Baptist, unlike Isaiah, does know the baby's name, and John tells us how entirely the demanding baby has turned into a demanding Messiah:

> "I baptize you with water," [says John], ". . . but [Jesus] who is more powerful than I is coming after me. . . . He will baptize you with the Holy Spirit and with fire. His winnowing fork is in his hand, and he will clear his threshing floor and will gather his wheat into the granary; but the chaff he will burn with unquenchable fire."
>
> (Matt. 3:11–12)

And then the demanding Jesus begins to preach and teach and here is what he says:

1. William Dix, "What Child is This," *The Presbyterian Hymnal* (Louisville, KY: Westminster/John Knox Press, 1990), 53.

"Whoever welcomes a child in my name welcomes me . . . If any one of
you put a stumbling block before one of these little ones who believes
in me, it would be better for you if a great millstone were fastened
around your neck and you were drowned in the depth of the sea."
(Mark 9:37, 42, au. trans.)

The demanding child becomes a demanding man who demands that we
pay attention to the children.

IV.

In America how are we doing with this demand, with these children?

I rely on information from the United Nations here, and of course it's not
perfect information, but it is sobering.

When it comes to child poverty, the thirty-five relatively wealthy nations
were surveyed by UNESCO. Ranking from best to worst, our country came
out thirty-fourth, underperformed only by Romania.

When it comes to the adequacy of child health care and the survey by
the World Health Organization, the United States came out twenty-seventh,
between Costa Rica and Slovenia.

If the hunger or poverty or illness is simply the unintended consequence
of our political decisions, then we are intending the wrong thing. If they are
collateral damage in the service of some larger strategy, then the strategy is
rotten at the core.

Isaiah in his time, John the Baptist in his, Jesus in our time, call us to justice. Isaiah talks of the demanding child; John of the demanding Galilean.
And the Galilean, threshing fork in his hand, points to the children.

V.

And there's one thing more that we learn when we keep on reading Matthew's
Gospel, when we move from the demanding baby to the demanding Baptizer
to the demanding Messiah.

When Jesus has come into his own as Messiah, indeed in the very last
speech of his earthly career, Jesus says: "Whatever you do to one of the least
of these you do to me. Whenever you harm one of these children, you harm
me. Whenever you receive one of these little children, you receive me."

The test of our faithfulness to Jesus is our compassion toward the least of
these—our compassion to our children. When we deal with them, we deal
with him.

The child who goes hungry now and will grow hungrier as the food stamp program is reduced: that's Jesus.

The child reduced to poverty, maybe because his parents are lazy but more likely because they've run out of luck. That's Jesus.

The child without insurance in a state that won't take more money for Medicaid: Jesus.

The name of every child killed in Newtown just a year ago—Jesus. The name of every child killed in South Chicago, day after day, Jesus.

Nelson Mandela. Of course he wasn't perfect, but he was probably as clear an example of human courage and reconciling hope as we will see in our lifetimes.

Read about one important change in his life: From a fairly conventional dismissal of AIDS as somebody else's problem he came to a passionate mission to reduce that awful scourge.

What changed his mind? He saw the children. Their suffering opened his eyes to the suffering of all the victims of that terrible disease.

He spoke a word to all those who thought that apartheid was unstoppable, that AIDS was inevitable, that injustice was just the way the world goes.

It's a word to those of us Americans who shake our heads at poverty and suffering and lousy health care for the poor and say that that's just the cost of doing business.

It's a word to those of us Americans who look at all the same suffering and wish it weren't so but throw up our hands because we haven't got much hope.

Here's what Mandela is reported to have said about the quest for justice; "Justice always seems impossible, until it is done."

VI.

"What child is this who laid to rest on Mary's lap is sleeping?"

This, this is Christ the King.

What child is this sitting in the long wait outside the emergency room because we don't provide insurance?

This, this is Christ the King.

What child is this in the coffin—shot in some absurd drive-by on the street or some appalling manifestation of mental disturbance at school or some absurd accident in her own home?

This is Christ the King.

What child is this going hungry in the richest country in the history of the world?

This is Christ the king.

What child is this, who, laid to rest
On Mary's lap is sleeping?
Whom angels greet with anthems sweet
While shepherds watch are keeping?
This, this is Christ the King,
Whom shepherds guard and angels sing.

The angels are still singing, but the shepherds have long since gone.
We are the guardians now.
Amen.

10

Bringing Our Lives to Light

ISAIAH 12:2–6
MATTHEW 2:16–18
LUKE 3:7–18

This sermon was preached at Trinity Presbyterian Church in Atlanta, Georgia on December 16, 2012, two days after the shooting at Sandy Hook Elementary School in Newtown, Connecticut. The shooting claimed twenty-six lives. The young man who was the shooter had killed his mother earlier that day and eventually took his own life.

I.

At eleven last night we turned on the local news and like most of us watched and listened to the horrible story of the slaughter of the innocents—thirty miles from our Connecticut home, fifteen miles from our children's home. Nothing diminished the pain even on the fourth or fifth watching of the day.

And then as the bad news went quiet for just a little while, and in order to get all the important news into the first five minutes, the camera panned to the weather person who—without missing a beat and entirely missing the context—smiled at us and said "A happy Friday to you all."

II.

Our Gospel reading from Luke seems almost as bad. Our passage seems to start with utter distress and pain.

John the Baptist said to the crowds who came out to be baptized by him, "You brood of vipers! Who warned you to flee from the wrath to come? . . . Even now the ax is lying at the root of the trees; every tree therefore that does not bear good fruit is cut down and thrown into the fire.

(John 3:7, 9)

And then when Jesus arrives on the scene, John the Baptist introduces him with much the same note of judgment: "He will baptize you with the Holy Spirit and fire. His winnowing fork is in his hand, to clear the threshing floor and to gather the wheat into his granary; but the chaff he will burn with unquenchable fire" (vv. 16b–17).

Then the camera pans to St. Luke the evangelist, who sounds uncannily like the meteorologist from last night: "So, with many other exhortations, John proclaimed the good news to the people" (v. 18).

"Good news?" Has Luke been paying the least attention to his own drama? How can this be good news?

I know as well as you that there was nothing good in yesterday's news, but in John the Baptist's angry speech—maybe some good news after all.

II.

In part John's speech is good news because it insists that what we do matters to God, and therefore it insists that we matter to God, too. God would not bother to judge if God did not bother to care.

Our failings grieve the heart of God and our trespasses awake God's anger precisely because we are God's people, the sheep of God's pasture.

William Muehl is a lawyer who taught for many years at Yale Divinity School and told an Advent story I'll never forget.

When Muehl and his wife were young, their small children went to the nursery school in the Presbyterian Church near their home.

As is the wont of small children in Presbyterian nursery schools, the boys made Christmas presents for their parents. The younger son's particular present was a small vase, which he had fashioned out of clay, shaping and glazing it with pride.

When his parents came to pick him up on the last day of school before Christmas, he was so excited that he came running across the classroom floor, wrapped present in his hand.

And tripped. And fell. And the pottery fell, too, and broke in tiny shards.

Muehl turned to his son trying to say the appropriate thing but failing altogether. "It doesn't matter," he said.

"Oh, but it does matter," said the mother and gathered the weeping child in her arms.

It does matter when our efforts go awry, when we shatter the gifts we intend for God, when we fall far from God's glory and from our calling. It matters, because we matter. The fact that God cares deeply about our losses and our stumbling means that God cares deeply about us—and that is good news.

III.

There is another way in which John's tough words can be good news. They ask a great deal of us, but they do not demand perfection.

Early in my life as a preacher I got in trouble with my congregation because I kept preaching on Albert Schweitzer and Dietrich Bonhoeffer and Mother Teresa.

"We need to hear about faithful Christians who aren't saints and heroes," they told me, and I've tried to remember that ever since. How about ways of being faithful and obedient that are not so far beyond our reach?

When the fairly affluent ask John the Baptist what they should do to serve God, he doesn't say, "Give it all up." He says, "Share." "Whoever has two coats must share with anyone who has none; and whoever has food must do likewise" (v. 11).

When the tax collectors ask John what to do, he doesn't say: "Stop working for the imperial government." He says, "Stop profiting at others' expense" (v. 13, au. trans.).

When the soldiers ask John what they should do to be faithful, he doesn't even say, "Lay down your arms and become pacifists." He says, "Don't use your power to extort wealth and don't use your authority to get others in trouble" (v. 14, au. trans.).

Now none of that is easy; but none of that is impossible, either.

We have the same problem with making faithful policies that we do in being faithful people. We think that unless we can go all the way toward a solution, we should go nowhere at all.

If we can't end war, why limit it? If we can't have universal health care, why try to do somewhat better?

If improved mental health care and stricter gun laws don't entirely protect all our children all the time, why bother?

Here's the good news. We are called to bother. We are called to work on interim solutions even when a complete solution seems far away. We are called to talk and not to posture, we are called to compromise and not pontificate. We are called to serve a perfect Savior—imperfectly. If we simply sit in our pews and wag our heads till the Kingdom comes, John the Baptist makes it clear that we will pay the price.

But we do not have to act perfectly in order to act at all. Half a loaf is better than none, and small steps are better than sitting around complaining.

There are things we can do; that is good news.

V.

And it is good news that when we obey—when we move toward sharing, when we move toward equity, when we move toward the day when the children in Newtown and the children in Atlanta and the children in South Chicago can walk to school without fear . . .

The good news that Luke makes abundantly clear is that when we join in that good cause and serve that good Kingdom, we do not do so alone.

This Jesus whom John announces, this Jesus whom John baptizes, all through these scenes has not said a mumbling word.

The first public thing Jesus says in all Luke's Gospel he says in the next chapter and he says it in church:

> "The Spirit of the Lord is upon me
> Because he has anointed me
> To bring good news to the poor,
> He has sent me to proclaim release to those who are in chains,
> And to let the oppressed go free."
>
> (Luke 4:18, au. trans.)

For Advent, for this week and next, we are allowed to sing, "Come, thou Long expected Jesus." But here's the good news. He will come, and then we sing a different song: "Lead us Lord, lead us in thy righteousness." "Jesus Still Lead on," "Lead on O King Eternal," and that old Baptist camp hymn that I still love: "Where he leads me I will follow, where he leads me I will follow, where he leads me I will follow—I will follow all the way."

So maybe Luke had it right after all: John the Baptist proclaims good news.

VI.

And one thing more, on Friday, Ed Lindsey, our state legislator, spoke to our Trinity men's breakfast.

He was concerned for so many legitimate causes—a better penal system, better education, and better health.

It was early in the morning and we did not yet know that we needed to talk about gun control and mental health as well.

At the end of his litany of good but not very hopeful causes one of us asked him: "Why can't more of these good causes succeed."

"Well," he said sadly, "we must never underestimate the power of the special interest groups."

Listen, beloved. We are a special interest group.

We are interested in justice.

We are interested in compassion.

We are interested in diminishing the awful violence that is turning this Promised Land into a wilderness.

We are interested in serving the coming Jesus—wonderful, counselor, the mighty savior, the everlasting Father, the Prince of Peace.

And it is time.

11

"Really?"

ISAIAH 65:17–25
LUKE 21:5–28

David preached this sermon on October 17, 2013, at Trinity Presbyterian Church in Atlanta, Georgia.

I.

When we preside at the communion table at Trinity, as in many Christian
churches all over the world, we often conclude the words of institution—the
words over the bread and cup—by quoting the apostle Paul: "For as often as
[we] eat this bread and drink [this] cup, [we] proclaim the Lord's death until
he comes" (1 Cor. 11:26).

At Trinity we don't exactly mumble the last phrase, "until he comes," but
we do move through it rather quickly and get back to the actual distribution
of the communion meal.

At another worship service I attend on a fairly regular basis, however, the
presiding clergy is determined to emphasize precisely what I'm inclined to
rush through.

"As often as we eat this bread and drink this cup, we proclaim the Lord's
death until he comes." Dramatic pause, then: "And he WILL come."

"Really?" I think, somewhat subversively. Fair enough to quote Paul who
expected Jesus to return very soon with trumpet sound, but that was long ago
when you could imagine Jesus returning to a particular place and a particular
audience and taking physical charge of the world. "And he will come," really?

Both our passages for this morning are filled with hope for the end of history. Isaiah pictures a world where there is no more weeping, when everybody will live to be at least a hundred, and instead of the wolf feeding on the lamb the wolf will feed with the lamb. And charming as we find the picture we are almost bound to ask: "Really?"

And for Luke the struggles between nations, the weeping, the dying, the endless injustice will come to a stunning halt when Jesus comes in a cloud with power and glory to establish the very new heaven and new earth which Isaiah has dreamed. And when I'm honest about it, I'm bound to ask: 'Really?"

II.

Rudolf Bultmann was the most influential New Testament scholar and one of the most influential Christian theologians of the twentieth century, and he said that in order to preach the Gospel to twentieth and of course twenty-first century people, we had to demythologize the Bible—we had to take out the bits that simply boggled the imagination, like the wolf and the lamb at a table together and Jesus arriving over Jerusalem on a chariot of clouds.

Bultmann was my teacher's teacher, and while we can argue about the details it still seems to me he has a point. I hope that we can talk about the great hope that lies behind our passage from Isaiah and our passage from Luke without thinking that we have to believe every detail of their predictions literally.

III.

To start with Isaiah, I don't think he takes his own predictions literally. He is a poet, and as a poet he tries to show us what kind of world God intends, what kind of Kingdom God yearns to bring.

A world where we are not withered by age and nature is not simply red in tooth and claw; where there shall no more be an infant that lives only a few days, and where Jerusalem—notice that—Jerusalem of all places—shall be the home of rejoicing.

Can we see that world? Not yet; can we dream that world; perhaps. Does God will that world? Isaiah believes so.

The prophets do not simply describe the world as we would read it in the AJC (*Atlanta Journal Constitution*) or see it on CNN or find it in our neighborhood. They draw a world that stands against our world as a goal, a guide, a lure, an enticement. They draw the world that God intends to assure us that however sad the world seems now God intends and builds toward a better world.

Now I want to move from the obviously poetic to a picture that's a little bit more of a stretch. A kind of Isaiah moment in the life of an American city.

You saw this on TV and if you didn't go find it on YouTube or have your younger and technically savvy friends find it for you.

Miles Scott is a five-year-old San Francisco boy who has leukemia. Just recently he moved into remission and they removed the tube that they'd inserted, and the Make a Wish Foundation discovered that Miles's wish was to be Batman for a day.

Rather, since he is only five years old, Bat Kid for a day. The word got out on the social media and tens of thousands of San Franciscans joined together to make this past Friday "Bat Day" in San Francisco.

There was a bat mobile and a bat costume and a senior batman to help the junior bat kid; San Francisco became Gotham City, the Mayor made a "batly" proclamation, and the *San Francisco Chronicle* issued a special edition as the Gotham City Chronicle . . . and the forces of evil were banished—the Penguin and the Riddler sent packing as thoroughly as Lucifer in that other great superhero story about St. Michael and the hosts of heaven.

Did San Francisco really disappear and become Gotham City? Well, not exactly. Was evil banished along with the Riddler? Well, not entirely. Was even Miles' leukemia conquered forever? We don't know.

But for a few hours another reality pushed up against the mundane reality of the City on the Bay. For a few hours a different vision enriched and revised the vision of life as usual.

A little bit like Isaiah and the children who don't die, and the old people who don't hurt from their old age and the carnivores and the herbivores munching away side by side.

Listen, beloved, sometimes what's real isn't just what we usually see and certainly not just what we usually measure. Sometimes what's real is what we dream toward, and what we work toward and what we pray toward. "For I am working to create a new heaven and a new earth," says the Lord our God.

IV.

And then there's the Gospel of Luke, Jesus coming on the clouds of heaven. And the creed that Pam will lead us in saying in just a few minutes: Jesus sitting on the right hand of God the Father Almighty. An image with an honorable history, but really? Does God really have a right hand? And is Jesus really sitting? And if so, where?

This is where Dr. Bultman got most busy with demythologizing.

Let me try it more tentatively.

Isaiah gives us a picture of a richer reality, not yet fully realized, but on its way—pushing against our reality, luring our reality into God's future.

Luke tells us that the reason we believe in that reality is not that we've added up the good things that happen in any year and they outnumber the bad things. It's not because on any given day we can be sure the world is getting better and better.

It is because God has shown us what God intends for the world, and what God intends for the world looks a lot like Jesus.

His mercy. His justice. His self-sacrifice. His loving suffering. His surprising triumph.

Not that long after Luke wrote his Gospel another Christian author, the writer of Hebrews, noticed that Luke's promise hadn't exactly come to pass, or Isaiah's either: we did not yet have a new heaven and a new earth; we did not yet have everything subject to the justice of God. We still had dubious us; we still had this complicated and often shady world in which we live.

Here's what that first century Christian wrote: "We do not yet see everything as God intends it to be; we do not yet see everything subject to God's good will, but"—says Hebrews—we do see Jesus" (Heb. 2:8–9, au. trans.). And when we see Jesus we see both who God is and what God intends.

We do not yet see a world where justice reigns: but we see Jesus who preached God's justice far and wide.

We do not yet see mercy for all sinners and restitution for those who go astray: but we see Jesus, good shepherd seeking endlessly for every wandering sheep.

We do not yet see the end of pointless human suffering: but we see Jesus suffering with us on the cross.

We do not yet see our way past decrepitude and destruction: but we see Jesus—gentle and triumphant, stronger even than death.

IV.

It is 1939, Marian Anderson, the great contralto, is scheduled to sing in Washington, DC, at Constitution Hall. Constitution Hall is owned by the Daughters of the American Revolution and the Daughters of the American Revolution decide that no African American artist will sing in their hall.

A number of people, including Mrs. Roosevelt, get to work and the concert is rescheduled for the Lincoln Memorial.

Thousands gather, and Marian Anderson sings.

Racism is rampant in America. The economy is absolutely bust. A terrible cloud of tyranny is rising over Europe and war is just around the corner.

Thousands gather and Marian Anderson sings:

> He's got the whole world in his hands,
> He's got the whole world in his hands,
> He's got the whole word in his hands,
> He's got the whole world in hands. . . .
> He's got you and me brother, in his hands. . . .
> He's got you and me sister, in his hands. . . .
> He's got everybody here in his hands. . . .
> He's got the whole world in his hands.[1]

Really!

---

1. "He's Got the Whole World," *Sing with Me* (Grand Rapids: Faith Alive Christian Resources, 2006), 26.

12

Rich toward God

LUKE 12:13–21

This sermon was preached at The Congregational Church of New Canaan, New Canaan, Connecticut, on March 16, 2014.

I.

There is a very old-fashioned word that appears twice in our fairly modern translation of this text. The word is "soul"—s-o-u-l.

In the worlds where I live and read the idea of a soul has had a kind of bad press.

In the world of biblical studies we are told that "soul" is a Greek idea, foreign to the religion of Israel and of Jesus. For Jews the human is all one thing, not bodies or souls but persons. The idea of "soul" crept into Christianity when people decided to supplement the Bible with Plato and it was a big theological mistake.

In the world of popular scientific studies we are told that our minds, souls and hearts are all so closely related to our brains—that we don't have any such thing as a separate soul. We are a bundle of neurological connections that one day will pretty much explain us altogether.

So I was helped a couple of months ago to read a fresh voice on this topic— David Brooks, a columnist for the *New York Times*. Brooks said that however we understand the soul theologically or physiologically, in actual practice we know exactly what a soul is. It is, he said, that aspect of a person that is spoken of at his or her memorial service and the quality that makes that person special and that we remember with gratitude.

When we think about that we realize that it's not so much a matter of theological categories or physiological theories. Whatever the theories tell us, we know that when someone dies it is fit and proper to tell the stories that show us a person we love. It is fit and proper to attend to someone's soul.

II.

So here is the problem with the rich landowner in the parable Jesus told. When he has laid up all his wealth so that nobody can get hold of it or take it from him, he doesn't just say: "In the black at last." Or even "what a good deal for my heirs." He says, "Soul, you have ample goods laid up for many years" (Luke 12:19a). He basically says: "Soul, you are all set."

Unfortunately for the self-satisfied landowner, as usual, God has the last word. "You fool! This very night your soul has been taken away from you" (v. 20, au. trans.).

Now one way to read that is that in that moment God intervenes and snatches away the man's life, destroys the man's soul.

But another way to read it is to say that by this time the poor fellow has no "soul" left. He's frittered away his soul piece in chasing after wealth and security and when he says: "Well, soul, you've got it all at last," the irony is that there's actually no soul left at all.

III.

Here is how Jesus describes the poor man's fate: "So it is with those who store up treasures for themselves but are not rich toward God" (v. 21).

It is so tempting to store up treasures for ourselves and not be rich toward God. It is so tempting to be richly committed to other things and to neglect our primary commitment to our God.

Sometimes it is riches that we're richly committed to. What we used to think were almost unimaginable luxuries we now think of as absolute necessities. Enough is never enough; too much is never enough. Our assets grow and our souls shrink.

Sometimes it's a kind of intellectual athleticism that we richly seek. We want desperately to know that we know more, or to show that we know more, or at least to persuade others that we are at the top of the competence game. One of my colleagues on the faculty of the Divinity School of the University of Chicago once said that he thought it was a good thing there was no Nobel Prize in religion because we were already self-important and competitive enough without it.

Sometimes we can put all our energy into the success of our children. Here I too can wander toward idolatry. But sometimes the lines between us and our children grow so blurry that we think our worth depends on their success—and we can define success in such a way that we threaten to damage their souls and our own. Our children are first of all God's children, and we love them best by trusting that God knew what God was doing when they were created.

The problem with all that is that we are richly obsessed with our success or our children's success and we all too easily say to ourselves: "Well, now my soul has made it," while alas our souls are sneaking out the back door of our attentiveness.

"So it is," says Jesus, "with those who store up treasures for themselves but are not rich toward God."

IV.

Here's something else, beloved, notice why Jesus tells this parable in the first place. He tells this parable because two brothers are fighting over their inheritance, competing for treasure.

That's what happens when we confuse our greed with our souls.

Seeking wealth, we too easily boast of our economic accomplishments or rely on the poverty of others to guarantee our wealth. And our souls diminish and die.

Seeking intellectual admiration, we insufficiently admire the contributions of others or embarrassingly talk too much about ourselves or awkwardly duke it out with our friends and colleagues. We may win the argument but the soul is shrinking.

Loving our children too easily turns into pushing our children. We alienate ourselves from our kids by trying to remake them in our image instead of God's. We have a hard time with the friends whose offspring did make it into the college that turned down our own child. We drive our children till they're tired of being driven. Even if the mission is accomplished the soul is eclipsed.

V.

Time to get rich toward God. Time to find our satisfaction in God and not in our sense of achievement. Time to find our satisfaction in love of neighbor and not in endless recitations of subtle competition.

I'm in Connecticut this weekend to record more of the Yale New Canaan Bible Study with Harry Attridge and to preach here this morning. But Mark Douglas and I are also in town in order to attend the meetings of the New Haven Theological Discussion Group. If that doesn't sound a little pretentious we've failed somehow—the "New Haven Theological Discussion Group."

A few months ago at the meetings of the group we heard a paper presented by Gary Green, a friend of mine for many years, who has recently retired as professor of religious studies at Connecticut College in New London.

Gary is by any standard an accomplished scholar. He has written books that everyone in our field is expected to read.

But somewhat surprisingly in this paper he talked not about his latest intellectual discoveries but about a deeper discovery, what he has learned since his retirement in his work in prison ministry.

Twice a week he gathers with a group of prisoners in one of our Connecticut men's prisons. Sometimes they are there just for talk, sometimes they join in worship.

Gary tells about how much deeper and fuller his own faith has become since he moved from the college classroom to the prison common room.

At the end of his presentation he played for us the recording of a song that he and the prisoners sing at their worship services while someone plays the guitar. The singer says that he was imprisoned behind bars, with no way of escaping, until Jesus forgave him. Now, he sings, "I'll never go back to that prison again."[1]

As he played the song, Gary choked up. We choked up.

We knew what we were hearing; we knew what we were seeing. We were seeing Gary's soul.

He was rich toward God.

To Christ be thanks and praise. Amen.

---

1. Sonya Isaacs and Rebecca Isaacs Bowman, "Prison," on the Boxcars, *All In*, Frontline/Mountain House Music Company, 2012.

13

On Being Christian: Why Jesus?

JOHN 6:60–71
ISAIAH 53:4–6

This is the first sermon in a series entitled "On Being Christian" at Trinity Presbyterian Church. This sermon was preached by David on September 14, 2014, when he was Theologian in Residence at the church.

I.

You will have noticed in the bulletin or in the Trinity Times that Pam and I have decided to try a sermon series for the next four weeks.

We draw our inspiration from the NPR program *On Being*, which asks what it means to be human and are calling our series "On Being Christian," and we're trying to ask what it means to be a Christian human.

In the old days the NPR program, hosted by Krista Tippet, was called *Speaking of Faith*, and it will be obvious that there is no way to speak about being Christian without speaking of faith.

What is more, I've discovered that there is no way for me to speak about "Why Jesus" without speaking of my faith. So it will soon be evident that while on one level I'm trying to ask "Why Jesus for the New Testament and the early Christians?" I'm also trying to say a few words about "Why Jesus for me?"

II.

In many ways my experience of seminary was different from that of most of my fellow students. Many of them came to seminary with a firm belief in the factual reliability of the Bible and a deep devotion to Jesus as the very revelation of God.

They were shaken to discover that the Bible was written over many centuries by many hands, that parts of the Bible contradicted other parts, and that it might be the Word of God but it was also the words of lots of fallible humans.

And they were shaken to discover that Jesus, whoever else he was, was very much a human being, flesh and blood, sometimes sounding very much like the rabbis of his time, often misunderstood and perhaps even sometimes misunderstanding.

My pilgrimage at seminary pretty much went the opposite direction from that of my slightly disillusioned classmates. I had grown up a classic liberal Protestant.

I knew perfectly well that the Bible was the product of human beings and even of human committees. What surprised me was that by the end of my seminary years I could also say that the Bible was the Word of God. We'll talk more about that in three weeks, but I'm just warning you.

And I knew perfectly well that Jesus was a first-century Jew with many of the beliefs and convictions of his fellow first-century Jews. I knew that we couldn't be quite sure what words in the New Testament he had actually said and which were the church remembering in faith. What startled and surprised and has since sustained me was the increasing conviction that Jesus represented and represents God; re-presents God; makes God present among us.

In many ways every sermon I have preached since 1967 has tried to say that, but today I want to speak very briefly of "Why Jesus" by saying a word about life and a word about death.

III.

A word about life.

When I was in seminary, as is still generally the case today, only Presbyterians were required to take New Testament Greek. The only Methodists and Episcopalians and Baptists who took Greek were the more nerdy members of our class.

So there I was sitting in Greek class and we were coming to the end of the semester. The great fun of coming to the end of the first semester was that at last we were able actually to read parts of the New Testament in Greek.

We started with the Gospel of John, which may have the most complicated theology in the New Testament but has the easiest Greek. Our teacher was Hiram Jefferson Lester, a graduate student who as far as we knew might or might not believe much of anything.

When it came time to read and translate the last verses of the sixth chapter of the Gospel of John, somewhat surprisingly Hiram Jefferson Lester read the Greek himself and translated into English.

"Many of [Jesus'] disciples turned back and no longer went about with him. So Jesus asked the twelve, 'Do you also wish to go away?' Simon Peter answered him, 'Lord, to whom can we go? You have the words of eternal life'" (John 6:66–68).

I noticed that Hiram Jefferson Lester's eyes were filling up. "That's why we're here," he said. He closed the New Testament. He closed the class.

IV.

Here is one reason why we're here.

> Not because Jesus was entirely unique. In many ways he echoes the prophets who were before him.
> Not because Jesus did miracles; even the New Testament agrees that lots of other people did miracles, too.
> Not that he was the wisest sage who ever lived. Benjamin Franklin was funnier and more practical.
> Not that he was the smartest philosopher of all time. Plato and Aristotle argued about deep things that never crossed Jesus' mind.

We are here because he has the words of eternal life. Eternal life in John's Gospel doesn't only mean life beyond death, it means real life, whole life, rich life, fulfilling life right here right now.

We are here because we have suspected the truth of Peter's confession, when we have searched everywhere and asked everything: "Where can we go? For you have the words of eternal life."

It is so easy to be Christian in a country that prides itself on its Christian values. It is so easy to think that Jesus is one more good thing like our favorite political party or favorite social club.

Last week a bishop of the Chaldean Orthodox church returned from Syria where his fellow Christians are being persecuted. "When I look at all this evil, I want to be like Rambo. But that won't do any good. . . . Our faith isn't a theory. It's not (just) a set of teachings. It's a person and we're called to be like him."[1]

"So Jesus asked the twelve, 'Do you also wish to go away?' Simon Peter answered, 'Lord, to whom can we go? You have the words of eternal life.'"

V.

That's a word about Jesus and life. Now a word about Jesus and death.

A terrible thing happened to this man who had the words of eternal life. He was arrested, convicted, put to death in a most terrible and shameful way.

Maybe he had predicted it, but if so nobody had paid much attention, so when he died those who had followed him were shocked. How could the one who gave them life be put to death? What was God thinking?

To find an explanation they looked to the Old Testament. They looked for words that would help them understand how Jesus' suffering could be a sign of God's goodness.

What they found was not a doctrine or even a sermon but a poem that uses imagery to talk about God's servant. What they found was Isaiah 53. And when they heard about the love of God's servant for humankind they believed that they had found words that point to Jesus Christ.

> Surely he has born our infirmities
> and carried our diseases;
> yet we accounted him stricken,
> struck down by God, and afflicted.
> But he was wounded for our transgressions,
> crushed for our iniquities;
> upon him was the punishment that made us whole,
> and by his bruises we are healed.
>
> (vv. 4–5)

Because this is a poem and not a proposition we may do better to sing it, as our choir just did, than simply to say it. And because it is a poem and not a proposition we cannot simply say exactly what it means.

---

1. Samuel G. Freedman, "As Iraqi Christians in U.S. Watch ISIS Advance, They See 'Slow-Motion Genocide,'" *New York Times*, September 6, 2014, https://www .nytimes.com/2014/09/06/us/as-iraqi-christians-in-us-watch-isis-advance-they-see-a -slow-motion-genocide.html.

But here is part of what the poem means. Jesus is not just Lord of the good days and the prosperous times. In Jesus Christ God is with us in our hardest times when life is painful and scary. Surely he has borne our griefs.

And here is another part of what the poem says: There is no place we can go where Jesus does not go with us. Not pain, not loss, not even—hear this— not even death, not even the shadow of death.

As many of you know, Steve Hayner, the President of Columbia Seminary, has been diagnosed with pancreatic cancer, and the prognosis is not good. During these few months Steve has posted his reflections on the web from time to time, and all of us are learning from him what it means to trust in the God who in Jesus Christ is with us in our suffering and our death. His reflections are publicly available and some have been published, so I trust I betray no confidence of friendship here.

In one recent posting, Steve asks himself whether he's depressed, and confesses that of course he gets discouraged and then goes on:

> Unfortunately in our culture, there is still a kind of shame connected with depression, as if we should never experience it. And after all, I'm the guy who signs every letter with "joyfully." But joy is dependent on who I am and how I am loved more than on my circumstances. It is happiness that takes the hit when circumstances go bad. Not joy. Our circumstances are just too variable to be the foundation of our daily feelings about life. It's way too easy to equate "blessing" with circumstances instead of with God's loving embrace![2]

Steve knows the letters of St. Paul. St. Paul surely knew Isaiah's hymn and he wrote his own:

> For I am convinced that neither death, nor life, nor angels, nor rulers, nor things present, nor things to come, nor powers, nor height, nor depth, nor anything else in all creation, will be able to separate us from the love of God in Christ Jesus our Lord.
>
> (Rom. 8:38–39, au. trans.)

Surely he has born our griefs.

VI.

Before he was a medical missionary, Albert Schweitzer was a scholar of the New Testament. His most famous book is called *The Quest of the Historical Jesus*.

---

2. Steve Hayner and Sharol Hayner, *Joy in the Journey: Finding Abundance in the Shadow of Death* (Downes Grove, IL: InterVarsity Press, 2015), 80.

He studied three centuries of scholarship written by serious and careful people trying to decide who Jesus is. At the end he discovered that our scholarship cannot capture Jesus and even our richest theology does not contain the richness of his grace.

Schweitzer said in his own way what the Gospel of John said in its way two thousand years before. We know him only when we follow him and discover that he still has the words of eternal life.

Here is how Schweitzer ends his book.

> He comes to us as One unknown, without a name, as of old, by the lakeside, He came to those men who knew Him not. He speaks to us the same word: "Follow thou me!" and sets us to the tasks which He has to fulfill for our time. He commands. And to those who obey Him, whether they be wise or simple, He will reveal himself in the toils, the conflicts, the sufferings which they shall pass through in His fellowship, and, as an ineffable mystery, they shall learn in their own experience Who He is.[3]

That is why Jesus.
Amen.

---

3. Albert Schweitzer, trans. W. Montgomery, *The Quest of the Historical Jesus: A Critical Study of its Progress from Reimarus to Wrede* (London: Adam and Charles Black, 1910), 401.

14

On Being Christian: Why Scripture?

ISAIAH 55
2 TIMOTHY 3

The senior minister at Trinity Church, Pam Driesell, and David did a series that took its title from the National Public Radio Program *On Being*. Their series was "On Being Christian" and they tried to address some of the fundamentals of faith for Christians who would understand themselves as "progressive." This sermon was preached there on September 28, 2014.

I.

During the past few months I have received several questions about why we say what we say after the Scripture is read aloud in Sunday worship.

The reader says, "The Word of the Lord."

And the congregation responds: "Thanks be to God."

That works quite well when the scripture is something we all know and love like the twenty-third Psalm, but it's harder if the scripture is puzzling or disturbing.

"God said to Abraham, take Isaac, your son, your only son whom you love and go to the land of Moriah and offer him there as a burnt offering" (au. trans.).

"The Word of the Lord," says the reader.

"Really?"

The response is especially problematic if it assumes that every word of Scripture is literally true, if "the Word of the Lord" means: "These are the infallible, inerrant, and uncontradictory words dictated by the Lord."

Now it came to pass that just after I had received one such query about the Word of the Lord that we went to worship at the church we attend when we are on vacation. The preacher of the day read the scripture, and when he was through he said:

"This is the Word of God
For the people of God."

And I began to understand something. When we say that we, the congregation, are the people of God, we are not saying that the congregants of Trinity Presbyterian Church are infallible, inerrant, and never contradict each other. What we are saying is that we are the people of God who have chosen to bear imperfect witness to God's perfect majesty.

And if we are the people of God, perhaps scripture is the Word of God because it bears imperfect witness to God's perfect majesty as well.

II.

I want to expand on that in two ways.

I want to talk about the Bible as a collection of stories. Then I want to talk about the Bible as the testimony to Jesus.

The Bible contains many kinds of literature but perhaps most important it is a collection of stories, or as the popular book of my childhood said: "The Greatest Story Ever Told."

What I have always loved about stories is that the best stories help me understand my own story.

The story of Robin Hood helped me think about good guys and bad guys and though I didn't know it at the time it planted the seeds of questions about being rich and being poor and about whether the people in power always use their authority well.

When I was even younger, Margaret Wise Brown's story *The Runaway Bunny* told me about a rabbit who talked about running away from home just to prove how independent he was, while his mother assured him that he could never run so far that he would be beyond her love.

That sounded a good deal like my mother, and some years later when I heard Jesus' story about a son who ran away from home but couldn't ever outrun his father's love, I had already begun to think about the kind of love that never lets go.

We love scripture because it is full of stories that tell us who we are, and especially because it is full of stories that tell us about who we are as people of God.

Did Jonah really get swallowed by a great fish? I don't know. Is it a bad idea to run away from God? You bet.

Did Moses really come down from the mountain with the Ten Commandments on two tablets of stone? I don't know. Does God really ask us to obey God's instructions not to kill, or steal, or commit adultery? The Bible tells me so, and I am forever grateful.

Isaiah says that the Word of the Lord brings forth life in us the way the rain from heaven brings forth life in our gardens. The Word nourishes; the Word nurtures; the Word shapes. The stories help us find our own stories.

III.

And something else: Scripture points us to Jesus.

Karl Barth was the most influential theologian of the twentieth century. He was influential in large measure because he stood firm against the German church's willingness to placate the Nazis, even though he had to leave his job and his town for his resistance.

The main reason he resisted the Nazis was because he thought you couldn't serve Caesar and Christ and you certainly couldn't serve Hitler and Christ, and he thought that because the Bible told him so.

When he was a young man, he heard lots of interesting sermons: Sermons about the state of Switzerland and then the state of Germany; sermons that expounded the great philosophers who try to help us understand the metaphysical foundations of the world. Sermons that praised poetry; sermons that praised nature

What he didn't hear were sermons that focused on the Bible and therefore what he didn't hear were sermons that focused on Jesus.

He wrote a great many volumes saying this in nuanced and helpful ways, but the heart of what he said was something about what it means to say, "the Word of the Lord," and why we might say, "Thanks be to God."

For Barth as for the Gospel of John, the real Word of God, the basic Word of God, is Jesus Christ. When we want to express ourselves we use words, and when God wanted to express God's self, God used words for a couple of millennia and then God expressed God's self in a Word made flesh; in the Word of God's love living and breathing among us—that was . . . that is Jesus.

In the response that Norman so properly chose to the scripture we read, we sing, not to the Bible, but to Christ, "Be thou my wisdom, and thou my true word."

But of course the only way to talk about the true Word was to use words, and the Bible, says Barth, is that collection of words that point us to The Word, to Jesus Christ.

We don't love the Bible because every word is literally true. We don't love the Bible because the Holy Spirit whispered every syllable into the ears of Matthew, Mark, Luke, John, Isaiah, and Amos. We love the Bible because the Bible gives us the words by which people like the prophets point ahead to Jesus Christ, the word of God incarnate. We love the Bible because the Bible gives us the words by which people like Paul and Matthew and Luke point back to the word of God incarnate, point back to Jesus.

Martin Luther told us that the Bible is the manger in which the Christ child is cradled. Some people think that denigrates the Bible. It's only a manger, wood and straw.

I think Luther lifts the Bible high: wood and straw bearing the very glory of God.

We don't worship the Bible any more than we worship the manger. But without the manger we'd never find the baby. And Him we worship indeed.

IV.

And that brings us to our New Testament text. In the Old Testament Isaiah talks about the Word of God nourishing us like the water coming down from heaven to nourish the earth.

In the New Testament, in the second letter to Timothy, the author talks about the word when it gets written down, about scripture. These are verses that my more conservative Baptist friends loved to quote at church camps in my youth:

In the King James Version: "All scripture is given by inspiration of God, and is profitable for doctrine, for reproof, for correction, for instruction in righteousness" (2 Tim. 3:16).

My friends thought that meant that God had pretty much dictated every word of Scripture verbatim, and that to doubt any word or syllable of Holy writ was to endanger one's faith.

There are a couple of ways I think we have to revise that reading. First of all, when 2 Timothy was written scripture meant Hebrew scripture—the Old Testament. Later we thought that the New Testament, including 2 Timothy, was scripture, but this letter didn't know that yet.

More important, later translations catch the heart of the letter's meaning better: Not "all scripture is given by the inspiration of God" but "scripture as a whole has been generated by the breath of God."

That is, in Holy Scripture the Spirit of God breathes over these mere words, as the Spirit brooded over bare creation, and brings the word to life.

God's Spirit breathes over scripture and brings order out of chaos and out of the chaos of our lives, as the Spirit brought beauty to the first creation.

A little bit like the story of Adam and Eve, it is not that God has dictated every syllable of scripture but that God takes this dust, this clay, and makes of it a living Word.

Scripture as a whole is breathed into life by the very breath of God:

> Breathed by God when it was written;
> Breathed by God when it is read;
> Breathed by God when we hear it, week after week.

So here's the deal. Do I believe that every word of scripture is inerrant, whispered by an articulate Holy Spirit into the ears of entirely reliable scribes. No, I don't. Never have. Never will.

Do I believe that Scripture as a whole breathes with the very life of God's Spirit? Do I believe that Scripture is the manger where the new born Messiah waits to be discovered, followed, worshiped? With all my heart.

So when the reader finishes reading even the most complicated biblical passage and says—not just of that passage but of the Bible as a whole—"This is the Word of the Lord."

Here's what I want to say: "Thanks be to God."

Amen.

15

The Things That Make for Peace

LUKE 19:28–44

This sermon was preached at Thousand Oaks Baptist Church in Berkeley, California, on April 4, 1971, Palm Sunday. In 1971 our country was in the midst of the Vietnam War and many were protesting our continued involvement. At around that time, Lieutenant William Calley was charged with the killing of twenty-two unarmed Vietnamese in the village of My Lia. He was court-martialed.

It's Palm Sunday again, and we know what we're supposed to be doing. We're supposed to be waving palm branches, shouting for joy, crying with the disciples: "God bless the King who comes in the name of the Lord. Peace in heaven and glory in the highest!" (au. trans.). That's what we're supposed to be doing, but somehow we're not up to it. We hear the disciple's words: "Peace in heaven and glory in the highest." Some comfort that is, we think. There may be peace in heaven and glory in the highest, but on earth we're a long way from glory, and as for peace—we've forgotten what it looks like.

In Southeast Asia we are embroiled—embroiled is too nice a word, we are ensnared, we are trapped—in a war none of us is quite sure how we got into, a war which all of us are quite sure we want to get out of. A nasty little war which got big without our noticing, which has dragged on forever, and injured and killed those we love and perhaps beyond repair the lives and livelihoods of countless Southeast Asians.

At home we are divided in so many ways: Black against white, poor against rich, young against old. Things have come to the point where two movies

I've seen in recent weeks, one set in affluent white America the other set in Harlem, try to make a queasy joke out of the fact that the next thing you know we may all be shooting at each other. Peace has never seemed farther away.

But the Palm Sunday story goes on, and at last we find ourselves in the picture. Jesus comes to the city. "And when he drew near and saw the city, he wept over it, saying: If only you knew even today the things that make for peace!" (vv. 41–42, au. trans.).

Amen to that. If only we knew.

We sit like poor Jerusalem, wondering whether destruction is just around the corner; wondering whether even now we may discover the things that make for peace.

What does Jesus mean by "knowing the things that make for peace?" Our text makes one thing clear. Jerusalem did not know the things that make for peace because they did not know the time of their visitation. That is to say, they didn't know what made for peace because they didn't know who Jesus was; they didn't understand what he was about. He kept preaching and shouting and staging demonstrations and doing everything else he could think of to make them pay attention, to make them understand. But they didn't, their eyes were closed. Now ahead lay his crucifixion and the destruction of their city; now in a terrible sense it was too late.

Pray God it is not too late for us. If it is not to be too late for us, then we must know the time of our visitation. We must know who this Christ is who comes to us; we must know what he means for our own lives.

So who is this Christ who comes? How does his coming show us what makes for peace? Luke's Gospel gives three important answers.

First, the Christ who comes is the king who puts all other kings in second place. We have been taught, in ways subtle and unsubtle, from the time we were old enough to understand, that our primary, ultimate allegiance is to our country. Now there is much that is good about country; I continue to believe that very strongly. And there is much to be said for loyalty to one's country.

But to think that one's loyalty is first of all to one's country is not good Christian doctrine; it is simple blasphemy. We have only one king and that is Jesus Christ; when we must choose between supporting our government and supporting his kingdom, we have no real choice.

Our Lord, after all, would never get any medals for good citizenship; he spent much of his time and energy disputing the laws of his own people and finally he was crucified because he disturbed the law and order of the Empire. Here is a terrible but inescapable fact. The Christian's first allegiance is not to his country or its laws: his first allegiance is to his Lord, who was a rebel and a lawbreaker.

A great, moving example for our time of a man who had to oppose his nation in order to serve his Lord was Dietrich Bonhoeffer. In a situation which to be sure was far worse than what we face in this country today, he joined in an attempt to overthrow the government, was arrested, imprisoned, and executed. As he awaited his execution, he wrote a poem, which included these lines:

> Who am I? They often tell me
> I would step from my cell's confinement
> calmly, cheerfully, firmly,
> like a squire from his country-house. . . .
>
> Am I then really that which other men tell of?
> Or am I only what I know of myself,
> restless and longing and sick, like a bird in a cage,
> struggling for breath, as though hands were compressing
> my throat. . . .
>
> Who am I? This or the other?
> Am I one person today, and tomorrow another?
> Am I both at once? A hypocrite before others,
> and before myself a contemptibly woebegone weakling?
> Or is it something within me still like a beaten army,
> fleeing in disorder from victory already achieved?
>
> Who am I? They mock me, these lonely questions of mine.
> Whoever, I am, thou knowest, O God, I am thine.[1]

That is the first way we can make for peace. To know that Jesus Christ is the One King of our lives; to know that whatever else we may be, we are first of all his.

Not only is Jesus Christ the one king who puts other kings in second place, Jesus Christ comes as our brother, who makes clear that we are all brothers with one another.

Luke's Gospel of course is the only one where Jesus tells the story of the Good Samaritan. The question which starts that story is: "Who is my neighbor?" And the point of Jesus' story is that our neighborhood is much larger than we thought. For the neighborhood includes not just the Jews, our own fellow-countrymen, but the Samaritan, the enemies whom the Jews hated above all others.

1. Dietrich Bonhoeffer, *Letters and Papers from Prison* (New York: Simon and Schuster, 1997), 347, 348.

This insistence that our enemy is also our brother is at the very heart of Jesus' message. The ease with which we forget that our enemy is also our brother, is I think, at the very heart of what has gone wrong in Vietnam.

Take the case of Lieutenant Calley. The distressing thing about the Calley case is not that an innocent man was condemned; the distressing thing is that one guilty man was condemned while so many other guilty men—ourselves included—apparently go free. Listen to what Calley told the court:

"(The Army) didn't give (the enemy) a race, they didn't give it a sex, they didn't give it an age," The enemy, he said, was never described to him as anything but "Communism."[2]

And there is the guilt we all share; our common incredible ability to dehumanize those with whom we disagree; to think of them only as the enemy or as communism. But the enemy is made of flesh and blood; it is composed of young men like our young men, with young wives and children; and communists are children of God, made in his image and in his likeness and to his glory.

And who Lieutenant Calley killed and we encouraged him to kill was not the enemy or communism, it was a mixed group of God's children, young and old and male and female; some of them, like us, perhaps dangerous, some of them, like us, perhaps innocent: But all of them human, altogether human.

Or take the "Body Count." Some of us realized how pathetic this war had become when instead of counting victories, ground won, land reclaimed, the government started giving us the numbers of the dead. What a terrible picture of us they must have had, thinking that we would be placated for the loss of our sons and our friends, for the waste of our money, for the endless stalemate and the frequent retreat, if only they could impress us with the number of dead Viet Cong and North Vietnamese. Somewhere I think we began to rebel against that. We began to remember that a death is a death, and that each man's death is a cause for our sorrow and not for our rejoicing; and when we saw the huge (and incredible) statistics of the enemy dead, we stopped thinking of them as the enemy dead, and realized that the figures tried to boast of how many human beings had died. As we were no longer heartened; we were appalled.

And then finally there was the ludicrous, awful day in 1968 when an unnamed officer stood over the ruins of a village and said to Associated Press reporter Peter Arnett; "It became necessary to destroy the town to save it," and we suddenly realized that not only had we forgotten the humanity of the so-called enemy, we had forgotten the humanity of the people we had

---

2. "Calley Testimony Excerpts," *New York Times*, February 25, 1971, https://www .nytimes.com/1971/02/25/archives/calley-testimony-excerpts.html.

supposedly come to save. We no longer cared about them as people. What we cared about were lofty-sounding principles: Commitment, National Honor. And if a lot of people, even the people we were fighting for, got killed in the process that was the name of the game.

At that point I think most of us had had it. Whatever we were supposed to be accomplishing over there, it wasn't worth the cost in lives, human lives, and in morale, human morale.

There are some posters around the city these days which show a picture of an American Prisoner of War; beside the picture is the question. "What if this POW were your brother?" And then at the bottom of the poster the reminder: "He is."

Indeed he is our brother; and so is the Viet Cong or the North Vietnamese prisoner of war our brother; and so are all the victims of this and every war our brothers and sisters.

Perhaps if we can remember that, if we can resolve that we will not again forget that our enemy is also our brother, if we will resolve to help our children understand that every human being is first a child of God and only much further down the line a North Vietnamese or a South Vietnamese or an American, a communist or a capitalist—maybe then, pray God, our nation will not be so callous with human life again.

So Jesus Christ comes as the King who puts other kings in second place; he comes as the brother who reminds us that we are all brothers; finally he comes as the rebel who breaks down the barriers between man and man. Luke's Gospel is full of stories of Jesus ignoring the barriers of his society, mixing in one ghetto as easily as in the other; eating one day with the establishment and the next with the outcast; refusing to be hemmed in. It is the letter to the Ephesians which captures in briefest terms this mark of Jesus' visitation: "For he is our peace, who has made us [all] one, and has broken down the dividing wall of hostility" (Eph. 2:14 RSV).

What a picture that is and what a judgment and a promise for our society. The dividing walls of hostility are all around us, but Christ comes and calls us to break them down.

A few years ago at Yale Divinity School we faced a demand on the part of the black students for a separate dormitory. At that time I supported the demand, thinking, frankly that this segregation would be a temporary matter, would help the Blacks to find their own identity and pride and then to move back into the larger community with the clear sense of their own worth and equality. As a matter of fact, something of that sort seems to be happening at the school, but I confess now that I think I made the wrong decision. I think now that I would urge my black friends not to separate in that way, not in a community which was avowedly Christian. I think that to promote

integration by means of segregation is about as unpromising as holding a war
to end war.

I rather think that as Christians we should bear witness to the unity we
have in Christ: that the black man needs of course to find his identity as a
black man, but that he also needs to find his identity as a fellow Christian
with the white man. Within the Church, at least, I no longer wish to support
separation, whether it comes from the black side or the white.

But of course our problem here in this church is not that we are confronted
by black separatists. Our problem is that you come on Sunday morning and
look at my white face, and I come on Sunday morning and look at yours. This
morning I am announcing my intention to join this congregation, so what I
say to you I now say to myself as well: I hope that we can find the ways to make
clear that in this church there are no barriers to anyone; that in this church
Christ is indeed our peace. I don't know how we can do that, but I don't think
a general willingness to smile at any Black who happens to come along is sufficient. I have been much impressed by the diversity of this congregation in
so many ways, but while we are as white as we are, we will not yet really be
a representative of the fullness of what it means to be one people in Christ.

And then, too, it will take more than good hearts and integrated congregations to break down the barriers in our society. The barriers are often
economic, social, and political. It will take, I suspect, drastic and sweeping
action if we are to save ourselves before it is too late. It will mean that concerned Christians will need to be active in changing institutions and not just
in changing hearts.

That is what the story in Luke tells us, as clearly as I can get it. That to
know what makes for peace is to know who Jesus is and then to follow him:
to follow him as the One King who puts all other loyalties in second place; to
follow him as the brother who reminds us that all men are brothers; to follow
him as the rebel who breaks down the walls between us.

Of course, the story doesn't end with Palm Sunday. It moves on.

It moves on first to Good Friday, to the terrible reminder that in the short
run goodness does not always triumph and faithfulness does not always succeed. To the cross, which reminds us that if we are to follow him we must do
so, not because it is practical to follow, or easy to follow, not even because we
are sure that if we follow all the problems of our world and society will end.
The cross reminds us that we are to follow only because he calls us to follow,
that if finally we fail, we fail in the best of company.

And then comes Easter Sunday: The reminder that when the forces of war
and division and hate have done their worst they have not done enough. The
reminder that God will be God: that He will establish his Kingdom, not today,
not tomorrow, but in his own good time, in his own good way, He will come.

So it is not up to us to decide the outcome of the struggle between the things that make for peace and the things that make for war. The outcome was decided on a Friday and a Sunday morning long ago. It is up to us to bear witness to the victory that is already won but not quite yet proclaimed. It is up to us to bear witness to the Peace that is already coming, but not quite here. It is up to us to be citizens of that great Kingdom which has come, and is coming and is to come.

I have been deeply moved in recent weeks to read some of the writings of Johann and Christoph Blumhardt, two German pastors of the turn of the century, father and son.

These two believed with all their hearts that the victory of the forces of peace was won and guaranteed on Easter morning. But they also believed with all their hearts that the Christian was called to join in the skirmishes which were going on, the last clean-up details, before the Peace could be declared. The father did battle with the forces of evil by a remarkable pastoral and healing ministry. His son did battle with the forces of evil by running for parliament and working for drastic social reform.

Yet both of them did what they did out of the faith that Christ was Risen, that his Kingdom was coming and would come.

So the son could write: "The Savior is on his way. He is not quietly sitting somewhere in eternity, waiting for a certain moment when He will suddenly plunge in. He is on the way. The coming of the Savior runs through Christian history, through God's working in the world, like a thread."[3]

And the father Blumhardt put in the hymn "Jesus' Victory Remains Forever":

Yes, Jesus wins! This is our faith indeed
And having faith, we join the fight,
And follow, Jesus, where you lead,
Even through darkness deep as night,
Till unto Christ all knees shall bow,
And evil's voice be silenced now.
Yes, Jesus wins!

Amen.

3. Christoph Friedrich Blumhardt, *Action in Waiting* (Walden, NY: Plough Publishing House,1998), 24.

16

Fear Nothing:
Meditation in Four Parts

MARK 16:1–8

While teaching at the American Baptist Seminary of the West, part of the Graduate Theological Union in Berkeley, California, David was interim pastor at Thousand Oaks Baptist Church in Berkeley. This sermon was preached on April 11, 1971, on Easter Sunday.

I.

And when the sabbath was past, Mary Magdalene, and Mary the mother of James, and Salome, brought spices, so that they might embalm him. And very early on the first day of the week they went to the tomb when the sun had risen . . .
  And [the young man] said to them: "Don't be afraid; you seek Jesus of Nazareth who was crucified. He has risen. He is not here."
                                          (Mark 16:1–2, 5–6, au. trans.)

It was a perfectly proper thing to do: to go to the tomb that morning. He had, after all, been a great man—worthy of a little good-hearted remembering, a touch of mourning, a pang of comfortable grief. Perhaps it was a little sentimental to want to anoint the body, to embalm it, to preserve him as long as possible as he always used to be. But there are appropriate times to be sentimental. And Easter morning was certainly such a time.

  So they would come to the tomb and take one last opportunity to give sway to their emotions; they would weep over what had been and would never be again; they would anoint the beloved body, bid him farewell, and be on their way back to business as usual.

Except that they had come to the wrong place. Or if it was the right place, it was the right place only because it was the place where they learned the astonishing news: "He has risen! He is not here!"

The tomb could not hold him; the embalming was beside the point; he refused to be relegated to the past they remembered with pious sorrow; he refused to be kept in the tomb where they had so lovingly, so cautiously laid him. He refused to stay dead.

It is a perfectly proper thing to do, to come to church this morning. Jesus was, after all, a great man, worthy of a little good-hearted remembering on the part of all Christians, or indeed on the part of all men of goodwill. Once a week for some of us, once a year for others of us, it seems only proper to give a nod in his direction. Good old Jesus is worth a little mass remembering.

And if there's a bit of sentimentality in that, well a little sentimentality is good for the soul. So we come, year after year, as we have always come, year after year, to embalm the body, to keep sweet Jesus just as he always was; the Jesus of our childhood that we knew so well, nothing threatening, nothing frightening, nothing alive about him. Safely and pleasantly dead. So we pause to do him homage for an hour, and then we go away.

But we have come to the wrong place. Or we have come to the right place only because this is the place where we hear the word: "He is risen! He is not here."

"He is not here." He is not confined to this church, this ritual, this place. He will not be contained in the pious tombs where we try to lay him. He is not embalmed by our sentiments. He is not the same old Jesus we have known and loved from childhood on. He is not the remembered pictures of the long-ago smiling figure with the cute children cuddling around his robe. He is not a departed hero whose valiant deed we honor. He is not contained in the sentimental memories of our childhood; of Easter lilies, Easter bunnies, Easter eggs, and Easter pageants. He will not be confined by our fond attachment to familiarity. He will not be contained by our piety. He is not here. He is risen.

He is not here; he is risen. He is not contained by the past in which we try to entomb him. He is not dependent on our old guilt; he does not need for us to cherish the memory of the things we did wrong in the bad old days in order that he may be our Lord. He is not dependent on the dogmas we believe, much less on the dogmas our parents believed before us. He is not dependent on our old saving experiences. He will not wait for us to retell for the hundredth time how we met the Lord. He has been in all those places at one time; he has been in our guilt, our dogmas, in our old experiences, but they cannot contain him. He is risen; he is not here.

II.

"But go; tell his disciples and Peter that he is going before you" (v. 7a RSV).

That is the promise to the frightened women. He is going before them. He will not be contained in the past, in their old sentiments or their pious memories. He insists on being a part of their future; he insists on being alive to them in what happens next and not just in what happened before. He is on his way toward the future, and they can only follow. He is going before you.

He is going before us. He will not be contained. He is going before us, outside the walls of the church. He is going before us into all the messed-up, confused, unpleasant, sinful, nasty, glorious world in which we live. He refuses to be confined to the religious life; he insists on being confronted in the fullness of life. He is going before us into all the places where people suffer and are in pain; he is going before us into all the places where people rejoice and are glad. He is going before us to suffer in people's pain and to rejoice in people's gladness. He is on his way; he is calling us to come along.

He is going before us. He will not be contained. He will not be contained by our desperate attachment to the past.

He will not be contained by our old guilt; we may still think it desperately important that we did some terrible thing long ago, but he does not; he no longer has time to help us nourish our old guilt. He has a whole future to be won. He goes before us.

He will not be contained by our old dogmas. We may still think it desperately important to get our creedal statements right, to polish the phrases, to argue with one another until we can all believe the same thing. We may think that that is terribly important, but he does not, he hasn't time for that; there is a whole new future to be won. He goes before us.

He will not be contained by our old religious experiences. He does not ask us what happened to us a year ago, or two years ago, or in our childhood, or on the day we were baptized. He does not demand our past credentials, but our future faithfulness. In that sense every Easter is a new beginning, and faith can only be renewed every morning. He is not back there in those old feelings of guilt, those old dogmas, those past experiences. He is going on before us.

III.

"He is going before you to Galilee; there you will see him" (v. 7b RSV).

Now that, of course, must have been a little disappointing. Galilee, after all, was just the old hometown. They had hoped that Jesus would bring the Kingdom of Heaven. Now that he has risen from the dead, the least that he could do was bring the Kingdom straightway, right there in Jerusalem, at the capital. A brand new king, in a brand new kingdom, and they his faithful, and properly rewarded, subjects. Galilee was nothing special. It was where they had worked and had their families, known all the small drudgeries, confinements, and disasters of common people in a common life. Why couldn't they stay in Jerusalem, why couldn't they enter a future which was altogether different from the past, serve the risen Lord in a brave new world. But no, it was back to Galilee. "He is going before you to Galilee; there you will see him."

"He is going before you to Galilee; there you will see him." He is going before us, outside the walls of the church. But he is not going only to great movements, thrilling historical dramas, holy and terrifying new events, major victories for the Kingdom of God. He is going before us to the drudgery of familiar jobs, familiar relationships, familiar fears; we will see him in small acts of kindness as well as in great movements for justice. He will meet us in the ordinary tensions of our regular lives. In all the familiar people; in all the familiar places; in all the familiar pains; he will be there. "He is going before you to Galilee. There you will see him."

"He is going before you to Galilee; there you will see him." He is going before us *toward* a future which will be new but not altogether new. He is going before us *into* the future which will be new but not altogether new. He is going before us into the future where we are free of our old guilt but where new guilt will surely rise to haunt us. He is going before us to a future where old dogmas are inadequate, but where we will still need to struggle with what it means to be faithful and will need to find words, however inadequate, to express our struggling. He is going before us to a future where the old religious experiences will not do, but where the experience of meeting him will not be some altogether new experience; where faithfulness will still look like faithfulness and fear like fear and hope will still be only halfway hopeful and love be mixed with selfishness. But He is going before us into that future; in all its newness and all its familiarity. He will be there. "He is going before you to Galilee; there you will see him."

IV.

"And they went out and fled from the tomb; for trembling and astonishment had come upon them; and they said nothing to any one, for they were afraid" (v. 8 RSV).

Of course they were afraid. In some ways it would have been easier to keep him dead. It would have been easier to come to him as a figure remembered from a distant past, embalmed in sentiment, honored with tears. Or it would have been easier if he'd told them that the future would be altogether new; if he'd promised them a Brand New Start in Jerusalem, or simply sent them packing to the Kingdom of Heaven without further ado.

But instead he told them that they'd have to leave the past, because he lived in the future; and then he told them that the future wouldn't be any great shakes either, except for one thing. He'd be there.

And of course we're afraid, too. We don't try to keep Jesus in the church or in the past out of sheer perversity. We keep him there because it's easier that way. We keep him there because the future scares us, and we think that maybe at least at one place in our lives, that place we call "religion," we can continue to live as we always have.

And we don't keep looking toward some blissful or exciting future out of sheer perversity. We look toward an impossible future because we're scared of a future where we'll have to deal with the same kinds of problems, the same kinds of people, the same kinds of us that we've known all along.

But in the midst of our fear, beloved, we can still hear the good news. Jesus Christ will not be bound to the church or the past; but that's all right. We knew secretly, honestly, that we couldn't live just in the church or in the past anyway. And Jesus Christ isn't going to give us a bright new altogether unrecognizable future, but that's all right. We knew when we left here we'd have to go back to Galilee, to the familiar world we know so well.

But the good news is this. Jesus Christ won't protect us from the future, and Jesus Christ won't clean up the future to make it comfortable for us. But He will go with us there. However fast we run into the future, He will outrun us. However far we run into the future, He will be there to meet us.

For here is the incredible good news of Easter. Jesus Christ has broken out of the tomb. He has broken the bonds of death. He has broken out of the confinement of the church, and out of the past. He has gone before us into a world and a future which are unsure and unsettling except for one thing. They are his world and his future.

He has broken the bonds which contained him; he has broken the bonds which constrain us.

He is free.

And so are you.

And so am I.

Happy Easter.

Amen.

17

Whether We Live or
Whether We Die

ROMANS 14:5–12

This sermon was preached at Thousand Oaks Baptist Church on
June 27, 1971. David served as an interim from 1970–1972, while
teaching at the American Baptist Seminary of the West.

All of us have moments when death is near and frighteningly real. For me,
such a moment came when I learned that Glenn Brown was dying of cancer.
Glenn had been the youth minister in the church where I grew up: he was
like an older brother to me. He was a young man, with a young wife, and four
children, and a promising career, and he was about to die.

Some months later, after his death, his wife showed me the pages of his
journal which was later published. Death was near and real again as I read
what Glenn had written in facing his own death:

> Today my doctor told me that I have incurable cancer.
> It was like hearing the sentence of death. As long as I
> have any life in me, I know that I shall hope for reprieve,
> but even in my hope I live as one under sentence.
>
> Actually, every man lives under a sentence such as mine,
> but everyone, just as I did (and still do!) tries to escape
> and hide from its threat and its imminence.[1]

---

1. Glenn Brown Jr., *Life Is a Gift: Journal and Selections from the Sermons of Glenn
Brown, Jr.* (Colorado Women's College, 1967). Quote was written on August the 8,
1965.

83

"Every man lives under a sentence such as mine." A sentence of death for all of us, all of those we love.

Then we look at this passage in the book of Romans. There are other passages in the New Testament which also speak of the meaning of death, some of them more familiar, and perhaps some of them more comforting. But I confess that this is the passage which means most to me.

> None of us lives to himself, and none of us dies to himself. If we live, we live to the Lord, and if we die, we die to the Lord; so then, whether we live or whether we die, we are the Lord's. For to this end Christ died and lived again, that he might be Lord both of the dead and of the living.
>
> (Rom. 14:8 RSV)

This passage tells us four things about death.

First, it reminds us that death is real. We die, says Paul, and Christ died. Every man must someday face up to the reality of death.

That seems simple enough: Yet we spend so much of our time trying to pretend that death is not real.

Some of you probably saw or read *The Loved One*. It is a grotesque, funny, unbelievable and sometimes uncouth story based on a grotesque, funny, unbelievable, uncouth and all too real cemetery in Southern California called Forest Lawn. Forest Lawn was conceived in delusion and dedicated to the proposition that death is not real. At Forest Lawn one must never speak of "The Loved One." The loved ones are buried on slopes called "Sunset Glade" or "Happiness Acres," covered by perpetually green grass and serenaded by perennially singing birds. The bodies are carefully boxed to remain intact eternally. And lest the loved one perhaps be unhappy about the creed or color of the corpse next door, Negroes are carefully excluded from the cemetery and Jews are buried in distant and unhallowed ground. Life goes on as cheerfully as usual, perhaps a little more cheerfully.

Or look at our words for death. We say: "Mr. So-and-So passed away." He "passed on." He "went home." He "took his rest." He "slipped through the veil." He is "on the other side." And only occasionally, under our breaths, do we dare suggest the truth: he is dead.

But of course, despite Forest Lawn and all our nice vocabulary, the simple fact is that men die: all men die.

We shall die, and whatever else that means, it means that our hearts will stop beating, our lungs will stop breathing, and our brains will no longer function. Life as we know it will be over, finally and forever done. Our bodies will decay, like the bodies of all dead things, and like all dead things we shall eventually be forgotten.

Those we love die, and whatever else it means that they die, it means that they are really gone from us. They are really with us no more. They do not hover about us with soothing words and comforting presence. They are gone, utterly gone. For a while we shall miss them; we shall be filled with loneliness. But in time we shall miss them less; the loneliness will fade. We shall find it easy not to think of them, except on those rare moments when a familiar sight, a remembered sound recalls them to us, and we feel again all the pain and sorrow of our loss. And we do not know which is worse, the pain at our remembering them or the guilt at our forgetting them.

That is the first thing we learn from our text; there is no avoiding it. Death is real, for all of us and for all those we love.

The second thing we learn from our passage is that there is a comfort for us in facing death: "If we live we live to the Lord; if we die we die to the Lord; so then, whether we live or whether we die, we are the Lord's."

Now in a sense that's a very modest comfort. It doesn't tell us at all what death will be like; it doesn't tell us what will happen to us when we die; it gives us no clue to what has become of our loved ones, where they are or what they are doing, if in fact they are anywhere doing anything.

But it is also a great comfort. For the most important fact about us is not the fact that we have this body or this mind; it is not the fact that we have these friends; it is not the fact that we have accomplished some good or achieved some success. The most important fact about us is simply this: we are loved and accepted by God.

And Paul says that death cannot possibly change that fact. Our bodies may die; our minds may die; our accomplishments and achievements may die; our friendships may be forgotten. But one thing will not die; our importance in the eyes of God will not die. Not even death can end his loving us: "Whether we live or whether we die, we are the Lord's."

You remember the point in Thornton Wilder's *Our Town*, where Jane Crofut receives a letter. The address on the letter is this: "Jane Crofut, The Crofut Farm; Grover's Corners; Sutton County; New Hampshire; United States of America; . . . Continent of North America; Western Hemisphere; the Earth; the Solar System; the Universe; the Mind of God."[2]

The point of what Paul says is this: that all of us, the living and the dead, have our address in the mind and love of God. Whatever else we may be, we are God's.

Not all the power of death can change that fact.

And that is a comfort when we face the death of those we love as well. For the most important thing which unites us to those we love is not that we see

2. Thornton Wilder, *Our Town*, act 1, part 2 (New York: Harper, 1960).

them or hear them or feel their presence; it is not even that we remember them. The most important thing which unites us to those we love is the fact that all of us are loved and accepted by God. And death cannot change the fact that all of us are his children. Death cannot divide us from those we love, because all of us belong to God.

There is a hymn we sing at funerals which speaks of the unity we have with those who are dead:

> Oh blest communion, fellowship divine!
> We feebly struggle, they in glory shine;
> Yet all are one in Thee, for all are Thine.
> Alleluia! Allelulia![3]

So Paul reminds us that death is real; then he tells us that even in death we are the Lord's. But this brings us to our third point. How can Paul make such a bold claim? How does he know that we live and die in the Lord? Here is Paul's answer: "For to this end Christ died and lived again, that he might be Lord both of the dead and of the living" (v. 9 RSV).

"For to this end Christ died, that he might be Lord both of the dead and of the living." Almost all of us have seen others we love face death. In a sense the most terrible thing for us is that we cannot share that death with them. We have shared so much with them. The joy of their health; the disappointments of the sorrows; the love for other people; even some of the pain and the frustration and courage of the final illness; we have shared that. But at the last, at that moment which we cannot avoid and cannot control; at the moment of their death, we cannot share with them. At the last they must face death all by themselves.

Yet though we cannot share their death with them, our faith is that Jesus Christ does share their death with them. Our Lord who shared human life also shares our death and the death of those we love. We do not die alone: "For to this end Christ died . . . that he might be Lord both of the dead and of the living."

And Christ not only shares death, He overcomes death: "For to this end Christ died and lived again, that he might be Lord both of the dead and of the living."

Like all men, Christ died, but death did not overcome him; death did not have the final word. Christ rose from death and by rising he showed once and for all that death cannot separate us from His love.

---

3. William Walsham How, "For All the Saints," *The Presbyterian Hymnal* (Louisville, KY: Westminster/John Knox Press, 1990), 526.

The Psalmist said it better than we ever could: "Even though I walk through the valley of the shadow of death, I fear no evil" (Ps. 23:4a RSV). Why fear no evil? Because death is not real? Not at all. Because death is really only a pleasant transition? Not at all. "Even though I walk through the valley of the shadow of death, I fear no evil, for thou art with me."

In Jesus Christ we see that God is with us; that he shares our death and overcomes our death. "Whether we live or whether we die, we are the Lord's. For to this end Christ died and lived again, that he might be Lord both of the dead and of the living."

But now our passage makes a fourth and final point. If everything we have said is true; if death is real; if we are God's even in death; if we know this through the death and resurrection of Jesus Christ; then that tells us something about the way that we should live:

"None of us lives to himself, and none of us dies to himself. If we live, we live to the Lord, and if we die, we die to the Lord" (Rom. 14:7–8).

"None of us lives to himself, and none of us dies to himself."

I once knew a woman who spent all the last years of her life thinking about her death. She had her final leave-taking planned down to the last detail. She had hired all her pallbearers in advance; she had made and remade her will at least three times a year for twenty years. She had chosen the funeral parlor, and the mortician, the casket and three appropriate hymns. She had virtually written the obituary for the papers and the eulogy for the preacher. The one obsessive concern for her life was that she would die in style.

I knew another woman who kept telling us that she could hardly wait to die. She was convinced that the sufferings of this present world would vanish instantly upon the moment of her death, and she would be transferred to some Hollywood Paradise beyond the Pearly Gates, where everything would be sweetness and light, and she would have a very comfortable pew near the throne of God.

All of us have known people who spend their whole lives mourning the loss of someone they loved; keeping his photograph prominently displayed at the devout shrine; making pilgrimages to the grave as often as most of us make pilgrimages to the grocery store; refusing to change the room of the one who died; living their entire lives in pious dedication to the past.

To all of these comes the clear word: "None of us lives to himself . . . [or] dies to himself." For what is it to spend our whole lives thinking about death? It is to live to ourselves because we are so afraid of dying to ourselves. It is to be so busy making sure that we have a sensational last curtain that we forget the whole play that goes before. It is to keep our eye so firmly fixed on the heavenly vision that we keep tripping over earthly needs which get in

our way. It's to mourn so exclusively for the dead that we forget that life is
for the living.

But if it is really true that even in death we are still God's, then we no longer need be so afraid of death. We no longer need try to escape it by careful
planning, or foolish dreaming, or self-pity. We can accept the fact that we die
and those we love die. We can accept the fact that whether we live or whether
we die, we are the Lord's.

And then we can come off it. Then we can stop being so worried about
death. Then we can do what we are called to do; we can live, not to ourselves,
but to the Lord.

We will not need to spend our time in worry about our leave-taking. We
will find enough to keep us busy here and now. We will not need to be concerned with what has happened to those we love; we can entrust them to the
care of God. We will not even need to hear sermons on death every Sunday
morning. We will be more concerned with hearing sermons on life, knowing
that our task now is to live to the Lord, and that in his time and in his mercy,
we shall die to the Lord as well.

I return to Glenn Brown. Faced even with the immediate prospect of his
own death, he realized that what mattered was his living. Given every good
excuse to worry about himself, he prayed that he might continue to live for
others. I want to read a prayer he wrote during the last weeks of his life; it is
the prayer fitting for a man who must learn to live even in the face of death; it
is therefore a prayer which is fitting for us all.

> O thou great giver of life, thou hast instructed me again in the limits
> of all things human, reminded me that thou art God, Eternal, ever-
> lasting, my Judge and my redeemer. It is too much for me to know. I
> would rather die in my sin, forget the brevity of my years, the partial-
> ity of my wisdom, the illusion of each security. But thou hast placed
> me under the sentence of death, given me the mission of sharing with
> others the reality of life, helped me see as in a vision the End. . . .

> Preserve me from my own fears for myself, the fear of pain to my
> body, the fear of being forgotten in death by my children and friends.
> . . . Keep me, in my mourning for myself, alive to the suffering of all
> men, aware in others of needs greater than my own, responsive to thy
> great love which encompasses me, lifting me out of terror and frustra-
> tion into the hope for a bright new day, through him who made all
> things new, Jesus the Christ my Lord. Amen.[4]

So say we all, AMEN.

4. Brown, *Life Is a Gift*. Quote from August the 8, 1965.

18

God Is at Work

PHILIPPIANS 2:12–18

This sermon was preached at Thousand Oaks Baptist Church, Berkeley, California, on July 18, 1971.

"Therefore . . . work out your own salvation with fear and trembling; for God is at work in you, both to will and to work for his good pleasure" (Phil. 2:12–13).

By any standards these are some of the least likely lines Paul ever wrote. If there is anybody who wanted to insist that we couldn't work out our own salvation, it was Paul. Salvation, he claims time and again, is always and only a gift from God. Salvation is none of our doing.

Yet if we look at the context of what Paul is saying, I think it can make a good deal of sense for us in our present situation. For the problem to which Paul addresses himself is the problem of a congregation come of age. In the old days when Paul was with them, they always had someone to turn to for advice or help or suggestions. Paul, if we know Paul, was only too glad to help them out with a few wise words for any situation.

But now he's impossibly removed from them: locked up in jail, able to communicate only by letter and that only when the messenger service is working well, which it hasn't been lately. So what he's telling them is that they need to grow up. That he can no longer be there to tell them what to do and how to do it on every crucial occasion; that they are to work out their own salvation.

And that's a word that we have to admit applies with a kind of frightening reality to our own situation.

That is some of what we feel in our personal lives when we reach maturity. When we were children we could rely on our parents to help us out in the difficult situations, could turn to them when problems became too hard for us to solve by ourselves. But as we grow up, time and distance and eventually death remove them from us. We often seek other figures who can have the same kind of authority we once gave our parents; teachers, or pastors, or friends. But again, time and distance and eventually death prevent us from relying altogether on any other person. Sometimes the mark of our maturity is to know that we must work out our own salvation; it is to accept our own responsibility for who we are and who we are to become. That is a frightening realization, but it is an unavoidable one.

Or take the case of our national political scene. The other night I was watching a panel discussion on the impact of "The Pentagon Papers," and one of the panelists summed up I think the most important result of the publication of those papers. We now know what perhaps we should have known all along, that our politicians are not invested by God with any special wisdom. That they are as fallible as we are, and that unlike us they have the special temptations which go with power. Part of the great American mythology has been that our leaders, unlike the leaders of other nations, are great selfless individuals with clear vision and high ideals. "The Pentagon Papers" have revealed that our leaders are mere and mortal men; they have reminded us that the citizens can never trust their destiny or their safety or their freedom to the good judgment of their leaders. If we are to work out our own salvation with fear and trembling, we shall have to learn a healthy amount of distrust; we shall have to insist that our leaders work for the welfare of the nation and for peace among nations; we shall no longer be able to assume that they are doing so.

And further this word "Work out your own salvation with fear and trembling" is a word for our life as Christians as well. Now this is very hard for me to say, since you know my own devotion to the Bible and to the traditions of the church, but one of the things that we have to face is the fact that the Bible and church tradition do not give us clear, explicit, incontrovertible guidelines for every situation in which we find ourselves. The Bible contains the word of God, but it does not consist of magic formulas for solving problems. The Bible does not speak directly to the problems of international relations in a nuclear age; it does not speak directly on issues of which it never heard: the drug problem, the generation gap, or women's liberation. On some problems, I confess, I think the biblical writers reflect too much the prejudices of their own time. That doesn't mean that the Bible doesn't have vast and helpful insights in dealing with a variety of problems, but it does mean that we can't use it like some Emily Post Guide to Etiquette for Christian Living. You can't thumb through the index, say, looking for "marijuana" and then turn to page 673 to see what the Bible has to say about that problem. In dealing with the problems we face, the Bible is an indispensable guide, but it isn't an iron-clad set of rules. We are still stuck with having to use our own insight, our own thoughtful, prayerful concern, our own imagination. "Work out your own salvation with fear and trembling."

Now if that were the end of Paul's word, it would be healthy and bracing, like a cold shower or a hard look in the mirror. But it wouldn't be the Gospel, and it would hardly be Paul. Paul goes on: "For God is at work in you, both to will and to work for his good pleasure."

God is at work in us both to will and to work for his good pleasure. When we work out our own salvation, with fear and trembling, what seems to us to be our own terrible groping in the dark may in fact be God's great leading into a new and wondrous light. What seems to us to be confusion may be part of His wisdom. What seems to us to be only our silly works, may be part of His great working in the affairs of men.

It may be frightening for us to give up on the counsel of a parent, a teacher, a beloved pastor. But it may also be for us a kind of mark of maturity; a kind of independence which allows us for the first time to be truly ourselves: that's an impossible goal, but it does mean that we can decide when we need help and when we can go it alone; it means that we can take the responsibility for our own decisions; it means that we can know a new maturity.

And in our political life, it may be frightening to learn that our leaders are men and not gods, but it is healthily frightening. May not God be recalling to us the true meaning of democracy, which assumes that leaders are sufficiently selfish and foolish that they must always be held in check by the will of a free people. May we not be coming to a new maturity in our national life, as we face up to the fact that as a nation we are capable of terrible mistakes, and that therefore we must learn to live, not as gods on the earth, but as one nation, among nations, working out our own salvation. Perhaps that new maturity is precisely the way in which God is at work among us now.

And it may be frightening to realize that the Bible and church tradition do not give us simpleminded answers to complex problems. But time and again in the history of the Church, God has worked precisely by facing us with new issues which cannot be answered in the same old ways.

The greatness of Paul's preaching grew out of the conflict between the old reliance on the Law of Moses and the new problem of how to preach the Gospel to non-Jews. The greatness of Augustine's theology came as a man wrestled with the relationship between the biblical work and the declining powers of the Roman Empire. The greatness of the Reformation came as Luther sought to apply the Gospel and the judgment of Christian faith to the problem of a powerful and increasingly corrupt church. The greatness of the Social Gospel came when Walter Rauschenbusch saw that the old answers of Christian fundamentalism were inadequate to the problems of industrial America. The greatness of the new reformation in this country came as Reinhold Niebuhr saw that the optimism of men like Rauschenbusch was inadequate to the dilemmas of capitalist society in a time of depression and war. The greatness of the black revolt came when men like Martin Luther King Jr. insisted that the Gospel was a Gospel of freedom which could not be bound to the racist culture which had too often pretended to have a corner on the Gospel; and some great renewal is now abroad, in this very time between, as we try to work out our own salvation; as we try to discover how to be faithful to our Lord and open to the cries of the oppressed for justice and of all God's weary children for peace.

This kind of faith that God is at work both to will and to work for His good pleasure was best expressed by the greatest of Americans. When Abraham Lincoln was leaving Springfield to go to Washington to take up the presidency in the most troubled time in the history of our nation, he spoke these words to his Illinois friends: "Trusting to him who can go with me and remain with you and be everywhere for the good, let us confidently hope that all will yet be well."[1]

That is what Paul is saying: even in the midst of having to work out our own salvation with fear and trembling, we can confidently hope that all will yet be well. For God is at work in us, both to will and to work for his good pleasure.

Finally, a word about the "fear and trembling" part of our passage. It's easy, though, to see why working out our own salvation should cause fear and trembling.

It is a scary matter to be told that you have to make your own decisions—in your own life, or as a nation, or as members of the Christian community.

But the point of the "fear and trembling" isn't so much that we have to work out our own salvation. What Paul says is: "Work with fear and trembling, BECAUSE God is at work in you."

"Fear and trembling" are good New Testament words for religious awe. They describe the way we are supposed to feel whenever God appears among us.

---

1. "Farewell Address at Springfield, Illinois" in *The Collected Works of Abraham Lincoln*, vol. 4, ed. Roy P. Basler (Abraham Lincoln Association, 1953), 190.

And what Paul is saying is that God appears among us, not just among us, but in us; that He's at work in our work.

That's an awesome responsibility; it means that the decisions we make, the things we do, the lives we lead, count not just for us, but for Him as well. That the way we decide to live, the future we set for ourselves as a nation, the way we seek to be the church in a changing world—these are also God's way of deciding, of making future, of living his life in a changing world.

But if God is really at work in us to work and will for His good pleasure, then the awe we feel can also be the awe of confident hope. Because we know that the final word about our actions will not be our word, but His word, that the final result of our actions is not our accomplishment, but His gift. That though we may seem to be wandering in great darkness, at the end of the dark valley is a great light; the light of his mercy extended to us all.

A couple of weeks ago I spoke about my grandmother, a truly remarkable person. She knew more than her share of difficulties: her husband was an invalid during most of their marriage; she had to raise five children, and teach school to make money during the depression, and care for her husband and manage to care for everybody else in her community as well. There must have been some rough times for her, some times when she wondered whether all her working might not be in vain. But when she died I heard at last of a poem which had been her favorite throughout those years. It was an expression of her faith, and in its own way an expression of the Christian faith. It is a sign of hope for us all, when we find ourselves having to work out our own salvation and wondering where God has gone:

"If but one message I may leave behind,
one single word of courage for my kind,
It would be this,
O brother, sister, friend,
whatever life may bring, or God may send— . . .
Take heart and wait!

Despair may tangle darkly at your feet,
. . . and hope once cool and sweet be lost,—
but suddenly, above a hill,
a heavenly lamp, set on a heavenly sill,
Will shine for you,
and point the way to go—
How well I know!

For I have waited through the dark and I
Have seen a star rise in the blackest sky,
Repeatedly . . . it has not failed me yet.

And I have learned . . . God never will forget
To light His lamp. If we but wait for it—
It will be lit!"[2]

"It will be lit": therefore, beloved, work out your own salvation, with fear and trembling, and faith and hope. For God is at work in you; His will shall finally be done.

So say we all. Amen.

Let us pray:

Father, help us to know your will, or if that is too much to ask, help us to do your will, unknowingly. Through Jesus Christ our Lord. Amen.

---

2. Poem attributed to Grace Noll Crowell.

19

How to Read the Bible

From 1973–1975 David served as Senior Minister of University
Baptist Church in Minneapolis, Minnesota. This sermon was
preached on November 6, 1975.

When I was teaching at Berkeley, I accepted the invitation to become interim
minister at the Thousand Oaks Baptist Church and as the time approached
for my first sermon to that congregation, I carefully polished my presentation and my delivery hoping that what I said would carry sufficient weight
to impress them. I presented the sermon and went somewhat nervously to
coffee hour waiting to see what kind of comments I would get from this new
congregation.

The first one to meet me at coffee hour was a young man who came up
and said, not very supportively, "I completely disagree with what you said." I
thought back over the various theological statements I made in the sermon,
thinking that they hadn't seemed to me very controversial and puzzled a little
bit about what he thought was wrong. Then he explained to me. "You said
that Mark wrote that the disciples had left their nets and followed Jesus," said
the young man, "but everyone knows it wasn't Mark who wrote that; it was
really the Holy Spirit and Mark was just like a pen in the Holy Spirit's hand."
Well, that was my first but not my last encounter with those Christians who
have moved from the valid view that the Bible is the inspired word of God to
what I think is the remarkable view that the biblical writers were somehow
just Dictaphones for the Holy Spirit.

I suppose that most of us are clearer that we don't buy that understanding of inspiration than we are on what we do think it means to say that the Bible is the inspired word of God. I want to do two things this morning. I want to suggest first of all what I think is a more adequate interpretation of the inspiration of the biblical word and then I want to make some practical suggestions for our own reading of the Bible.

I.

So the first part of the sermon raises this question. What do we mean by saying that the Bible is the inspired word of God? And for the center of my thinking about the inspiration of the Bible I take that very familiar text from the prologue to the Gospel of John: "And the Word became flesh and dwelt among us, and we beheld his glory, as of the father's only son, full of grace and truth" (John 1:14, author trans.).

Now what does this familiar verse suggest to us about the inspiration of scripture? On the one hand I think it reminds us that the heart of God's inspiration to us isn't a bunch of words (not even the words of the Bible). The heart of God's inspiration to us is the WORD MADE FLESH in Jesus Christ. And the Bible is important not because it contains the words dictated by the Holy Spirit, but the Bible is important because it bears witness to Jesus Christ, who was God's revelation of God's self. The Bible is the record of faithful people who are trying to understand what it means to say that the word became flesh in Jesus Christ. The Old Testament is the story of that history out of which comes Jesus Christ. The Gospels are the attempts of faithful people to understand the meaning of Jesus' life and ministry. Paul's letters are Paul's attempt to relate the meaning of Jesus' death and resurrection to the founding of new churches.

The writers of the Bible were not inspired because God whispered in their ears telling them what to write. The writers of the Bible were inspired because by faith they tried to understand God's mercy to Israel and God's great mercy in Jesus Christ, and by faith they tried to show what that mercy meant for people who needed it.

On the other hand, not only is the Bible the witness of the Word become Flesh in Jesus Christ, the words of the Bible need to become flesh in our lives, too. They need to become not just old-fashioned history or impossible rules. They need to become part of our own life experience. In part that suggests that we are to bring our own experience to bear upon the scripture. We are to raise the question, "How does who we are, what we do, help us make sense of the Bible and what the Bible says about Israel, about Jesus Christ and the

Church?" But equally important, we are to bring scripture to bear on our own experience. We are to try to see ourselves, our needs, our questions, our hopes in a different light because of what scripture tells us about God in Jesus Christ.

This past week we were at a campus minister's meeting which somehow got into a discussion of the work of the psychologist (Lawrence) Kohlberg. Kohlberg, I take it, has developed a scale by which we're supposed to be able to measure people's moral development and I noted that the discussion among the campus ministers did a good job of trying to relate our own contemporary experience to the New Testament, because the question came up—"Where would Jesus fit on Kohlberg's scale of moral development?" The point for us is not just that we're supposed to see the scripture through our own experience. The point is also that scripture helps us to rethink, to reshape, our experience in the light of Jesus Christ.

So the importance of the Bible isn't that it bears the words dictated by the Holy Spirit. The importance is that it bears witness to the Word made Flesh in Jesus Christ and made flesh again in our own lives.

Now there are a couple important theological implications of this view of inspiration of Holy Scripture. The first implication, as Norman Perrin says so well. (Norman Perrin is the head of the New Testament department at the University of Chicago. I have a strong suspicion that in the years ahead more and more of my sentences will begin "as Norman Perrin says so well.") Anyway, as Norman Perrin says so well, "The first thing to be said about the New Testament is that it is both a book and a collection of books. . . . As a book it is a single entity of primary importance to Christians. As a collection of books it is a variety of documents of different literary forms and sometimes of different religious viewpoints."[1]

That is, because the New Testament and the whole Bible record different people's attempts to struggle with the meaning of what God has done and what God has done in Jesus Christ, different books of the Bible sometimes represent different understandings of what God's revelation is all about. Some find that threatening. I find it freeing, because it means that even in the Bible there's not just one way to come to faith. There's Mark's way and Luke's way and Paul's way, and so there can be our way, too.

And there's also an important implication of the view that inspiration means that the WORD MUST BECOME FLESH. The implication is that the words of the Bible must become flesh in every generation and that means that every generation of the Church has to reinterpret scripture to meet its

1. Norman Perrin, *The New Testament: An Introduction* (New York: Harcourt Brace Jovanovich, 1974), 17.

own needs. Augustine interpreted scripture in a highly allegorical way to try to understand the relationship of the Church to the Roman Empire. Luther interpreted the scripture in a metaphorical way, applying Paul's words about works of the law to the whole system of indulgences in the Roman Church of which Paul had never even dreamed. In the nineteenth century, Christian liberals tried to reinterpret the Bible in the light of the scientific understanding of their day while fundamentalists came up with a brand new idea that every word of scripture is inherently and literally true. All of these were new ways of trying to relate scripture to our situation, trying to relate scripture to a historical situation. And that, of course, is what we're called upon to do for our time and for our situation.

II.

Well, that's the end of a kind of theological understanding of the inspiration of scripture and its implications for us. Now I want very briefly to make five practical suggestions on how to read the Bible.

The first suggestion is a suggestion about which translations to use and why. Like most of you, I started with the King James. The King James Version is full of magnificent poetry, but I don't think it's very helpful theologically. The language is archaic, and since the time of the translation of the King James Version we have found new manuscripts which very often made it easier for us to come closer to an understanding of the original text itself. Both the Revised Standard Version and the Jerusalem Bibles are scholarly careful attempts to do as accurately as possible a word-for-word translation of the texts and I would commend those to you as perhaps the best study Bibles. The New English Bible and the translation called "Good News for Modern Man" (which we should certainly retitle "Good News for Modern People") are a little more deliberately interpretive but I find them good reading and an excellent source for regular devotional use of the Bible. The so-called Living Bible is called a paraphrase of the Bible. What it actually is is often a rewriting of texts from a so-called evangelical bias. I take it as one of the ironies of recent biblical scholarship that the so-called literalists have played faster and looser with scripture than the modernists every dared or wanted to do. As Kurt Vonnegut would say, "So it goes."

Well, that's a word about translations. The second thing I want to say is this: When reading the Bible, try to get a sense of the whole context of what you read. Over a period of time try to read a whole book and not just a verse here and a verse there. The problem with devotional material like "The Secret Place" is that you really never get a sense of the concerns out of which they grow. My own practice in Bible reading is to try to read through a whole book of the Bible, not of course at one sitting, but over a period of time. Just take some of it each day, and I think that way one can get a much richer sense of the special concerns and interests and theological ideas of the writer of the book you read.

The third suggestion is this. When reading the Bible, try to get a sense of the concrete situation to which your passage was addressed. If we don't see the Bible as dictated by the Holy Spirit as eternal truth, but as the attempt of faithful people to understand God's revelation in a concrete situation, then it's important to try to understand the concrete situation to which that word was addressed.

For example, that familiar passage that we all know and love, 1 Corinthians 13 on the meaning of love, was not just dictated by Paul as a timeless truth, it's his attempt to deal with a very specific problem within the Corinthian church—the problem of people speaking in tongues and being unduly proud of that gift. And so when the chapter begins "though I speak with the tongues of men and of angels and have not love" that's speaking to the concrete problem which Paul faces. And it is only in understanding those concrete problems that we can come to an understanding of the reality of the text itself.

Now this is the place where commentaries can be a real help to us. I wish there were more good commentaries for non-scholars, but I can at least commend to you the introductory articles in the *Interpreter's Dictionary of the Bible* as a good place to start in understanding the point and meaning of the various books of the Bible.

My fourth concrete suggestion is this. When reading the Bible, try to see how the words of the Bible apply to your concrete situation. Try to see the way in which the words made sense in the situation of Corinth, can also make sense in the situation in Minneapolis in 1975. Try to find the ways in which those words can become flesh for you—can touch your world, your needs.

The best way I know to do that is to read the text with some care, understand it in its own situation and then back off and do some kind of creative daydreaming over the text until you get some sense of the place where it touches your life as well.

Finally, and perhaps self-evidently, when reading the Bible I suggest that you pray about what you read. The faith of the Church is that the Holy Spirit didn't die after John of Patmos put the last period on the Book of Revelation, but that God's Spirit continues to inspire faithful people even in this day. Pray to God for guidance, for understanding, and for insight. Guidance, understanding, insight will come.

As we come to this Thanksgiving season, I suppose that all of us go back and recall all those various stories of the Pilgrims and Puritans we have enjoyed through our lives. One of the favorite Pilgrim sermons of mine was a sermon which John Robinson preached. Robinson had been the Pilgrim pastor while they were in Holland. He was not staying and seeing them off to a new world. As he took his departure from them he summed up what it was that he wanted them to remember in words which I think still have meaning for us today. This is what Robinson said:

"When God reveals something to you by another minister of his, be as ready to receive it as you have ever been ready to receive any truth by ministry. For I am very confident that the Lord has some truth and light yet to break forth out of His Word."[2]

That's why we continue to read the Bible, because we believe that the God who there bears witness to Jesus Christ, through Jesus Christ will cause yet more light and truth to break forth out of His Word.

So say we all. Amen.

2. John Robinson, "Robinson's Farewell Address to the Pilgrims upon Their Departure from Holland, 1620. The Account by Edward Winslow in His 'Hypocrisie Unmasked,' Printed in 1646," Ould South Leaflets No. 142, https://oll.libertyfund.org /titles/robinson-words-of-john-robinson-robinsons-farewell-address-to-the-pilgrims.

20

Enemies

LUKE 6:27–36

This sermon was preached on February 13, 1977, at Hyde Park
Union Church in Chicago, Illinois, where David served as Senior
Minister. The church was a dually aligned American Baptist and
Congregational Church.

I.

At first I thought the others were my enemies;
I spotted them standing among the crowd.
The whole town had come out to listen to him speak,
including that unwelcome band of hypocrites,
my enemies, somehow imbued with new religious fervor,
repenting much too late, if you asked me.

There stood Thaddeus, my brother Thaddeus,
the one I would love so much.
Then he got drunk one night and told me all things
he thought I ought to know about myself.
And I could not forgive his knowledge or my own.
Since then we have avoided one another,
and avoided family get togethers, save at
funerals or weddings, when he and I
invariably sit as far from one another as we can
and scowl.

And there is Martha, who for years and years
was always my most trusted confidante;
I told her all the deepest and the silliest
desires of my heart, until one day
in sudden indiscretion she betrayed my confidence
and told another what she'd sworn she'd never tell.
Now I can barely speak to her, since I can never
trust her with my private thoughts
and since we know each other far too well for trivia.

There's Malachi, who slandered me.
Bile-monger, gossip, vile-tongued wretch.
What right had he to judge my projects or activities?
He is no paragon of virtue, yet he condemns others
as if he were God. He had no right to be here;
he has no right to come hear this preacher Jesus;
no right to act as though he gave the slightest weight
to finding and obeying the commands of God.

And there is Simeon. We argued viciously
over an issue which seemed life and death back then,
but which I admit I've quite forgotten now.
Since then, although we've both been utterly polite,
we've never dared to speak of anything that mattered to us,
either one. And we have learned the fine art
of evasive looks; we can stand face to face
and never meet each other's eyes.

And there stands Lydia; with her I guess no one's to blame.
We once were sure that she and I would marry,
and then, sometime later, were both sure that we would not.
As to what happened in between, you can take her version
or else mine.
But anyway, as dead romances do, ours died with a special bitterness.
You cannot hope so much without enormous disappointment.
Now I cross the street to keep from meeting her;
I change the subject when someone mentions her name.

And Joshua—how hard!—see, one day, to my vast astonishment,
the silence simply fell between us,
and I am not sure, not even now,
just where that silence came from, what it means.

So there they stood, scattered among the crowd, my enemies.
How all my grudges came to haunt me, seeing them.
I'd tried so hard, so long simply to forget them all,

and there they were, one after one, bold as you please
standing before the preacher Jesus, waiting for his word.

II.

Then I thought Jesus was my enemy.
What right had he to know my mind?
Was he some kind of sorcerer or god
that my most hidden needs and wishes,
my most secret angers and my private sores
were his domain? What right had he to speak to me,
as I nursed my grudges, my alarms:
"Love your enemies," he said.
"Do good to those who hate you."
"Bless those who curse you."
"Pray for those who abuse you."

The autocratic master, stern authority;
giving me orders as if I were under his command:
"Go love your enemy! Be reconciled!"

Oh yes, I thought. I'll just go to my brother,
and I'll say: Thaddeus, listen here, I think you wronged me
by your honesty; perhaps I wronged you by my hurt.
Thaddeus, I'll say, you are my brother, and you are my friend,
Can we be friends and brothers once again?
Why should I go to him? What right does he have to receive
mercy, forgiveness of me? A cruel, a selfish brother,
thinking he can simply tell me all my faults,
excused by our relationship, his drunkenness.
I will not go.

I thought, well, maybe I should turn to Martha,
after all, we all have faults, and her loose tongue
is something I'll just have to live with.
Then I thought again how cruelly she'd betrayed me,
and I knew she was not worthy of my love.
So then I thought of Malachi; all right, he slandered me.
Let bygones be bygones, but then, I thought,
He slandered me; demeaned me; by what right
did he belittle my life, shrink my soul?

That is how I thought I knew that Jesus was the enemy,
He asked of me what I would never do:
"Go love your enemy," he said, "Be reconciled

to your brother, forgive your friends."
But just when I started on my way,
my pride prevented me: "Look here," I said,
"I'm much too good to ruin my life with the likes of them."

Then Jesus spoke again: "God is kind
to the ungrateful and the selfish," he proclaimed.
He meant (I know) "Are you more good than God?"
Will you bear grudges even God won't bear?
Not even my enormous ego could sustain that claim.
Perhaps; perhaps, I could move toward my enemies,
If only I could overcome my pride.
And so I thought about his words again:
"Love your enemies, do good, expecting nothing in return."

"Expecting nothing in return," that word
struck home again.
Suppose I went to Simeon, with who I argued,
and I said: "The argument wasn't that important after all,
I can't even remember what we argued for?"
Suppose he said: "Oh yes it was important,
you were altogether wrong, you're stupid;
you're mistaken. Go away!" How could I bear the
shame? How could I bear the hurt of that again?

"Expecting nothing in return."
Suppose I turned to Lydia, whom I had loved,
And said: "Look here, of course we disappointed
one another, you and I, but can't we find some way
to share together, now and then?"
Suppose she said: "I cannot bear you now;
I never could; from first to last our love
was nothing but a vast mistake!" How could I
bear the shame? How could I bear the hurt of that again?

"Expecting nothing in return."
Suppose I turned to Joshua; all by myself
ended the silence which we both began,
and said: "Listen, what's happened to us?
Can't we find some words to bridge this sudden loneliness?
Suppose he simply turned away, still silent,
dreadful, full of scorn. How could I bear the shame,
how could I bear that silence, once again?

Jesus, my enemy, spoke on: "Love your enemies,
do good, expecting nothing in return.
For God's your Father," Jesus said.

"With God you have no shame, for God is patient,
merciful with you. Whatever other shame you bear,
God's mercy takes you without shame.
However stupid, foolish, worthless, or alone you think you felt,
God is your father, you're God's child.
Take courage, take mercy; reach out to those you even dread,
and do not be afraid of shame."

III.

So I discovered that I was the enemy.
It was my pride or shame which has prevented reconciliation.
I am myself the one who builds and mans the barricades
between myself and those I used to love,
between myself and those I long to love.

It is myself who stands afraid and blessed
before the word of Christ.
It is myself who stands before his judgment.
He tells me that I am not good enough to let my pride
stand in the way of reconciliation.
It is myself who stands before his mercy,
He tells me that I am not bad enough to let my shame
stand in the way of love.

I am the enemy; and so I stand, abashed, afraid,
and pray for victory over that tyrant, sneak,
that foe, myself, who can be vanquished—
will be vanquished—by the triumphant mercy of my God.

Amen.

21

Hoping Not to Hinder the Spirit

JOHN 13:31–35
ACTS 11:1–18

This sermon was preached at Trinity Presbyterian Church on April 28, 2013, at a time when the church was discussing inviting the children in the Agape Tutoring Program (that predominately served children of color) to join the congregation at their weekly Thursday night church dinner. The response to the idea was mixed—some thought it a great idea, others were on the fence, and a few were against it for a variety of reasons.

I.

Jesus is giving his farewell speech to his disciples. Here is what he says: "By this everyone will know that you are my disciples, if you have love for one another" (John 13:35).

For many years I preached about once a month at the Congregational Church of New Canaan, Connecticut. Until she died last year at the age of one hundred and two, Janet Robbins was always there, sitting in the third pew at my left.

Janet was entirely alert but nearly entirely deaf, so while she followed the service in her bulletin she was not very good at hearing the voices of the congregation around her.

Week after week the prayer of confession went something like this. Janet and everyone else would start out together: "Almighty God, we have sinned against you and against one another . . ." but as the prayer went on Janet fell just a little bit behind so that after ninety seconds the prayer ended like this: 224 people would say: "And help us to amend our ways, through Jesus Christ our Lord."

Then all 224 remained entirely silent while Janet finished at her own pace in a voice that all could hear: "And help us to amend our ways through Jesus Christ our Lord."

And then 225 people said: "Amen."

Two hundred and twenty-five people showing that they were disciples by the love they showed that beloved disciple, Janet.

When that earlier beloved disciple wrote his gospel he was probably not writing for a congregation of 225 people; much less for a congregation of eighteen hundred.

And in some ways it was probably easier for the fifty or sixty people in his congregation to love one another than it was for us in the larger congregations that followed. At least it was easier for them to know one another.

II.

But the fact that there are so many of us and so few of them does not make the commandment any less a commandment, not just a suggestion, but a demand: "I give you a new commandment, that you love one another" (v. 34).

Still for us as the people who are Trinity Presbyterian Church the commandment suggests some celebrations and a couple of suggestions.

I think we can celebrate the ways in which this congregation grows in love toward one another. Conversations around the supper table on Thursday night or around the breakfast table on Friday morning are at least as much being church as the seminars or the speakers that follow.

The choirs are groups of friends gathered in love to praise God. And the men's support groups, and the women's support groups, and the spirituality growth groups, and the Bible studies where we get to know scripture better but each other better too.

Trinity Serves is a way of helping our neighbors but also a way of growing in neighborliness toward one another.

In that we rejoice. In a church I previously served, one of the pillars of the church, Louise Perkins, said: "People say that there's an in-group at this church, and they're right, but everybody is welcome to join it."

We've got a lot of in-groups here and everybody is welcome to join. Let us know, ask around, and show up.

III.

Sunday morning is harder. There are so many of us and we're nervous about forgetting that name we should remember or extending a hearty greeting to the couple who have been coming to this church for thirty-five years.

> Sunday morning friendliness is harder but it's not impossible.
> Wear those name tags. Look your neighbor straight in the tag and call them by name.
> Talk to two people you don't know before you greet your best friends.
> Show people the secret passage to coffee hour.
> When the registry comes back down the pew, don't be ashamed to look at the names of the other persons in your pew. And don't be shy about telling others your own.

In the overall scheme of things all this courtesy may not seem like a very big thing, but it is a very big thing. It is church being church, Christians being Christians, doing what is the main thing to do: Loving one another.

IV.

The blessed apostle Peter was there when Jesus gave that last speech about loving one another. And for all his foibles he proved to be pretty good at keeping that commandment.

His love for that original circle of Jewish disciples was strong and clear and his love for all the other Jewish people who joined the Christian Church.

When the Spirit fell on a multitude of Jews at Pentecost and brought them into the community of Christian believers, Peter was thrilled. These were people he could love!

He got less thrilled when the Spirit just kept going. While Peter was welcoming Jews into the church, the Spirit was out recruiting Gentiles, too.

So when Peter tried to keep the church homogeneous God sent a dream where a whole tablecloth of food came down from heaven, including stuff Peter thought he could eat and stuff he was pretty sure he couldn't.

"You can eat it all," said the voice in the dream. "What God has made clean you must not call profane" (Acts 11:9, au. trans.).

Peter knew full well that this wasn't a dream about eating; it was a dream about loving. If the Spirit was out rounding up Gentiles for the church, who was Peter to call them profane? So Peter gave a speech to his fellow Jewish Christians where he confessed how wrong he had been. "If . . . God gave [the

Gentiles] the same Spirit that God gave us, when we believed in the Lord Jesus Christ, who was I that I could hinder God?" (v. 18).

V.

And now perhaps the word of God gets a little harder to hear and a little harder to obey. Peter was great at being loving and hospitable and downright friendly to people pretty much like himself. When the borders got more porous it was harder to be so welcoming.

Let's face it, beloved, we at Trinity Church are a little demographically challenged. I don't think we want to be, but we do look, dress, and eat pretty much alike.

Maybe the Spirit is pushing us, too.

You'll have your best guesses about where the Spirit is leading us or nudging us or shoving us.

Here's a good start. Next fall we will no longer have Thursday suppers in one room while our friends from the Agape Community Center meet at another. We will eat together, break bread together, look like church, together.

I believe with all my heart that in the years ahead we will find more and more ways to let the Spirit have the Spirit's way among us. And they'll know we are Christians by our love.

VI.

And one thing more. Not straight from our text but an extension of our text. Our church can continue to be what it has always been at its best, a parable of what the larger society might look like. Open hearts here might help encourage open hearts in the larger world beyond our doors.

Xenophobia is abroad in our land: The fear of the stranger, the fear of the foreign. Not hatred but fear.

The question of national security is complicated and subtle. The question of a fair immigration policy may even be more complicated than I realize.

We have all been pondering the terrifying bombings at the Boston marathon, wondering if there is something we should learn.

Here is what is clear to me. Those sad events tell us one thing about a fair or sane immigration policy. If we're already fearful of strangers, those events can stoke our fear.

But if we are on our way to an immigration policy that is compassionate and just, those deplorable events do not change our quest one iota.

VII.

If our church can be a parable of hospitality to the larger world, there is a story that is a great parable of hospitality to our church.

At the beginning of World War II in the little village of Le Chambon in France, the reformed church chose, not after a vote of anybody, but just one step at a time, chose to be a place where Jews from all over Europe could be sheltered in relative safety as the Nazis took over France. Talk about xenophobia; Nazism was fear of the other at its destructive worst.

Two words from those days in Le Chambon. Translate them to our church and to our time.

When the Vichy mayor came to try to persuade the Pastor André Trocmé to betray the Jews he was sheltering, he tried to assure Trocmé that the Jews were polluting the pure heritage of France and would be better with their own kind.

Here is what Trocmé said: "We do not know what a Jew is. We only know men."

When the first German Jewish refugees, who had heard of Le Chambon, presented themselves at the parsonage asking for help, here is how the pastor's wife described the event, years later, remembering:

"A German woman knocked at my door. It was in the evening and she said she was a German Jew, . . . that she was in danger, and that she had heard that in Le Chambon somebody could help her. Could she come into my house? I said, 'Naturally, come in, and come in.'"[1]

God's Spirit urges us on. "Naturally, come in, and come in."

Amen.

---

1. Philip P. Hallie, *Lest Innocence Blood Shed* (New York: Harper and Row,1979), 120, 103.

22

Wrestling with God

GENESIS 32:22–32
ROMANS 9:1–5

Sermon preached at Trinity Presbyterian Church in Atlanta, Georgia, on August 3, 2014.

I.

In the years of my youth I went for a week each summer to the Thousand Pines Baptist Camp in the San Bernardino Mountains of California. It was a great time to enjoy the beauty of the mountains, fellowship with other teenagers, and all those Baptist songs that we sang at camp but never on Sunday at First Baptist Church of Los Angeles, or for that matter, Trinity Presbyterian Church of Atlanta.

By my third or fourth year I had figured out that there was also a not very hidden agenda for the camp. The hope was that separated from home and family, in an unfamiliar place surrounded by new friends and old songs we would at some point during the week have a personal experience of the living God.

Our leaders called that personal experience of the living God "receiving a blessing." And on Friday night, always the last night of camp, we gathered around a campfire and were invited, yea, encouraged to share aloud with others exactly when that week we had experienced God: To say just when we had received a blessing.

In many ways the purpose of camp was to duplicate the famous experience of Jacob in the book of Genesis at Bethel when he falls asleep and sees angels ascending and descending and hears the voice of God saying: "Jacob, you are blessed, and all your descendants shall be blessed."

We even had the right camp song to recapture the blessing: "We are climbing Jacob's ladder." And better yet, "Every rung goes higher, higher."

We loved the story of Bethel but we didn't pay much attention to the story of Peniel, the story that comes a little later in Jacob's history. The story we read this morning.

In our story Jacob is blessed once again, but this time the blessing isn't the final moment of a dream it's the final outcome of a struggle. And what he gets is not simply a blessing; he also gets a wound.

II.

We all need the second story as well as the first. Whenever we come down from the mountaintop experience at camp or, from the enthusiastic beliefs of our youth, whenever we discover that the life of faith isn't all blessing and light but sometimes darkness and hurt.

So here is that story; and here is that side of God. Here's how we sometimes have to wrestle the blessing.

Notice that when Jacob meets God he's all alone.

> "The same night he got up and took his two wives, his two maids, and his eleven children and crossed the ford of the Jabbok. He took them and sent them across the stream, and likewise everything that he had. Jacob was . . . alone."
>
> (Gen. 32:22–24)

Sometime God finds us in our fellowship but sometimes in our solitude. The saints like Saint Francis and Saint Clare and Thomas Merton and Dorothy Day chose loneliness voluntarily.

For the rest of us the loneliness is often imposed: The end of a romance, the end of a job, the end of a marriage, or the loneliness of death.

"What I miss most," said a friend of mine whose wife had died, "is someone to talk to. I turn to share something with her and she isn't there." Jacob was alone.

III.

Notice also that when Jacob meets Jesus he has to wrestle with God. We have to read through to the end of the story to realize that the mysterious wrestler is God, but we see the wrestling from the start.

"Jacob was left alone; and a man wrestled with him until daybreak" (v. 24).

We get so consumed with the idea that the way to meet God is quiet piety that we forget that sometimes the way to meet God is honest striving.

Jacob: "I will not let you go until you tell me your name" (v. 26).

Job: losing everything, family, property, health: "Why have you made me your target, when did I become such a burden to you?" (Job 7:20, au. trans.).

Jeremiah, the great prophet discovering that a prophet's life is not a happy one:

> Oh LORD, you have seduced me, and I was seduced. You have overpowered me and you have prevailed. I have become a laughingstock all the day long.
>
> (Jer. 20:7, au. trans.)

The Psalmist, seeking to live the life of faith but wrestling with despair: "My God, my God, why have you forsaken me?" (Ps. 22:1).

Jesus the servant, seeking to live the life of faith but wrestling with despair: "My God my God why have you forsaken me?" (Matt. 27:46).

Beloved when you find yourself bereaved, bereft, betrayed sometimes the right and faithful word is: "Let it be to me as you have chosen." But sometimes the right and faithful word is: "How can you do this to me?"

God can take it, this I know,

For the Bible tells me so.

IV.

Notice further that though Jacob gets God's blessing he never does learn God's name. "Then Jacob asked him, 'Please tell me your name.' But he said, "Why is it that you ask my name? And there he blessed him" (v. 29).

You've heard this before and you're about to hear it again. For the Jewish people to name something is to claim it, control it, and understand it. Adam and Eve name the beasts and take dominion over them. Sarah and Abraham name their son "Isaac"—laughter—to remind them that they had laughed at the promises of God.

When you name a child you have found the words to claim who that person is, who you want her to be.

In the Old Testament nobody gets to name God. God is too big and too mysterious for our naming. God's name isn't even God; that's a kind of cipher, a code for something bigger than our best words.

Jacob says: "What's your name?" and the wrestler says, "I won't tell you my name, but I will give you a blessing and what's more I'll give YOU your name to show who's knowable and who's not. You are now Israel. That means you are the one who strives with God."

Moses says: "What's your name?" and the voice from the burning bush says something like: "I am who I am" or "I will be who I will be." To this day devout Jews never say aloud the phrase that the voice spoke to Moses because God is mystery.

For the most influential theologians of the twentieth century, what we worship, whom we worship is a mystery. For Paul Tillich, "the ground of being," for Karl Barth, "The Entirely Other."

Entirely real, entirely knowing, never entirely known; God without a name, not because God is not real, but because God's reality is far bigger than our ability to name.

So here's the tricky thing we learn from our passage: if you feel sadly alone, are angry about it, blame God, but if you aren't at all sure who the God is whom you blame, then you are just where Jacob is when the blessing finally comes.

V.

The blessing finally comes, but does not come alone: Along with the blessing, always the wounding. "The man . . . struck [Jacob] on the hip socket; and Jacob's hip was put out of joint. . . . The sun rose upon Jacob as he passed Penuel, limping because of his hip" (v. 25, 31).

Along with the gratitude, the permanent limitation. Dancing the holy dance of blessing, but always with a limp.

What got injured when Milton Mackaig wrestled with the mysterious God was his pride. Milton was the most pillarly of the pillars of the church where I grew up, and he loved that church just the way it was.

Just the way it was was entirely composed of white people, and when a black mother and daughter sought to join the church, Milton led the group who voted no. Milton led the group that won the vote.

The man who had been minister of that church for twenty-two years quit. "If I've preached all these years and that's what you got out of it, I've failed," he said. Though, of course, he'd faithfully tilled the ground that would one day bear fruit.

The new minister came, my father as it happened, and preached and preached and taught and taught and argued and argued. When another black man, Neil Rose, asked to join the church, Milton Mackaig, after a painful separation from his old supporters, after suffering a major wounding to his pride, voted yes.

Neil Rose not only joined the church, he joined the choir. When he was robing for service one day someone came into the men's robing room and beat him badly.

The next week when the Sunday service began we looked back as the choir processed, and there marching down the aisle, the first pair of the baritones were Neil Rose with his beautiful voice, and next to him, joining the choir for the first time ever, perfectly robed but painfully flat— Milton Mackaig.

Right there for God and all the people to see; mind changed; pride injured—soul healed. Of course he was marching, of course he was limping.

He had wrestled with God and he had lost and he had prevailed.

Just like Jacob: Wounded. Blessed.

Amen.

23

Watching with Hope

MARK 13:24–27
ISAIAH 64:1–9

This sermon was preached the first Sunday in Advent on November 30, 2014, at Trinity Presbyterian Church in Atlanta, Georgia. David served as Theologian in Residence at the church.

I.

I grew up in an American Baptist church before American Baptists were influenced by the liturgical revival. The liturgical revival was an attempt to help people like American Baptists pay more attention to issues like the church calendar—to start celebrating the second Sunday of Advent instead of "Pension for Retired Ministers" Sunday. More and more Baptists began decorating their pulpits and their stoles with the proper liturgical colors. And we started using pretty much the same scripture readings that Lutherans and Episcopalians had been using for years.

There were two ways especially in which we differed from our Lutheran and Episcopal neighbors.

The first difference was that we didn't know you weren't supposed to sing Christmas carols until Christmas Eve, and so inspired by the music at Macy's we were perfectly glad to sing "Joy to the World" at least three weeks prematurely.

The second difference between us and those more formal churches was that while we knew Advent was a time of waiting it was clear that what we were waiting for was the babe in the manger, not the Son of Man returning in clouds at the end of time.

It came as something of a shock as I grew more interdenominational in my interests to discover that Lutheran and Episcopalian churches always watch for two great events during Advent: they wait for Christ's first coming, in the manger. And they wait for Christ's second coming, in glory, at the end of time.

Looking back on those days when Advent was all about the manger, I suspect that our pastor, who was also my father, was not just avoiding the ecumenical readings. We didn't read those texts about Jesus' second coming because my father didn't much believe in them.

Somewhat remarkably after sixty years or so I remember one of his sermons where a visiting preacher asks a wise old farmer (wise old farmers figured prominently in sermon illustrations in those days): "Do you believe that Jesus is coming again?"

And the wise old farmer, undoubtedly channeling his preacher, responded: "I never knew he went away."

II.

That is not an unfaithful or even an unbiblical response. It pretty much mirrors what the Gospel of John says about Jesus' second coming. He comes again into the hearts and minds of believers. About the end of time John is remarkably silent.

But Mark is not silent, nor Matthew, Luke nor the apostle Paul. Nor, let it be said, Jesus. Though it is very hard to sort out just who believed what when, it is quite clear that none of those people would have been embarrassed by the text we read from Mark's Gospel.

> The sun will be darkened/ and the moon will not give its light/and the stars will be falling from heaven/and the powers in the heavens will be shaken. Then they will see 'the Son of Man coming in clouds' with great power and glory.
>
> (Mark 13:24–26)

So there it is, not just for Episcopalians and Lutherans and more conservative evangelicals, but right there at the heart of the New Testament time after time.

III.

Despite the strangeness of the language and the drama of the picture, as we come to this season of watching for Christ, I think that our passages for this morning help to deepen our hope.

Most obviously the text from Mark helps us distinguish Christian hope from astrology or fortune-telling. Jesus himself tells us not to read history the way Madame LeRue reads your palm. "Just look at this; I can tell you exactly what's going to happen when."

Here's Jesus on his own return: "But about that day and hour no one knows, neither the angels of heaven, nor the Son, but only the Father" (Matt. 24:36).

So the people who chart the situation in the Middle East as a clue to the date of Christ's return dare what Jesus himself would never dare. And those who look to the prophets or to Mark or to the book of Revelation as a kind of giant puzzle to be solved entirely misunderstand the shape of Christian hope.

Christian hope says that when we watch for God to finish history, we know who we watch for, but we don't pretend to know the date.

IV.

But here's the thing, beloved, we do know who is in charge of history.

Many years ago, Krister Stendahl, who was a New Testament scholar and then Dean at Harvard Divinity School and then the Bishop of Uppsala, came to speak to ministerial students at Yale Divinity School.

"Don't assume that what most worries our people is whether each of them will get to heaven, what worries our people is whether history has any meaning, any purpose at all."

For all the complications of its language and the apparent foreignness of its pictures, this passage from Mark provides Jesus' answer to the great prayer of Isaiah:

> "O that you would tear open the heavens and come down . . .
> to make your name known to your adversaries,
> so that the nations might tremble at your presence!
> (Isa. 64:1–2)

Here is one fundamental hope of Advent. That we watch and serve and pray believing, knowing that the God who shook the nations by sending a baby in a manger, who harrowed death by raising Jesus from the dead, that same God has not let go of the history in which we live.

Therefore we hope.

IV.

When we think of our own history in this time and this place at least two things get in the way of our hope: fear gets in the way of hope; despair gets in the way of hope.

When it comes to foreign affairs, to our relationship with other nations, fear gets in the way of hope.

I finally realized a couple of weeks ago what an odd word "terrorist" is. Nobody can make himself or herself a terrorist. He or she can be dangerous, annoying, deadly but nobody can be a terrorist unless . . . unless . . . we are terrified.

If we're terrified, terror wins. If we're hopeful, assured, sane, sober and even slightly smart, we win.

Of course, an unspeakable thing happened on 9/11/2001 but a whole number of inexcusable things have happened since we started paring away at the protections and the liberties and the compassion that mark us at our best.

If we watch in hope we know that history is finally in God's hands. If we watch in hope we know that the best way to be faithful is precisely not to be scared out of our wits and our witness.

The gates of hell will not prevail unless we concede our rights one by one. The war on terror is fought within our own hearts. We watch with hope.

V.

And the other enemy of hope is despair.

We will have different interpretations about whether all the events in Ferguson, Missouri, in recent weeks serve justice. We can say sadly that they do not serve hope.

You don't just need to watch the streets. Watch the polls. We live out different realities. In many of our cities white and Asian Americans are fairly confident that the law works; African and Hispanic Americans testify that often it does not.

In my hometown in 1968, in an area of south Los Angeles called Watts, there were terrible riots and testimony from the citizens that in their neighborhood the police were there neither to serve nor to protect.

Last week we were in California again and again watched a report on Watts. It is still a neighborhood too often steeped in poverty and driven by anger. Fifty-six years; so little change.

In the light of such evidence it would be easy to despair. But in the light of the promise of the Gospel we watch with hope. Watching is not just waiting. Watching is not passively keeping our fingers crossed and whistling in the dark.

This year the story from Watts was just a little different. It was about a youth baseball league in Watts, founded, run and coached by the LA cops. About the first small breach in the old wall of prejudice and distrust.

The baseball league has not changed the world or even the neighborhood. It is a start, like the mustard seed that becomes a great tree, like the manger that holds a savior, like the candle we lit this morning in the midst of whatever darkness tempts us to despair.

VI.

Watching is trusting in God; watching is also always working with God. When he talks about the coming end Jesus says to his disciples what he says to us: "Wake up."

> Wake up not because we're desperate but because we're faithful.
> Wake up not because we are so filled with fear but because we are so filled with hope.
> Wake up because the promise of the Gospel is not just a promise for each of us but a promise for the world in which we live. Be faithful; be hopeful; stay awake; get to work.

Our passages this morning are not prediction; they are poetry. Another poet tries to catch the hope with other words that may bring comfort too: Thornton Wilder in his play *Our Town*. The two lead characters are discussing a letter that came to a member of their community, a letter sent by a former minister who clearly uses even the postal service as a chance to preach.

Here's how the envelope read: "Jane Crofut; The Crofut Farm; Grover's Corners; Sutton County; New Hampshire; United States of America; . . . Continent of North America; Western Hemisphere; the Earth; the Solar System; the Universe; the Mind of God."[1]

The Mind of God. That is where we are. That is who we are. Watch in hope.

Amen

---

1. Thornton Wilder, *Our Town*, act 1, part 2 (New York: Harper, 1960).

24

Can Anything Good Come Out of Nazareth?

JOHN I

This sermon was preached two days after the celebration of Martin Luther King Jr.'s birthday, on January 17, 2015, at Trinity Presbyterian Church in Atlanta, Georgia.

I.

We have just come through Advent, Christmas, and Epiphany: Shepherds hurrying; angels announcing; and magi bowing. All of us singing:

> Joy to the world!
> The Lord is come:
> Let earth receive her king.[1]

We have just come through Advent, Christmas, and Epiphany, and it seems so obvious to us: Here he is, King of Kings and Lord of Lords.

But perhaps because he doesn't pay any attention to the shepherds or the kings, the Gospel writer John suggests that to the first, about to be disciples, it wasn't so obvious that this man from Nazareth could be the Messiah at all.

---

1. Isaac Watts, "Joy to the World!" *The Presbyterian Hymnal* (Louisville, KY: Westminster/John Knox Press, 1990), 40.

Philip found Nathanael and said to him: "We have found him about whom Moses in the law and also the prophets wrote, Jesus son of Joseph from Nazareth." Nathanael said to him: "Can anything good come out of Nazareth?"

(John 1:45–46)

What now seems to us so obvious was at the first entirely surprising. If God was to send a Messiah, a King, the Messiah would almost certainly not come out of so unlikely, uninteresting, out-of-the-way place as Nazareth.

How can someone from a town so out of the way turn out to be the way, the truth, and the light?

II.

This is not the only time that God uses a surprising person from a surprising place to live out God's will. It happened long ago. Elijah the great prophet came from Tish, a town so obscure no one knows where it is. He was pitted against the power of the religious establishment—the priests of Baal and against the power of the political establishment, the disastrous Ahab and his equally disastrous wife Jezebel. No one believed that Elijah could prevail against such odds. Could anything good come out of Tish?

God used a surprising person from a surprising place in these last few years, Malala . . . from Swat in Pakistan. She wrote a blog, which called the attention of many Pakistanis to the plight of girls seeking to be treated as humans despite the oppressive stratagems of the Taliban. The world began to pay attention. Can anything good come out of Swat?

Our own church began as a new church plant in Northwest Atlanta and soon founded a school. Under the leadership of Allison Williams, Trinity became the first private school in Atlanta to integrate and a brand new church showed our city a better way.

On WABE last week the story of the Georgia family where the teenage daughter came home from school deeply concerned by the plight of the poor. "We need to give more," she told her father. "What are you willing to give up?" he asked. "For instance are you willing to move into a smaller house?"

Somewhat surprisingly she said "Yes." Somewhat surprisingly her parents agreed. They live with half the space and give what they save to help feed the hungry and house the homeless. Out of a teenager's surprising response came a family faithfulness that forces me to stretch my own imagination.

III.

Can anything good come out of Nazareth? Martin Luther King Jr. himself was originally a surprising man in a surprising place. By now we have so often heard and celebrated the story of the growing civil rights movement in this country and especially the story of the Montgomery bus boycott and the Montgomery Improvement Association that we forget that for the earliest actors in the story it wasn't obvious at all that Martin Luther King Jr. would emerge as the movement's greatest leader.

The standard line is that the surprising and reticent Rosa Parks was so tired one day that she simply refused to move to the back of the bus, and a movement was born, with Martin Luther King Jr. just standing in the wings well prepared for his moment.

But the fact is that Rosa Parks had been waiting for this moment, working hard for the NAACP, taking training in community organizing, biding her time. No one who knew her was surprised when she refused to move.

But Dr. King was a surprising spokesperson for social change. He had always looked like a budding scholar. He was, after all, DOCTOR King. He didn't have an honorary doctorate but a real PhD earned at a real university by the young man who got into Morehouse without having to graduate from high school and was first in his class at Crozer Seminary.

What everybody expected was that young Dr. King would preach sermons that sounded more like a PhD seminar than like a Baptist homily and bide his time until Morehouse or Crozer or some other distinguished institution called him to come teach philosophical theology.

Even the night of the first community meeting it was not that Dr. King stepped forward to fulfill his destiny. He was the host pastor for the meeting called to consider a response to the events with Rosa Parks. So of course he had to say a few words. When he was through speaking it was obvious that the man had gifts for causes even greater than the causes of philosophical theology. Something really good came out of Nazareth.

King was as surprised as anybody, and some days understandably he was disillusioned and disappointed. In the first lesson for today Elijah bemoans the fact that he is suffering for God. In one of his early sermons, Martin Luther King Jr. remembers his own such doubts

Late at night he was asleep in the manse in Montgomery and was awakened by a phone call, threatening and mean. He went down to his kitchen put his head on the table and prayed:

I am here taking a stand for what I believe is right, but now I am afraid. The people are looking to me for leadership, and if I stand before them without strength and courage they, too, will falter. I am at the end of my powers, I have nothing left.

And yet King still believed the promise that God could bring something good out of Montgomery.

Here is how King remembered the answer to his prayer.

"At the moment of distress," King wrote, "it seemed as though I could hear the quiet assurance of an inner voice, saying, 'Stand up for righteousness, stand up for truth, God will be at your side forever.'"[2]

"Can anything good come out of Nazareth?" By the surprising mercy of God the answer is yes, again and again and again.

IV.

One thing more. This week for the first time I realized that in John's Gospel that question is the prologue to the deeper question. Not just, "Can anything good come out of Nazareth?" but, "Can anything good come out of Calvary?"

The fact that the Messiah came from Nazareth was a surprise. The fact that the Messiah was crucified was a disaster.

All that promise, all that hope, all that bright assuredness hung on a cross to die. It seemed so sad, so hopeless.

And yet there is still the promise. Can anything good come out of Calvary? For the New Testament and perhaps most emphatically for the Gospel of John the answer is Yes. Great good can come, has come, will come out of Calvary.

When he has Jesus crucified Pilate puts a sign above the cross. He puts it to mock Jesus but it really praises Jesus. It names the crucified one in all the great languages of the world: This is "Jesus of Nazareth." He is "the King of the Jews" (John 19:19).

From the cross Jesus cries out what is the clearest word of triumph in John's Gospel. "It is completed" he says (v. 30 CEB). That is not a cry of loss; it is a claim of victory.

Dealing with the mystery of the cross Christians have often claimed from the beginning of time God's plan was that Jesus would have to die for us in order to bring us to God.

2. Martin Luther King, Jr., *Stride toward Freedom: The Montgomery Story* (Boston: Beacon Press, 2010), 114.

I do not pretend to know the eternal mind of God, but I can tell you how the story worked. Had Jesus not been crucified but simply preached wisely splendid wisdom till he died at a ripe old age, Jesus would most likely have been forgotten. At best his sayings would have been appended to the real Bible as a kind of afterthought like Ben Sirach or the Wisdom of Solomon.

Can anything good come out of Calvary? Our faith came out of Calvary.

IV.

That brings us back to Martin Luther King Jr., whose life we celebrate today. Was it God's plan from the beginning that King should be martyred so that we would pay attention to his message? Here I am more bold. I don't believe that for a minute.

Could God use King's martyrdom for the sake of the justice and equality in which King believed? God could; God did; God does.

Can God use what look to us like defeats, losses, setbacks, and disasters to move history toward God's own purposes? God can. God does. God will.

Tavis Smiley, in his dramatic retelling called *The Death of a King*, reminds us that King's popularity was fading fast at the time of the visit to Memphis where he lost his life.

He had frustrated his closest followers by insisting on paying attention to Vietnam as well as to Memphis. He had frustrated all of us who worked for racial equality but weren't so sure about economic equity.

Smiley tells us that the polls the week of King's death indicated that 75 percent of the American people had turned against his leadership and that 57 percent of his own people considered him irrelevant.

Now—after his martyrdom, we are still far from fulfilling his dream or understanding his vision. But it is not insignificant that schools are closed tomorrow and that soon his statue will stand on the capitol grounds a few miles from the church he and his father served.

This is a good day to remember the way King ended that sermon about the frightful night in Montgomery when his life was threatened and he turned to God.

Here is what King preached:

> (God's promise) will give our tired feet new strength as we continue our forward stride toward the city of freedom. When our days become dreary with low-hovering clouds and our nights become darker than a thousand midnights, let us remember that there is a great benign power in our universe whose name is God. Our God is

able to make a way out of no way and transform dark yesterdays into bright tomorrows.

This is our hope for becoming better people. This is our mandate for seeking . . . a better world.[3]

To which we all can say: Amen.
Amen

---

3. Martin Luther King, Jr., "Our God Is Able," in *Strength through Love* (Philadelphia: Fortress Press, 1981), 114.

25

The Acceptable Time

JOB 38

2 CORINTHIANS 6:1–11

This sermon was preached on June 21, 2015, at Trinity Presbyterian Church in Atlanta, Georgia. The shooting referred to in this sermon happened at the Emanuel African Methodist Episcopal Church in Charleston, South Carolina. On June 17, a young man (21 years of age) walked into the church, joined a prayer group, and then proceeded to shoot and kill nine members of the church and seriously wound three others. The young man was a white supremacist; the victims were African American.

By midweek the preparation for this sermon was well under way. We would talk about the difficulty and grace of knowing acceptable times: acceptable times for me to retire; acceptable times for this church to accept its growing and changing ministry.

And then suddenly after the shooting in Charleston this week became an entirely unacceptable time and the sermon changed.

My gratitude for you has not changed; my prayers for the years to come, unchanged. But the focus of the sermon could not stay the same.

This is Father's Day. Somewhat interestingly my father never preached on the themes of Father's Day, but he did preach many memorable sermons.

One sermon came in the midst of a controversial election season in Los Angeles when a group of community leaders, especially people of faith, had come together to support a new slate of candidates for the school board. The issues would seem old fashioned now, but then it seemed that the educational hopes for Los Angeles children were at stake.

When my father's name appeared prominently in the ads for a new school board he got a number of letters and phone calls urging him to get out of politics and stick to the gospel.

Here is pretty much what he said in the next sermon he preached. "What Gospel do you read? I read the gospel that says in as much as we hurt one of the least of these, we hurt our Lord. I read the gospel that says if anyone harms one of these little children it would be better for that person to have a millstone hung around the neck and be cast into the deepest sea."

So partly in honor of my father but mostly in honor of the gospel, here are a few thoughts for this unacceptable week . . . thoughts that I believe are deeply grounded in the word of God.

II.

First a few words about the text from Job. I am officially the theologian in residence at this church but every pastor is really a theologian in residence, and after a week like this people ask theologians absolutely rightly: How can God let these things happen?

And every theologian should know enough to answer: "I do not know."

There's something a little weird about the word theologian, anyway, a scholar of Theo-logy. Bio-logy is the study of living things; it works best when we use a microscope or dissecting tools to look at the details of human life. Psycho-logy is the study of the human consciousness; it works best when we take careful empirical measurements or when we spend long hours gathering the trickiest details of another person's life.

But THEO logy . . . the study of the living God? Who would dare to be a theologian; who would dare to claim to have the right tools, or enough evidence, or know enough of the secrets of the almighty to be a theologian?

Job, as you will remember, was the first theologian in residence. He was resident on a dung heap, which didn't help, and he spent thirty-seven chapters trying to psychoanalyze his Creator.

At the end God would have none of it.

> Then the LORD answered Job out of the whirlwind: "Who is this that darkens counsel by words without knowledge? Gird up your loins like a man, I will question you, and you shall declare to me: Where were you when I laid the foundation of the earth? Tell me, if you have understanding. Who determined its measurements—surely you know!
> (Job 38:1–5)

Listen beloved, when we theologians have thought our hardest and done our best and spoken most eloquently we have only touched the aura of the edge of the hem of the garment of the majesty of God.

Just when we prepare to write most copiously or speak most loudly we should be most humble. There is so much we do not know.

Does God desire such pain, such suffering? Of course not.

Does God demand such awful sacrifice? I don't believe that either.

Then "Why?" I do not know.

III.

There is a great line in the Epistle to the Hebrews. "We do not yet see the fullness of the counsels of our God, but we do see Jesus" (Hebrews 2:8–9 au. trans.)

That is what Paul tells us in 2 Corinthians again and again. The reason Paul says that this is the acceptable time is not because it is either an easy or a pleasant time. He says that he himself has suffered "in afflictions, hardships, calamities and beatings."

It is the acceptable time because it is the time in which God in Jesus Christ offers forgiveness, guidance, courage, that old-fashioned word: salvation . . . which doesn't just mean getting to heaven, it means serving the heavenly goods on earth.

Look out when theologians tell you they can explain exactly why Jesus had to suffer so that we might come closer to God. But listen to the old, old story and trust the old, old assurance: that awful time of his death was also the gracious time when God got just as near to us as breathing; hurt with our very hurts, wounded with our very pain.

The most unacceptable time is the time in which God accepted us most deeply.

When Martin Rinkart wrote his great hymn "Now Thank We All Our God" he was not sitting at Holden Beach watching the pelicans dip over the waves. He was sitting in a town devastated by the thirty years war having lost most of his family and the strength of his nation.

He sat under the shadow of the cross and wrote:

Now thank we all our God
With heart and hands and voices,
Who wondrous things hath done,
In whom His world rejoices;

Who, from our mothers' arms,
Hath blest us on our way
With countless gifts of love,
And still is ours today

IV.

But notice one thing more. It is not just that Paul accepts God's mercy in Jesus Christ, Paul calls us to join in his ministry—all of us. "I speak [to you] as to my children—open wide your hearts" (v. 13 NIV).

In this most unacceptable time we accept God's mercy by opening wide our hearts.

We pledge to grow in understanding. We pledge to move from stereotyping and generalization and put downs, to listening and knowing and raising each other up.

Tom Jones said that this week he learned like the rest of us that Memorial AME church in Charleston was the church where Denmark Vesey had tried to stir South Carolina slaves to rebellion in the early nineteenth century. For Tom as for most of us Vesey was always held up as a terrible example; for the people of that church in Charleston, he was a hero. We begin by beginning to understand.

We have begun conversations with the other Trinity Presbyterian Church, the one in Decatur, where the membership is almost entirely African American and they are trying to understand their new neighbors, who are almost entirely Hispanic.

Pam and I have begun those conversations and Jane and Pam will carry them on. We have no idea where they will lead, but Paul's admonition is not bad: "I speak as to my children—open wide your hearts."

V.

Open wide our hearts not just of understanding, but of reconciliation: forgiveness. Did you see who showed up at the first hearing for the young man who killed all those Christians; the families of the Christians. Not talking about closure or restitution or the great biblical injunction of taking an eye for an eye, an injunction, incidentally, which our Lord said had absolutely no place in the practice of his disciples—us.

They were talking about mercy, about forgiveness.

They were living out the acceptable time of God in the midst of unacceptable hatred and violence.

Not that many months ago I stood right here after Newtown and addressed the ease with which we can get guns and use guns to enforce our prejudices or enact our hatreds or indulge our manias.

The last words of the sermon, as I remember it, were: Enough! This church under the leadership of Jamie Brownlee and Pam Driesell and Matthew Ruffner and a host of others have said that loudly and clearly and will continue to say it, thanks be to God.

But not nearly enough has changed, and the cry "enough" turns into a more plaintive cry: "How long, O Lord."

VI.

All this is far removed from the sermon I started to write as the week began.

I think it is the acceptable time for me to retire. I have had no special visions and no word from on high, just the deepening conviction that it is time to live another way.

Robert Frost reminds me that I have promises to keep and miles to go before I sleep, but I've kept most of my promises, and there are not that many miles left.

Now is the acceptable time for Trinity to open your hearts to a complicated, fearful and angry world as time after time you have opened your hearts to Carol and to me.

This is not my last sermon; this is not even my last sermon here.

But it's my last sermon for this time.

May the words of my mouth, the meditations of our hearts, and the courage of our actions be acceptable in the sight of God, who is our rock and our redeemer.

Amen.

26

Two Returns

LUKE 15:1–3, 11B–32

This sermon was preached at Trinity Presbyterian Church on March 13, 2016. The "Agape children" referred to in the sermon are the children who participate in the tutoring program called "Agape," which was started by church members and which meets at the church. The day ends with the children having dinner before their parents come to pick them up. It was suggested that the church, which had a congregational dinner on Thursday evenings, invite the Agape children to join us for dinner. While many members supported the idea and volunteered weekly to help serve the meal, there was a very small group who felt that the Thursday night dinner was for "our" families and should not include the Agape children.

I.

After my first year in Divinity School I returned to my home church, the First Baptist Church of Los Angeles, to preach the morning sermon.

I chose every seminarian's favorite parable, the parable of the Prodigal Son, and I did what pretty much every seminarian does, I waxed eloquent about the Prodigal—his wasteful but exciting journey to the far country, his edifying move toward existential self-awareness when he found himself in a pig sty, his long and penitent journey home.

But then like pretty much every seminarian I gave very short shrift to the older brother, out there in the field. "Self-righteous," I said. "Self-satisfied," I said, insufficiently aware of the doctrine of original sin.

Then a sermonic flashback to the prodigal's party, the fatted calf, the general rejoicing. Organ swells up with "Just as I am" and we move to the benediction.

After church the chair of the church's board of trustees, Milton Mackaig, and his wife invited me out for lunch. We hadn't gotten far into the meal when Milton came to the point. "I think the older brother always gets mistreated in these sermons." He said, "I've tried to be a good husband and parent, a good citizen, I've given time and money and lots of effort to this church, and the parable I like best in the New Testament is when the master says to the very responsible servant: 'Well done, good and faithful servant, enter into the joy of your master.'"

From that day until this I have always tried to give a more sympathetic account of both brothers—as of course Jesus does in the parable. And I went back to the parable this week to see what we could say briefly about each of them.

II.

Notice to start with why Jesus tells this parable. He is responding to the criticism of his opponents that he eats with tax collectors and sinners. The criticism that sets him off on his storytelling is this: "This fellow welcomes sinners and eats with them" (Luke 15:2).

"All right," says Jesus, "Let me tell you what kind of a fellow I really am. I'm a fellow like the shepherd who goes and seeks the lost sheep. I'm a fellow like the widow who turns the house inside out looking for the lost coin. I'm a fellow like the father who goes looking after two sons."

III.

I'm a fellow, says Jesus, like the Father who welcomed the son returning from the far country. Full of himself, proud of himself, the son treated the father as if he were dead while he was still very much alive.

Grabbed his goods and headed to the far country—that place we all know which is just as far from home as we think we can possibly go.

Wasted his substance, the story says, dribbled away his goods and his goodness and woke up one day in a pig sty surrounded by animals his father had told him were unclean.

Then, because he felt guilty or because he felt hungry or because like most of us he found it hard to distinguish between the two he came to himself: came to himself, looked at himself in an imaginary mirror; stepped outside himself and saw this poor imitation of himself—jealous of the pigs because they had enough to eat.

And then began the long return. Mumbling to himself the little speech he would try on his father. "Father I have sinned against heaven and before you; I am no longer worthy to be called your son" (v. 21b).

Along the long road until at last the farm house comes into view, wondering what kind of welcome he'll receive until, before he can even start to mumble his speech, he sees the old man hitch up his skirts or pull up his trousers, come eagerly down the porch steps, stretch out his arms, welcome him home.

Who is this fellow? They ask of Jesus. He's the fellow in whom God reaches out to us when we are in the farthest country we can imagine—the country of unfaith or unhope, the desolate place of disappointment or disaffection or despair.

The fellow in whom God takes our imperfect repentance for perfect repentance and gets the music playing and the banquet baking.

IV.

And also, says Jesus, I am the fellow who is like the father who comes down off the porch a second time to go and find the elder brother.

The elder brother is coming down the road, too. I just noticed that this week. The elder brother is coming down the road, and the father heads out to welcome him, too. And now the question isn't whether he will return to the father but whether he will turn to the brother.

"Listen!" says the older brother. "For all these years I have been working like a slave for you, and I have never disobeyed your command; yet you have never given me even a young goat that I might celebrate with my friends" (v. 29).

And now notice what the father doesn't say.

He doesn't say: "Shame on you. You've always been self-righteous and self-satisfied, so just stand out here and stew."

He says: "Son, you are always with me, and all that is mine is yours" (v. 31). He says just what Milton Mackaig always wanted him to say: "Well done, you good and faithful servant, enter into the joy of your father."

But then he also says: Come in, join the party.

The older brother stammers on: "But when this son of yours came back you killed for him the fatted calf." This son of yours.

The father will not let him get away with that. "Your brother . . . not just my son, but my son and therefore your brother . . . your brother was dead and is alive again, he was lost and is found."

Jesus is the fellow in whom God greets us when we come back from the far country and brings us to the one whom he calls father.

Jesus is the one in whom God greets us when we stand affronted and aloof and brings us the ones whom he calls "brother," "sister."

"That son of yours is such a bleeding heart liberal"—your brother
"That daughter of yours is such a hopeless conservative"—your sister
"Those refugees of yours are so ill-fitted to be in America"—your brothers and sisters
"Our children don't really feel very comfortable with the Agape children"—who are also our children

V.

There is a back story on Milton Mackaig, the man who quite rightly saw himself as the elder brother. I may have told it here before, but while you weren't looking I turned seventy-five, so I've earned the right to repeat myself.

Some years before I preached the sermon on the Prodigal Son at the First Baptist Church of Los Angeles, the first African American family ever had applied for membership in that congregation.

After a very long and contentious debate, the congregation voted down their application. The man who had been pastor for twenty-two years resigned in sorrow. One of the leaders of the opposition was Milton Mackaig.

After a long interim the church called my father to be its pastor and a few years after another African American came forward to join the church: his name was Neil Rose. And because lots of people had prayed and argued and listened to my father's sermons for three years, this time the congregation voted to welcome Neil as a member.

Neil not only joined the church, he joined the choir. But after his first Sunday, someone came down to the choir room while Neil was putting away his music and beat him rather soundly.

Of course the word spread, and people were worried about Neil's safety and about the church's unity. The next Sunday as the choir processed we looked back and to our relief saw Neil in his proper place, with his beautiful baritone voice. And next to him, for the first time ever in a choir robe, Milton Mackaig in a brand new place, with a fairly awful baritone voice.

Some years later at the farewell dinner for my parents, Milton Mackaig spoke. "I have learned a lot from our pastor," he said, "but most of what I learned is what it means to say that in Jesus Christ we are all brothers and sisters."

VI.

Younger brother, younger sister.

Older brother, older sister.

Jesus is the one in whom God brings us to God's self when we have stuck ourselves in some far country of the soul.

Jesus is the one who brings us to our brothers or our sisters when we stand outside the party in some odd conviction of our own specialness.

In Jesus Christ God has brought us all home from afar. In Jesus Christ God invites us all to join all our brothers and sisters in one amazing party.

For God's sake, let's go in.

27

"The Word Became Flesh"

JOHN 1:1–18

In his later years, David's father, Gene E. Bartlett, served as Senior Minister of the First Baptist Church of Newton, in Newton, Massachusetts, until his retirement. David preached this sermon on the occasion of his retirement on December 21, 1980.

I.

Today marks not only a celebratory event for this congregation; it is also a celebration for our family. Therefore I hope you'll forgive me if I begin with a familial word.

For years the five Bartlett children have been regularly subjected to the fundamental occupational hazards of ministers' children: we have been used and reused in sermon illustrations. Perhaps it is appropriate for this rite of passage if we pass the torch to the next generation of long-suffering preacher's kids and use my father's grandchildren to make a point.

Our children are still very small but already very mobile, so our Christmas tree, traditionally decorated with bright and breakable delights, untraditionally sits in the middle of a playpen, designed to keep the Christmas beauty visible but unreachable. Presents which might otherwise sit tantalizingly underneath the tree are hidden in closets behind locked doors. And last week we brought out our favorite crèche from Nigeria, its figures carved in marvelous but fragile detail from thin wood—a crèche we found only after several years of searching and purchased at some expense.

Naturally we wanted to share the crèche with the children, but naturally we didn't want them to destroy what we had sought long and greatly cherished. So as I held the children more or less in tow, my wife brought out each of the carved figures from its box and explained to the children: here was the shepherd, here some sheep and a goat; here the angel; here the wise men; here Mary, Joseph. After she introduced the children to each figure, I carefully placed the figure in its appropriate place, on a very high mantelpiece, not out of sight but very much out of reach.

Finally, from its careful packing Carol unwrapped the manger with its small, fragile figure. Here was the tiniest piece of all. I watched the children with particular care. Least of all did I want the infant to be dirtied or damaged or broken.

"This is the baby Jesus," said my wife, placing the manger on the mantelpiece.

The ceremony ended with everything safe, and we went about our business or our play until the next morning when Benjamin, who is almost two, came in from his bedroom to survey the Advent wonders, canvassed the tree, and then moved toward the mantelpiece, pointed his finger, and with proud recognition exclaimed: "Baby Jesus in the air."

That of course is where we would keep him, left to our own devices and intuitions. Jesus in the air: where he could not be dirtied or damaged or broken. Jesus in the air: a benign ideal, not burdened with particularity or history: nor ever quite knowing the pressures, the compromises, the disappointments or the dirt of real humanity.

And certainly (if we were to write the story) Jesus not finally broken at the hands of folk who thought that they were only doing what was best.

But what we celebrate this Christmas is God's astonishing unwillingness to be cautious; God's unwillingness to protect divinity from the corruptions and the pains of humankind. God's astonishing insistence that "Jesus in the air," Jesus without risks or dirt or loss, is no sufficient savior, no sufficient picture of the love of God.

And so the Word became flesh: got entangled with curious hands, grubby fingers, almost unintentional brutality. For us, the great confession says, and for our salvation.

II.

John's Gospel suggests more than that as well. In ways appropriate to the special recognition of ministry on this Sunday, John's Gospel suggests that the incarnation, the enfleshment of God goes on. In John's Gospel more than any other the community of faith, the church, becomes the place where God's love and mercy and judgment are rescued from the air, where Christ is still present in the dirt and compromise and fragility of human action.

And even today, the Christmas promise, that Word comes close as flesh, is a promise for the church as well.

Because God's Word comes close as human flesh, we are not surprised that it is subject to the vagaries of flesh. We are not surprised that the human words of the best sermons, for example, are sometimes misstated and sometimes misunderstood. We are also not surprised that sometimes when the preacher is least satisfied the Word is most present; that what was not quite meant becomes the healing word, that what was said brokenly helps make life whole.

Because God's Word comes close in human flesh, we are not surprised that the church's fellowship does not look exactly like the heavenly council and that no one would confuse the debates of congregations in Chicago or Newton with the celestial harmony of angels. But we are also not surprised that among fragile egos, occasional rivalries, and necessary compromise, God's own rich fellowship does reach out. That we grow closer to each other than we had ever thought to be. That when one of us suffers, the others suffer and in the joy of one we all find reason for exceeding joy.

Because God's Word comes close in human flesh, we are not surprised that the church does not enter the world of political concern unsullied. We are not amazed when our best laid plans go ever so slightly awry, when we discover that there is no gain without loss and no victory without someone being victimized. But we are also not surprised when here and there our witness counts: some structure budges slightly; some law moves toward broader humanity.

What has shown most strongly in my father's ministry, in my parent's ministry, that ministry we celebrate today, has been that strong commitment to the Word enfleshed in church, and in the local church. Words my father wrote in his journal twenty years ago speak rightly of his ministry in and for local churches, perhaps, I may say, especially of the deeply happy ministry he and my mother have shared in this church:

> [I confess] the definite bias of a great affection. After these years, there seems to me no greater honor that can come to a man [now he'd say no greater honor that can come to a person] than the invitation, "Come, be our pastor." What this offers, of course, is not a guarantee, but a tremendous possibility. It is a possibility to be involved for life,

your life, the life of others, and, I believe, the life of Jesus Christ in our world . . . in the abiding sense that in the relationships with the church Christ becomes most real.

III.

And that brings me to a final suggestion. In John's Gospel more than any other the disciples as individual Christians, as individual ministers almost, represent, re-present, Christ's incarnation.

Now there are dangers in that kind of suggestion, dangers that ministers, or more probably parishioners, will think that the clergy should somehow be little Christs. Close to home, indeed, one can recall the dangers of too glowing praise even for a minister as praiseworthy as my father.

On a similar occasion some years ago in Los Angeles, as Dad was ending his ministry there, one of the more eloquent and even flowery laymen had asked to deliver the morning prayer. After some minutes spent commending my father to the care of the Creator and commending the Creator on the creation of my father, the prayer moved to a dramatic and unavoidable climax:

"All this we pray in the name of the God of Abraham (pause); Isaac (long dramatic pause) and BARTLETT."

I doubt if Jacob in the heavenly court was offended by his omission, but Bartlett, sitting behind the pulpit, was visibly embarrassed.

It is important not to confuse the pastor with the patriarch or the preacher with that greater one whom he proclaims.

Nonetheless, the richest ministries, the ministries we remember and celebrate, do show forth congruity between the Gospel they preach and the Gospel they live. In such ministries the Gospel is never enfleshed perfectly, as it was in that great Incarnation Christmas celebrates, but you can sense the Gospel always struggling to be born. You can catch glimpses of the Word, the Word of love and justice and compassion, not only in what the preacher says but in what the preacher lives.

So while we rightly and centrally celebrate the one true incarnation of God's Word in Jesus Christ, it is not inappropriate to celebrate the ways in which the Word is modestly enfleshed, generation after generation, century after century in faithful Christian ministers.

It is not inappropriate to be glad for the integrity of your pastor, who is my father and my pastor, who does live what he speaks with remarkable congruity. And if the manger is the one great sign of God's goodness to us, the ministry we celebrate is an appropriately humbler sign of that continuing, smashing goodness.

Fourteen years ago my father preached the ordination sermon which began my ministry. He closed by quoting an anonymous devotional writing called "The Cloud of Unknowing." The words with which he initiated me into my ministry were these: "Continue faithfully in your work, and I promise you God will be faithful in His."

I was grateful for the words; I am more grateful for my father's ministry, which has enfleshed them all these years.

Amen.

28

More than Conquerors

ROMANS 8

This sermon was preached at Yorkminster Church in Toronto, Ontario, Canada, on August 17, 2014.

One of the great privileges of being a teacher is that you have the opportunity to gain wisdom and insight from your students. But today I want to quote the very first doctoral student I ever taught. His name is Stan Smith. Stan was so inspired by my New Testament courses that he almost immediately left PhD studies and headed for the parish, but in our years together he reflected once on this great verse from Romans 8:37: "In all these things we are more than conquerors through him who loved us."

What Stan noticed was that as you read Romans you realize that Paul isn't saying: "We are more triumphant than other conquerors" or "We always beat the competition." What Paul is saying is that our lives are not a matter of conquering at all.

We are more than conquerors because we are other than conquerors. Conquest is not our business.

The Gospel is our business, pastors and laypeople alike, we are about the good news of God's love for us in Jesus Christ.

Here's the thing about conquerors: Conquerors need to conquer because they need to show that they are important, worthwhile, winners.

That I suppose is why Alexander the Great wept when there were no more worlds to conquer. That is why we sometimes weep when we can't manage to conquer even the lesser territories we take on. Maybe we're just not worth much of anything.

But here is what Paul says. If our worth does not come from our achieve-ments but from God's love for us, then we are more than conquerors because we are freed from the conquest game. That's why Paul's whole sentence goes like this: "In all these things we are more than conquerors through him who loved us." We are more than conquerors because we don't have to prove a thing. We are already worthwhile, valuable, loved.

II.

Of course for Paul the proof of this love was Jesus Christ who was himself preeminently more than a conqueror precisely because he refused conquest.

Paul had looked for a Messiah who would triumph over Rome and its pow-ers. The one thing the Messiah could not do was be defeated by those powers. The one thing the Messiah could not do would be to get executed by those powers. So that crucified Jesus, that conquered Jesus—he could not be Mes-siah and Lord.

The great revelation that came to Paul on the Road to Damascus was this: the one who was conquered was greater than the conquerors.

Because that cross, which looked so much like a sign of defeat was instead the profound and acting out of the enduring, suffering, inescapable love of God.

"What then shall we say to this?" asks Paul. "If God is for us, who can be against us?" (v. 31 NABRE).

Christ the conquered is more than conqueror.

III.

The church is also more than a conqueror, because when we are true to our-selves we are not finally about conquest at all.

I realize that I am not especially qualified to talk about the social situation of the church in Canada, though I do eat regularly at Tim Hortons and my brother is a hockey agent and I smiled knowingly when Mr. Obama told Mr. Trudeau to enjoy his youthful black head of hair while it lasted.

I grew up in the '40s and '50s of the last century, and in the United States we were all very excited about the church triumphant. At the beginning of the century lots of more liberal Protestants like you and me started a new maga-zine for other mainline Protestants and called it boastingly *The Christian Cen-tury*. The magazine is still going but it's a lot more modest than it used to be.

More evangelical Protestants started a journal called *Christianity Today* which continues to publish helpful articles even though for many of the coming generations it might better be called "Christianity Yesterday."

When the National Council of Churches dedicated its new headquarters in New York City the Protestant churches were so influential that President Eisenhower came to town to speak at the ceremony.

More evangelical Christians were even more optimistic about the triumph of the faith. The Southern Baptists of my youth began a massive evangelism campaign whose slogan was: "A Million More in Fifty-Four and Every One a Tither."

More people joined the churches in those years than at any time in the history of our country—before or since. We did not worry about being more than conquerors because we were so obviously on our way to triumph.

Now there are those who are very worried about the decline in numbers of your denomination and my denomination and the mainline churches are now called the old line churches.

In our country at least many of the most successful churches are successful precisely because they preach a gospel of success. The more faithful you are the more God will bless you—which means increase your income. And the higher your income, the more obviously are you blessed. And there is a corollary: the bigger your church the more obviously faithful because you are so clearly prospering. Super conquerors.

But the Gospel reminds us that we are not in the conquest business. We do not know if the church will grow bigger or richer in the years ahead. We do not know which denominations will flourish or whether denominations themselves will wither away.

What we do know is that we are called to be the servants and the proclaimers of the love of God in Jesus Christ, and as long as we do that, the gates of hell will not prevail against us.

Nor the gates of apathy; nor the gates of discouragement.

We are more than conquerors through him who loved us.

IV.

And then a word about church leaders, too. That remarkable group of the faithful who actually give their Saturdays to a synod meeting. The ministers who toil over preaching and pastoral care, the faithful who take on the Christian education of our children; those who sing in the choir, those who balance the books. Not one of those services a high profile, financially rewarding option. But here's the deal:

When we are faithful we are more than conquerors, too.

When Paul wrote Romans there were no seminaries, no ordinations, no elders, and no official clergy. All that was to come.

But there were apostles, preachers like Paul, and Paul was already in trouble. In one of the churches he had founded, just after he left, a whole host of hotshot preachers came in, flashier than he, more articulate, masters of persuasion and wizards of church growth.

"Paul writes pretty good letters," they said, "But as a preacher and expert in churchly success, he's no conqueror."

Paul called his wandering successors "super apostles" and he didn't mean it as a compliment.

The church at Rome has never met Paul so when he introduces himself to the Romans he says: "I am Paul, I am a servant of Jesus Christ, I am set apart for the Gospel" (1:1 au. trans.).

I am more than a conqueror because I'm not in the conquest business; I am more than a success because I'm not anxious about succeeding.

"I am not anxious about success I am eager for the gospel," says the apostle.

All of us church leaders can learn from Paul on that.

I hope that it's not just because I'm an aging curmudgeon but I've noticed a kind of shift in ordination and installation services through the years. Too often more and more emphasis is placed on the wonderful qualities of the new minister and not enough emphasis on the redemptive qualities of the gospel.

You sometimes feel as if we might just as well give up reading scripture and read the new minister's resume instead.

Or the welcoming of new members. It's great to say a few words about each new member, but probably not so good to linger longer over the lawyer while short-circuiting the postal carrier or the retired teacher or the loyal spouse.

Two weeks ago my divinity school had its annual reunion, and gave out awards for alumni and alumnae of the year.

Now like Saint Paul I'm going to criticize bragging while I brag, but it gets better, I hope. One of the awards went to the new presiding bishop of the Episcopal Church in the United States. One went to a theologian who has just published a massive and massively impressive two-volume study of how Christians understand human life. One went to a woman who had founded one of the most impressive equal rights groups in our country. One went to a classmate of mine who had been dean of a major divinity school, president of two first-rate universities and head of the International Rescue Organization . . . though I was not the least bit jealous.

I remarked to my spouse afterward that I looked forward to the reunion when the alumni awards went to another of my classmates who had been a Methodist pastor in small churches in Minnesota for forty years, or to the woman had singlehandedly revived the dying Kentucky Council of Churches or to the classmate who had never gotten ordained, had gone into the family business, but spent every weekend leading the youth group of the local church—year after year after year.

Because what's wonderful and gracious about those people is that they are every one of them more than conquerors. More than successful: because not worried about success. More than superstars: because they are servants of the Servant.

Paul's final claim in this chapter of Romans shows us the good news that we proclaim. Paul's final claim in this chapter gives us the promise that enables us to be church, to be ministers, to be elders, to be Christian, to be faithful.

> For I am persuaded that neither death nor life, nor angels, nor rulers, nor things present, nor things to come, nor powers, nor height, nor depth, nor anything else in all creation will be able to separate us from the love of God in Christ Jesus our Lord.
>
> (vv. 38–39, au. trans.)

"For I am persuaded that neither death nor life . . ."
(Not the days when church life is exhaustingly lively and not the days when it is deadly familiar; not the days when the world thinks we count for a lot and not the days when the world thinks that faith is way past its expiration date.)
"nor angels, nor rulers, nor things present, nor things to come"
(Not the pretty good values that get in the way of the truly good God; not the government at its most helpful or its most intrusive; not the economy at its most flourishing or its most punishing.)
"nor powers, nor height, nor depth, nor anything else in all creation"
(Not the power of prejudice or the power of fear. Not the height of winning, not the depth of loss; not trying to conquer, not learning to fail.)
None of that "will be able to separate us from the love of God in Christ Jesus our Lord."
None of it. None.
Amen.

29

This We Believe: Who Is God?
Maker of Heaven and Earth

GENESIS 1:1–7, 26–28
PSALM 8

This sermon was preached on October 17, 2009, at The Congregational Church of New Canaan, New Canaan, Connecticut. This sermon was the first in a series entitled "This We Believe," preached once a month at the church's request.

In 1961 Gene Bartlett, my father and Jonah Bartlett's grandfather, wrote a book called *The Audacity of Preaching*. Were he alive to revise the book today he would have to add at least a footnote on the audacity of preaching a series of sermons called "This We Believe."

It is audacious, maybe even foolish, to take on such a series because the topic so exceeds the ability of any preacher to explore its meanings. It is also audacious because I don't claim to speak just for myself but to try to articulate what we as Christians have believed through the years and continue to believe today.

The point of the series is that the Christian business isn't so much a solo as a symphony. It has been played through the ages by a vast orchestra on diverse instruments, and we play it still. I think if we listen carefully we can catch some of the symphony's themes.

One more warning: When I look at the great themes of the Christian symphony, both today and during the months ahead, I will always begin with the Bible. There are a number of reasons why that is so, but that's another sermon. Stick with my metaphor and just presume with me for today that the Bible is the score for our common symphony, though it leaves plenty of room for improvisation and variation and surprise.

I.

At any rate, the first theme of the symphony is clear enough. If we were a creed-saying church we would say every Sunday, "We believe in God, the Father Almighty, Maker of Heaven and Earth." Since we are a Bible reading church, we open the Bible and the first words are clear enough. "In the beginning God created the heavens and the earth" (Gen. 1:1 RSV).

There is no way to capture the depth and variety of what Christians believe about creation, so I have tried to focus this morning on four central claims.

> First, creation is not about proof but about praise.
> Second, creation is not about ancestors, it's about images, about us being made in the image of God.
> Third, creation is not just about then but about now.
> Fourth, creation is not just about Adam and Eve. It's about Jesus.

First, then, creation is not about proof, it's about praise.

A few years ago on an October day I was walking through downtown New Haven. It was one of those October days when you can't imagine wanting to live anywhere besides Connecticut. Leaves turning; sky absolutely blue; clouds absolutely white; everything as fresh as the first morning in Eden.

I started to walk past a man walking the other way. Somewhat surprisingly for New Haven, he stopped to say: "Good morning."

"Good morning," I replied. "It's a beautiful day."

"Yes," he said. "It makes you proud to be an American."

It wasn't quite clear where he was going with that, but it was perfectly clear where he was coming from. On a day that shines like glory we want to glorify something—we want to glorify someone.

E. E. Cummings was a poet of the first part of the twentieth century. He was not overburdened by orthodoxy, but looking at his own New England day he captured better than the passing stranger what the Bible says:

> i thank you God for most this amazing
> day:for the leaping greenly spirits of trees
> and a blue true dream of sky;and for everything
> which is natural which is infinite which is yes."[1]

So many of the debates about the book of Genesis, and the belief in creation, assume that Genesis was written to answer the question "How was the

---

1. e.e. Cummings, "I Thank You God for Most This Amazing," in *Complete Poems 1904–1962*, ed. George J. Firmage (New York: Liveright Publishing Corp., 2013).

world made?" But maybe Genesis was written to answer this different question: "Whom should we thank?"

The poet, Cummings, gives his own answer:

> how should tasting touching hearing seeing
> breathing any—lifted from the no
> of all nothing—human merely being
> doubt unimaginable You?"[2]

I've not read Richard Dawkins latest book, only the reviews and the ads, but the impression I get is that this so-called "new atheist" is asking a familiar question: "We stand in awe before the majesty of what?" His answer is "In awe of evolution's process." Our answer is: "We stand in awe of God's person." The hymn we sang this morning captures it, too. Not "How can we reason about our origins?" but "How do your creatures say Thanks?"

In the beginning, God.

II.

Now a second claim. Creation is not just about ancestors, it's about images, about humankind being made in the image of God.

Look, as we celebrate the 200th anniversary of Darwin's birth, we know that he was onto something. We got here in ways that were more complicated and more prolonged than the writers of Genesis would have dreamed. And it is not just that we have dominion over the animals; we have an ancestry to share with them. But what we claim as Christians is that there is not just one true story about who we are; there are at least two true stories.

One story says that we are descended by a complicated and contentious process from the earliest one-celled animals. The other story says that we are made in the image of God—male and female. Maybe both stories are true. Bear with me while I try a kind of analogy.

Suppose you are trying to explain to your children or grandchildren why you fell in love with and married the person you married.

Here is one true story. You were driven by a deep primal urge for the procreation of the species. That urge has Darwinian roots and is absolutely essential if Homo sapiens are to survive on the earth. Furthermore, you were the victim of raging hormones. The next thing you knew: a wedding ring.

Here is another true story. Let another poet tell it. Elizabeth Barrett Browning, invalid, alone and lonely until Robert came to call:

2. Cummings, "I Thank You God for Most This Amazing."

> The face of all the world is changed, I think,
> Since first I heard the footsteps of thy soul
> Move still, oh, still, beside me, as they stole
> Betwixt me and the dreadful outer brink
> Of obvious death, where I, who thought to sink,
> Was caught up into love and taught the whole
> Of life in a new rhythm.[3]

Now tell me, which story are you going to tell your children and your grandchildren?

There are two stories about creation, too. Of course we evolved through the millennia, our own species among the species of the earth. But just as truly—even just as obviously—the psalmist has it right as well: "What is man that you are mindful of him? Or woman that you visit her? You have made us a little lower than the angels, and crowned us with glory and honor" (Ps. 8:4–5 au. trans.).

And God said, "Let us make humankind in our image, according to our likeness" (Gen. 1:26).

III.

Here is the third claim. To say that God is creator of heaven and earth is not just to talk about then but to talk about now.

Listen to the psalmist again: "What is man that you are mindful of him, or woman that you visit her?"

There is a philosophy called deism, beloved of many of our founding fathers and mothers. It says that long ago God set the world ticking like a clock and then retired to wherever God retires to. Some contemporary scientists say that God started it all off with a big bang, but then as far as God was concerned, the party was over.

Genesis 1:1 is just the beginning of a great collection of books that starts with God and ends with God and is obsessed with God all the way in between. And God returns the favor. God is obsessed with us. Maker of heaven and earth and also lover of heaven and earth.

The spiritual says it: "He's got the whole world in his hands." And the poem says it: "And God said 'I'm lonely; I'll make me a world.'" And the hymn says it: "O love that wilt not let me go." For Jews and Christians and

---

3. Elizabeth Barret Browning, Sonnet 7, in *Sonnets from the Portuguese and Other Poems* (New York: Dover Publications Inc., 1992), 26.

Muslims, too, faith in God as maker of heaven and earth has always also been faith in the God in whom we live and move and have our being.

Where I think the new atheists often get it wrong is that they think that faith in creation is a hypothesis we think up in our heads and then test against the evidence. Faith in creation is the strategy by which we live our lives. It's the trust by which we get up in the morning and the confidence with which we go to bed at night.

"God saw everything that he had made, and behold, it was very good" (v. 31 RSV). Can you prove it? Not really. Can you live it? You can. You do. You will.

IV.

Now my last move is the trickiest. I know that, so at least you cannot say "That's really tricky, Bartlett" and be telling me something I don't already know. Here we go: To talk about creation is not just to talk about Adam and Eve but to talk about Jesus Christ.

Long ago I was edified and terrified when I read a series of volumes called *Church Dogmatics* written by a Swiss theologian, Karl Barth. Barth wrote three huge volumes on the doctrine of creation, but the heart of what he said is this: Most of us don't believe in God as a gracious creator just because we look at the world and are persuaded that a good God made it. Most of us believe in God the creator because we look at Jesus Christ. When we see Christ's goodness we can turn back to the world and say: "Listen that looks good, too."

For Barth Jesus is the lens through which we view the world, and when we view the world through him we see the world as the creation of a good and loving God. Barth wasn't the first one to think this up. When John wrote his gospel he said that when God made the world God made it according to a plan, and the name of that plan was Jesus Christ—Christ was the blueprint for creation.

Many years ago Kenneth Scott Latourette taught history at Yale. He talked once about a really low period in his life when he had no faith in anything. He went to spend the night in the mountains near his home in Oregon. He was lying out at night looking at the distant and impersonal stars. Then he thought about his father, his father's goodness and integrity, and he thought to himself that the power that created his father was not a force of indifference but a God of love, and that that same God must have also created the world.

It's not a perfect argument, but it's not altogether distant from what we as Christians believe. The God whom Jesus called "Father" is also God, the

Father Almighty, Maker of Heaven and Earth. The beauty and love we see in Jesus Christ we can see in the created universe, because before we had really surveyed the universe, we had seen our savior's face.

But all that sounds a little bit like a proof, and I want to go back appropriately, to the beginning. "Look," I said when we began, "Creation is not about proof, it is about praise." It is not so much that we preach about God, the maker of heaven and earth. It is much more that we sing:

> Praise to the Lord, the Almighty, the King of creation!
> O my soul praise him, for he is thy source of thy health and salvation.
> All ye who hear, now to his temple draw near.
> Join me in glad adoration.[4]

---

4. Joachim Neander, "Praise to the Lord, the Almighty," *The United Methodist Hymnal* (Nashville: The United Methodist Publishing House, 1989), 139.

30

This We Believe: Who Is God? Liberator, Governor, Judge

This sermon is the second sermon in the series "This We Believe," preached on November 8, 2009, at The Congregational Church of New Canaan, Connecticut.

I.

Bernard Meland taught theology at the University of Chicago for many years in the middle of the twentieth century. He was rightly admired for the way in which he tried to combine theology with philosophy and for the way in which he paid close attention to the latest developments in science and not just in religious studies. He was in addition a genuinely kind and generous man.

Of the writings of his I have purchased through the years only one of them still sits on my bookshelf eternally unopened. The title of that book is: *Write Your Own Ten Commandments*.

Now since I haven't opened the book I can only comment on the title, but it strikes me that the title indicates at once what is best and what is most problematic about American Protestant thought in the last fifty years.

What is best is that Christian thinkers like Meland are always trying to make sure that the claims of the tradition are relevant to contemporary people. They are never satisfied simply to say: "The Bible says . . ." or "John Calvin says . . ." or even "My pastor says" and then to assume that that ends the discussion. They want to show how religion can still make sense.

What is trickier is that many of us who are American Christians have been deeply influenced by the myth of the Lone Ranger. We're Lone Rangers because for us the question is not what Jews or Christians believed in the past—it's the present that counts. We're alone because the question is not what other Christians believe right now, it's my convictions that count.

So I'll write my own ten commandments, and you write your own Sermon on the Mount and I promise not to inflict my laws on you if you won't inflict your principles on me.

We are looking together once a month all year long at what we can believe together, not only together with each other, but together with the church through all the ages. Not of course that you and I believe exactly the same thing; not that either you or I believe exactly the same thing as ancient Christians like St. Francis or St. Claire. But we are part of one great family and we have one great family story; you tell it your way, and I'll tell it mine, but it's our story.

And they are OUR commandments. Not my own commandments and not your own commandments and not even Professor Meland's commandments; they are our commandments.

Now when I started planning this series it was clear enough what the first claim should be: We believed in God the Creator. Then it seemed sensible to move from the book of Genesis to the book of Exodus and there we find God the liberator and God the governor, the law-giver. I tried that title on some friends and they suggested that we'd better face up to the fact that we've got God the judge as well. Right there in Exodus.

So there were the three moves for the sermon: liberator, governor, judge.

II.

The law-giver, governor part is the most obvious. The big thing God seems to do is give a bunch of laws by which we're supposed to live. But the truth is that even before God hands down the laws he reminds Moses who God really is:

> "I am the LORD your God who brought you out of the land of Egypt, out of the house of slavery."
>
> (Exod. 1:2)

In the biblical story, in the Christian faith, liberation comes before obligation.

Notice what God did not do. God did not sidle up to Moses at the burning bush and say: "Hello; I've got a bunch of rules for you. Follow these commandments and someday I'll let you out of the house of bondage."

God spoke straight to Moses: "I have come to liberate my people from their bondage."

Straight out; free gift.

When African American slaves read the story they knew who Moses was, first and foremost, and who God was, too. God was the one who set people free: "Go down Moses, way down in Egypt's land, tell old Pharaoh: let my people go."

And if we think that song was just about Israel twenty-eight hundred years before, we just haven't been paying attention.

In the Biblical story God is wholly against slavery and wholly in favor of freedom.

> If somebody's in bondage to political oppression: Let my people go.
> If somebody's in bondage to addiction: Let my people go.
> If somebody's in bondage to ambition—we've got to work harder and harder so that we can do better and better—Let my people go.
> Bondage to poverty: God's fighting that.
> Bondage to wealth: God's fighting that, too.

The theology of liberation got started in Latin America just after Bernard Meland was writing in North America, and it spread to those who felt oppressed by race or income or gender or sexual orientation or disability. It said that God had a preferential option for the poor, which annoyed a lot of us who weren't that poor, but what it meant was partly this:

"I am the Lord your God, and here's what I'm up to. I am bringing you out of whatever Egypt is trying to destroy your soul and whatever house of slavery has chained your heart and whatever poverty beats down your body."

III.

But then, of course, after the word about liberation, the laws. "I brought you out of the land of Egypt out of the house of bondage: THEREFORE. No other Gods; don't kill; don't steal; honor your father and mother."

But get this very clear. God doesn't say: "Do all this good stuff so that I will liberate you." God says: "Do all this good stuff because I have liberated you."

Live out your freedom. Live out your gratitude.

Look, it's a little like the difference between giving your children an allowance and giving them a wage.

If you give them a wage, you say: "Here's what you have to do to earn enough money to do the fun stuff." Of course that's really all you mean by it, but sometimes it can feel like: "Here's what you have to do to become a member of the family. Here's what you have to do to earn our love."

If you give the allowance, you say: "You're part of the family. The money is just a sign of that; just a sign of saying what is ours is yours. But here's how you respond to that. You live out your membership in the family. You live out your freedom. You live out your gratitude."

Either way there are rules, expectations. But one set of rules is driven by anxiety: Can I please them? And the other set of rules is driven by gratitude: How do I thank them?

Let me try it one other way. The two greatest earliest Protestant Reformers were Martin Luther and John Calvin.

When they wrote worship services, they both included in the worship the reading of the Ten Commandments and the prayer of confession of sins.

Luther had the pastor read the Ten Commandments first. Then everybody in the congregation would notice how badly they had done in keeping the commandments and would turn to the prayer of confession and throw themselves on the mercy of God.

Calvin had the people pray the prayer of confession first. And of course for Calvin as for Luther there was plenty to confess. But then after they had confessed their sins and the pastor had promised them the pardon of God, the pastor read the Ten Commandments . . . to show them how to be grateful. Now that you know you're free, do this. To show them how to live out the mercy they had just received.

I know denominations aren't what they used to be, but it may be worth noting that the Congregationalists who were your spiritual ancestors in Great Britain and the Baptists who were my spiritual ancestors in the Netherlands were all pretty much Calvinists. That meant they thought that God gave us the law not just to show us how sinful we were but so that we could show God how grateful we are.

IV.

God the liberator, God the governor, God the judge.

Well of course; there's no way out. Once you have the law you've got to have the judge. Even when we obey the law out of gratitude we can't escape the reality of judgment. Moses talked a lot about freedom but a lot about judgment too. Jesus talked a lot about God's love but a lot about God's judgment too.

But here's the thing. The purpose of God's judgment is not to punish the sinner but to defeat sin. The purpose of God's wrath is to clear the way for God's mercy.

Surely when we say that God is our Father in heaven or our Mother in heaven we don't just mean our encourager, though we do mean that. If your parents were anything like mine they were also those who disciplined you. So when we pray our Father in heaven we pray "Oh you in heaven who discipline us, your name is holy."

Our text from Exodus even shows us something of what judgment looks like. The children of Israel are all afraid of the special effects—the thunder, the lightning, the trumpet and the smoking mountain.

But Moses says an oddly contradictory thing:

> "Don't be afraid, for God has come to put the fear of God upon you, so that you may not sin."
>
> (Exod. 20:20, au trans.)

"Fear of God"—what an odd phrase. When I was still in elementary school our family moved to a new community and a new church. As is always the case with the pastor's kid some of the members graciously took on the role of informing me about the quirks and qualities of the other members.

Early in our days there one friend pointed to an elderly gentleman standing and chatting in the narthex. "That's Harry Openshaw," he said. "Now he's a true god-fearing man."

"God-fearing," I thought. Must be hard to get up every morning scared of God and go through the day wondering what God is doing to do next.

But I learned more about Harry Openshaw. He had been a missionary to China, continuing to minister courageously until the Communists finally forced him to leave. He had lost a beloved wife to illness but kept his faith. When our church was caught in conflict over whether to integrate he had braved the wrath of more powerful members of the church by standing quietly and steadfastly for the Gospel.

Then I began to get it. Just because Uncle Harry (I'd gotten to know him pretty well by now) just because Uncle Harry was God-fearing, nothing else could get to him. God fearing was a way of God trusting. Knowing that God and God alone was our judge and our governor is a way of knowing that nothing else has any right to get to us—to make us afraid.

Maybe judgment isn't being zapped or injured or losing something we love. Maybe judgment is being afraid of everything but God. Afraid of losing status, afraid of losing love, afraid of losing security, afraid of the market or the divorce court or fading popularity or failing health. Maybe we're not afraid of judgment; maybe being afraid IS judgment.

Except when we fear God; except when we reverence God. ("Reverence" may be a more helpful translation of the word.) Except when we love God so completely that worshiping God and serving God's children is not only what is required it is what we desire.

Except when we reverence God; when we accept completely that obeying God is not our harshest obligation, but our greatest joy.

To God be thanks and praise.

Amen.

31

This We Believe: Who Is Jesus? The Word Made Flesh

JOHN 1:1–18

This is the third sermon in the series "This We Believe" preached at The Congregational Church of New Canaan, Connecticut on December 13, 2009.

I.

When I was six or seven I appeared for the first time in a Christmas pageant. I was not much of an actor, but you will not be surprised to know I was pretty much of a talker, so I was assigned to be one of the narrators.

I stood in the middle of the chancel of the First Baptist Church of Evanston, Illinois, and recited the words I had memorized from the King James Bible:

> And there were in the same country shepherds abiding in the field, keeping watch over their flock by night. And, lo, the angel of the Lord came upon them, and the glory of the Lord shone round about them, and they were sore afraid.
>
> (Luke 2:8–9)

Now when I grew older and when the newer translations came along I realized that what Luke meant when he said the shepherds were sore afraid was that they were terrified, very afraid.

But at seven years old I thought I knew exactly what Luke meant; they were sore afraid, so afraid that their sides hurt and they were short of breath. Sore.

Many a day I was sore afraid, because each weekday afternoon I set out on the road from Orrington School to my home on Lincoln Street and many weekday afternoons I was waylaid by the Bogen gang. Tom and Mike Bogen and their cohort of tiny thugs loved to hide in the bushes along the road, and as I walked by to rush out from the bushes, grab me, and throw me to the ground. I was often sore afterwards; I was always sore before, sore afraid.

The Christmas stories are about God overcoming fear. In Luke's Gospel people are afraid of the powers that might oppress them . . . their own Bogen gang.

In Matthew's Gospel people are afraid of losing their way. They always worry about wandering astray . . . like the poor magi who almost don't make it to the manger.

In John's Gospel people are afraid of the dark. They're afraid that from birth to death we wander around lonely and ignorant and when we die we just die into deeper darkness.

So the Gospel writers tell Christmas stories to show us how God overcomes fear.

In Luke, Jesus is the mercy of God, a baby lying in a manger whose mercy is stronger than the strongest king.

In Matthew, Jesus is the wisdom of God; he shows us the way even more clearly than the star guides the wise men.

But in John—in John's Gospel Jesus IS God.

II.

So while Luke starts with the manger and the shepherds and Matthew starts with Mary's house and the wise men, John starts at the very beginning—the beginning of all creation. And while Luke and Matthew tell Christmas stories, John sings a Christmas carol. He gives us a poem about the birth of Christ.

John's poem says that even when creation began God the creator was all mixed up with God the savior. Now the word John used for God the savior was the word "Word."

I know that sounds like the beginning of a comedy routine. "What's John's word for the Savior? . . . Word . . . That's what I just said."

And it's not just that God the creator was all mixed up with God the savior, when John started to talk about creator and savior he got a little bit mixed up, too. In one sentence he says: "The Word was with God." And in the next sentence he says: "The Word was God."

At the end of his Christmas story John says something complicated but not really mixed up at all: "The Word became flesh and dwelt among us, and we have seen his glory" (John 1:14 ESV).

III.

Here's the amazing deal. Here is John's Christmas carol. It is absolutely true that at Christmastime God sent Jesus to save us from the powers that oppress us. And it's absolutely true that at Christmastime God sent Jesus to show us the way from all our wanderings.

But one thing more says John. At Christmastime, God sent us God's own self, to be the light in the midst of our darkness.

A few centuries later the church tried to figure out a way to describe how it could be that Jesus was a man who delivers us and guides us and could somehow also be God dwelling with us.

And the formula the church came up with said that Jesus was very God and very man or in more contemporary language, Jesus was entirely God and entirely human.

Now I want to use a homely analogy—homely in two ways: kind of down home, but also about looking kind of plain.

Some years after my debut as the narrator in the Christmas pageant I was still standing up in front of people and making speeches. And it came to pass that one day I gave a speech in front of another group of church people in another town, and one of the women who heard the speech was not impressed. So she wrote a note to my parents in which she managed to insult all three of us at the same time.

And here is what she said. She said: "Unfortunately young David has inherited his father's looks and his mother's brains."

Leave aside the slander for the moment—my father was very distinguished looking and my mother is very smart—but what this ineffable person was saying was that she thought she could divvy me up between my father's part of me, the looks, and my mother's part of me, the intellect.

To this day I have seminary students reading New Testament stories who try to figure out what's the God part of Jesus and what's the human part of Jesus. The human part of Jesus wept when Lazarus died, but then fortunately the God part of Jesus raised Lazarus from the tomb. The God part of Jesus walked on the water but the human part of Jesus must not have recognized the disciples because he was about to pass them by when they cried out and got his attention.

That's not the way John wants to tell the story or Jesus to interpret it. Entirely God and entirely human: not one thing one minute, and another thing the next.

IV.

Very smart and faithful theologians have tried from the third century into the twenty-first to explain how Jesus could be both human and divine.

Here is a simple attempt which leaves out a great deal but may help us on the way.

In Jesus Christ we see what it really is to be human; and in Jesus Christ we see what it really is to be God. Jesus is not human one minute and divine the next, but both those things truly, all the time.

Jesus is compassionate because God is entirely compassion and because at our most human we are compassionate too.

Jesus gets angry at injustice because God is just and because humans who are made in God's image strive toward justice, too.

So, says John, we don't really have to turn our backs on Jesus to find out what it means to be fully human. Jesus shows us that. And we don't have to sneak behind Jesus to see what the God who sent him looks like because Jesus shows us that, too.

V.

In this same passage, in this same Christmas carol, John says it in another way, perhaps not quite as richly but a little more clearly.

"What came into being in Jesus was life, and the life was the light of all people. The light shines in the darkness, and the darkness has not overcome it" (John 1:3–5).

Remember I said that in John's Gospel what we're afraid of is the darkness—the darkness of loneliness, the darkness of confusion, the darkness that awaits us at the end of life.

Except for Jesus. Except for the light that keeps shining in the darkness. Except for the moment when God sees how much we fear the darkness and God lights the light; God sends the light; God is the light.

A woman I knew when I was a child told the story about her own childhood Christmas. The children in her family were excited by the new toys they got at Christmas day and took them out to play with them in the snow. But the day was short, and the dark fell quickly and they came dashing into the home to get warm, leaving the toys.

Their mother noticed that the toys were still lying in the yard, and being a mother sent the children forth to gather all the gifts they had scattered carelessly about. But when they went out to the dark, she stood on their home's front step, holding a lighted candle. And calling out again and again and again: "I am here." "I am here." "I am here."

The Word became flesh and dwelt among us; we have beheld his glory.

The light shines in the darkness, and the darkness has not overcome it. Does not overcome it. Will not overcome it.

Merry Christmas. Amen.

32

This We Believe: Who Is Jesus?
Teacher and Healer

MARK 2:1–12

This sermon is the fourth in the series "This We Believe," preached at The Congregational Church of New Canaan, Connecticut, on January 10, 2010. Samuel Sandmel, who is mentioned and noted as a Jewish scholar, was a colleague of David's at the University of Chicago Divinity School and a dear family friend.

I.

Indulge me while I talk for a minute about the series of sermons we've been sharing. We're talking about what we believe—not what I believe but what we believe together as Christians, most days anyway. We started talking about God the creator and judge and then it was time to talk about Jesus. It was also the week of the Christmas pageant, so of course we began the sermons on Jesus by talking about the great Christmas theme, incarnation—the word became flesh.

Yet for many of us, me included, our interest in Jesus did not begin with the belief that he was God incarnate but with a commitment to the power of his teachings.

Thomas Jefferson worked very hard to be both a rational, enlightenment thinker and a kind of Christian, and his solution was to compile his own version of the New Testament. In the Jefferson version Jesus teaches many wonderful things and makes many strenuous demands, but he does not claim to be God incarnate, and he does not die for the sins of humankind, and he does not rise again from the dead. Indeed Jefferson cuts out all the miracles, so he would have liked the first part of this sermon's title, Jesus the teacher, and he would have found the second part of the title, "Jesus the Healer," not very believable.

To this day in our country at least even the most strenuous secularists acknowledge that Jesus had much to teach us. And in the ever enriching interfaith dialogue, very important Jewish scholars like Samuel Sandmel and Michael Cook and Amy-Jill Levine have acknowledged not only that Jesus was a great teacher, but that he was a great teacher who had much in common with the great prophets of Israel like Amos and Micah.

For the Hindu Mahatma Gandhi, living as he did under the power of a Christian empire, Christianity had no appeal whatsoever, but he loved Jesus as a teacher and learned from him.

And in Islam, Jesus is neither the greatest nor the last of the prophets—that is Mohammed—but he is a great prophet nonetheless, quoted with approval and heard with interest.

II.

So here we seem to have a starting point where what we believe as Christians is very close to what people of other faiths and people of no faith at all believe. When springtime comes we'll look together at what Jesus the teacher demands of us, but this morning I want to look at what Jesus the teacher promises us.

We look at that dramatic passage where four of his friends bring a paralytic to Jesus for healing. And when the crowd is so great that they can't get in, they go to the roof, knock a hole in the roof, and let the paralytic down through the hole. Jesus must have been surprised, what with plaster coming down on his head and this bedridden man lowered in front of him.

But then the friends and the paralytic are surprised when Jesus doesn't start by saying what they obviously want to hear: "You are healed." He says what he obviously thinks he needs to say: "Your sins are forgiven."

One way to summarize the good news we find in all the Gospels and in Paul's letters, too, is that simple phrase: "your sins are forgiven."

Now the word "sins" is so rich in meaning and possibility that I could spend all morning defining and describing sin, and indeed some of our Puritan ancestors thought that was as good a way as they could imagine to spend a Sunday morning.

But I want to try one definition of sin and then tell one story to show what sin looks like. The definition of sin is this: "Sin" is the distance we put between God and ourselves. "Sin" is the distance we put between God and ourselves.

Here's the story. My siblings and I are visiting my aunt and uncle and cousins in Los Angeles. We have been promised that that afternoon the adults will take us to the Los Angeles zoo. But first, in the morning, my uncle Fred is laying the cement for a new sidewalk outside his house. Now my brothers, sisters, and cousins will all gladly testify that I took my role as eldest among them with a seriousness that bordered on the pathological.

So as Uncle Fred was laying the cement, I was marching up and down in front of the new sidewalk warning off my younger relatives: "Don't step in the cement or we can't go to the zoo."

Two steps forward; the announcement, and then one step back. Time after annoying time until—you guessed it—one step forward: "Don't step in the cement or we can't go to the zoo." Then two steps back. Into the wet cement. Devastated, I ran to my uncle's car, threw myself on the front seat and locked the door.

And here's what the sin looked like. Of course it looked like proclaiming one thing with my mouth and doing something entirely different with my feet. And it looked like trying to be the boss of my brothers and sisters and cousins. But mostly it looked like me, locked in the car—separated from everybody else and especially separated from Uncle Fred.

And here's what forgiveness looked like. It looked like my uncle, knocking firmly and kindly on the door of his own car.

III.

When Jesus says to the paralytic: "Your sins are forgiven" we don't actually know the paralytic's history . . . where he may have gotten it wrong all the time he was bragging about getting it right.

But we do know about his distance. We know how far they had to bring him to Jesus; and how hard they had to work to get him there; and we know that before Jesus ever said "Your sins are forgiven" he said something even more amazing: He said: "My child."

"My child, your sins are forgiven." Two ways of saying the same thing. "My child . . . MY child."

But notice what a brave thing Jesus says. He does not just say: "God is a forgiving God, so I'm pretty sure God forgives your sins." He says: "Your sins are forgiven."

And here's where the scribes get annoyed. And here's where Mr. Jefferson would have to change the text to fit his Bible. Mr. Jefferson would say: "Wait a minute, now he's not just a teacher, Jesus is doing something more."

The scribes say: "No one can forgive sins except God alone." Mark loves to throw in little dialogues like this. The technical word for these dialogues is "irony." "Irony" is when somebody says just the right thing for just the wrong reason.

They think they're mocking him, but the fact is they're naming him: "No one can forgive sins but God alone." You've got it. So if this man just forgave sins, then this man, this Jesus IS God for us; God with us; God forgiving us.

Suppose Uncle Fred had sent one of my siblings or cousins to the Ford station wagon where I had locked myself. "Uncle Fred is in a forgiving mood; come on out."

But Uncle Fred came himself. Knocked on the door. Probably didn't say, "I forgive you," since he was a taciturn kind of guy. Probably said: "Come on out; let's go to the zoo." Which meant: "I forgive you."

See Jesus the teacher doesn't just teach forgiveness, he does forgiveness; in the first century and in this century, too.

Think of it this way; it's an anniversary of a relationship with somebody you love. Suppose she sends a note, suppose he sends a note that says: "Happy anniversary; I'd really like to hug you." Not so bad; but how much better when you get the hug.

Jesus isn't just the teacher telling us how much God would like to hug us; Jesus is God's own embrace. Jesus does not just talk about God's forgiveness. Jesus IS God's forgiveness."

IV.

And then one thing more that really would have annoyed Mr. Jefferson. After Jesus not only teaches about forgiveness but forgives, Jesus not only teaches—he heals. He performs the miracle. He tells the man on the stretcher to get up and walk; and the man walks, he runs, he dances—right there in front of the crowd, where everyone can see.

A few weeks ago when we were having our brunch conversation after church one of you asked me to say what I believed about miracles and I said a few things and then said, "Stay tuned" because I knew it would come up today.

Here's what I believe about miracles, what I think we can believe even in the twenty-first century.

I don't believe that illness is usually a result of sin. I don't think that when our bodies suffer we need to ask what our souls have done wrong to get us in this mess.

I do believe that medicine is an enormous gift and part of the world that God has given us.

But I do believe that our minds and our souls and our bodies are so mixed up that we cannot say: "Oh that's just my body," or, "that's just my spirit," and I know that sometimes when my spirit is awry my body shows it. And I would not be surprised if someone who was paralyzed in all kinds of ways was liberated by the news that her sins were forgiven, his sins were loosed.

And I do believe that God is bigger than our categories and that one thing God likes to do time and time again is surprise us.

When Jesus the teacher wants to look at a mystery, that is something that is both puzzling and surprising and graciously true, he tells parables.

I want to close with a parable that in this case is a true story of my friend David Gray.

David Gray is about my age, and when we were young we played squash together, or rather we were on the squash court together; he played and I suffered. He is married and, in those days, his three children were still very young.

He and Margy were building a new house. The garage roof wasn't finished so on a rainy night he climbed up on the roof to put a tarp over the opening to protect the garage beneath. And slipped and fell and broke his spinal cord and was paralyzed.

> He had the very best medical care one can imagine.
> He had a church that cared about him and a wife and mother and kids and friends who pretty much went full time trying to find a way to help.
> Those of us who love him would have borne him to Jesus, pushed through any crowd and knocked open any roof. Our prayers pounded on God's roof for weeks.
> He did not walk; he does not walk.
> For a time he despaired; he does not despair.

The annual Christmas letter came last week; there they all were—wife, children, grandchildren. David not only returned to his career, he used his gifts as a psychologist and author to advocate for people with handicaps. He became one of the architects of the Americans with Disabilities Act to provide justice for millions of his fellow citizens.

In those first weeks how we prayed that Jesus would say: "Rise, get off that bed and walk."

What Jesus did say seems simpler but finally meant much more: "My child." He said. "My child."

Is David cured? Not really.

Is David loved? Absolutely.

Is David whole? More than we ever would have dreamed.

To Christ, therefore, be thanks and praise. Amen.

33

This We Believe: Who Is Jesus?
The Crucified Messiah

MARK 15:25–39
ROMANS 8:31–39

This is the fifth in the sermon series, "This We Believe," preached at The Congregational Church of New Canaan, Connecticut, on February 14, 2010.

I.

I want to start with an illustration that is a good deal more sensational than the rest of the sermon.

Former Senator John Edwards has been in the news a great deal lately, not alas because of his political convictions but because of his marital troubles. And the word used to describe his situation in story after story is the single word: scandal.

His behavior has been a scandal for those who were devoted to him, who followed his political career, because it has been deeply disappointing. Not at all what they had expected or hoped.

And his behavior has been a scandal for those who opposed him, because it has been sadly satisfying. It opens the opportunity for criticism, mockery, ridicule.

The apostle Paul says that the crucifixion of Jesus Christ is a scandal. In our time that's hard for us to understand because as Christians we quite rightly sing: "In the cross of Christ I glory" or "Lift High the Cross!" How can this be a scandal?

But think yourselves back to first century Palestine.

Suppose you had decided to follow Jesus, believing that he was the promised Messiah. And it's looking pretty good: very wise teachings, astonishing miracles, a triumphal march into Jerusalem, and then within the course of a few days, terrible reversal. Jesus arrested; Jesus convicted; Jesus—the Messiah—hung on a cross. He wasn't hung on the cross like an ordinary criminal. That's much too easy. He was hung on the cross AS an ordinary criminal. Judged and convicted.

Not at all what we had expected, or hoped.

Or suppose you'd been opposed to Jesus from the beginning, suspicious of his pretensions and doubtful of his power. Now his conviction becomes sadly satisfying. Just what you always expected: "Some Messiah this is!"

You can understand why the passersby wag their heads at him and say: "You saved others; you can't save yourself."

You can understand why Saul of Tarsus, that outstanding citizen, could hardly stand the fact that some of his community were actually still trying to defend this crook.

You can understand why he sets out to prosecute those annoying Christians, to make them pay for their shameful allegiances.

Because the whole thing is a scandal.

II.

Early Christians knew it was a scandal. All the gospel writers knew it was a scandal. Saul, who astonishingly turned into Paul and joined the church he had persecuted—he knew it was a scandal, too.

But there it was. So they ended up believing two scandalous things.

Thing number one: Jesus is Messiah, God's own son.
Thing number two: Jesus was crucified as an outlaw.

Then they prayed and thought and searched scripture and tried to find a way to talk about how both those things could be true at once.

And because that claim—that Jesus is not only the Messiah, he's the crucified Messiah—is so enormous and so scandalous no one from that day until this could come up with a perfect explanation. What they came up with is what Professor David Tracy of the University of Chicago calls "fragments."

Put all the fragments together and you may have something of great beauty, like a stained glass window or a Byzantine mosaic.

By themselves they always, only, give us part of the picture.

III.

Here are two fragments—one from Mark's Gospel and one from Paul's letter to the Romans—that give us a piece of the picture—a step or two toward understanding, a step or two toward faith.

In Mark's Gospel, more than any of our other Gospels, the scandal of the cross is absolutely clear. It is clear not only that Jesus suffers but that he suffers in such pain and such disgrace that he cries out to God, "My God, My God, why have you forsaken me" (15:34b).

Luke takes the same story, Jesus on the cross, and he knows that Mark's telling of the story is scandalous. So in Luke's Gospel instead of crying in anguish: "My God, My God, why have you forsaken me," Jesus speaks out in fidelity: "Into your hands, O God, I commit my spirit."

But Mark's fragment is an essential piece of our faith. There is a verse from a hymn we used to sing in the Baptist church: "Jesus knows our every weakness."

What Mark tells us is that Jesus knows human experience at our best and at our worst, when we are most comforted and when we are without comfort.

What Mark tells us is that in Jesus Christ God enters into every human experience. In Jesus Christ God even knows what it is to feel the absence of God.

It's a fragment. I know that. One fragment tells us that sometimes God relieves suffering. And that's true. There are other fragments that talk about our relationship to God. One fragment tells us that God blesses us abundantly; and that's true. One fragment says that in Christ God shares our burdens and suffers our losses. That's Mark's truth.

Joseph Lowery followed Martin Luther King Jr. as the president of the Southern Christian Leadership conference. Lowery is a retired pastor in Atlanta and I heard him talk one time about his dismay at the so-called prosperity churches that are not only springing up in Atlanta, they're growing, flourishing.

The prosperity churches seem to say that what God is up to in the world is to make everything all right. Making everything all right means clearing up every problem, and healing every illness, and finally improving everybody's lifestyle.

And Lowery wonders: Where in all that is the cross? Where is the God who suffers with our suffering?

We all know, these are my words and not Lowery's; we all know that sometimes the faithful don't get blessed, sometimes we get bludgeoned.

Lowery's friend and colleague Martin Luther King Jr. prayed during one of the hardest times of his life that God would take the pain away, and the only assurance he got was that God would be there in the pain as well.

IV.

And that brings us to the other fragment for this morning. Now it's not Mark, it's Paul who believed that the cross was such a scandal until he learned that the scandal was also a gift.

When he was still Saul he had believed that the cross was the proof that God did not love Jesus. But when he became Paul, when he became an apostle, he discovered that the cross was the proof that God does love us.

Those arms outstretched on the cross, Paul says, those arms are of course the arms of the man Jesus, but they are also the very arms of God, embracing us, holding us, claiming us for God's own.

Mark shows us Jesus on the cross crying out in separation from God. Paul shows us Jesus and says that God reaches out in that same cross to end the separation. In life and in death, in triumph and in suffering, in health and in sickness, claiming us for God's own.

"For I am persuaded . . ." says Paul, and he's looking straight at the cross. "For I am persuaded that neither death, nor life, nor angels, nor rulers, nor things present, nor things to come, nor powers, nor height, nor depth, nor anything else in all creation, will be able to separate us from the love of God in Christ Jesus our Lord" (Rom. 8:38–39, au. trans.).

V.

We stand before mystery now. We try to discover not just what any one of us believes, least of all what I believe, but what the church seeks to believe, century after century.

We talk in fragments. Mark's fragment about an abandoned Messiah. Paul's fragment about the God who does not let us go.

Here is another fragment to help us see those fragments, that portion of the whole.

Nicholas Gage is an American journalist who was born in Greece during World War II. At the end of World War II, the communists took over Greece and they set to work to eradicate democracy and any who supported democracy.

Nicholas has written a book called *Eleni*. Eleni was Gage's mother. She and Gage's father decided that the only way to provide safety for their children was to smuggle them out of Greece to the United States.

So the father went first to establish a home, and then one by one Eleni made arrangements to smuggle her children out of Greece to their new home in the United States.

But just after the last of the children had been sent safely away, a neighbor who knew what Eleni had been doing reported her to the Communist authorities.

And they arrested her, and tried her, and found her guilty, and took her to a hill outside the village where a firing squad awaited her.

When they got to the top of the hill, Eleni said one last thing: "My children!" she cried, sad, defiant.

And then they fired.

On his own hill, Jesus, arms outstretched, crying to God, claiming us for God.

"My children."

> For I am persuaded that neither death, nor life . . . , nor anything else in all creation will be able to separate us from the love of God in Christ Jesus our Lord.

To Christ be thanks and praise. Amen.

34

This We Believe: Who Is Jesus?
The Risen One

I CORINTHIANS 15:1–11

This sermon is the sixth of a series on "This We Believe" at The
Congregational Church of New Canaan, Connecticut, on March
14, 2010.

I.

Calendars can be tricky. This morning we've got at least three calendars going
at once. There's the secular calendar, and it is the fourteenth of March, the
first day of Daylight Savings Time. Then there is the liturgical calendar: this
is the calendar by which much of the church marks the seasons and celebrations of faith, and by the liturgical calendar this is the fourth Sunday of Lent
. . . right in the middle of the time of preparation for Holy Week and Easter
Sunday.

And then there is the Congregational Church of New Canaan calendar,
and suddenly, perhaps uniquely, it's Easter.

It's Easter because that's where we are in our series of sermons. We've
been talking about Jesus Christ, his birth, his life, his death, and so now of
course it is time for his resurrection.

But it is also Easter because for the church every Sunday is Easter Sunday.
Getting the time right was very important for the first Christians. Jesus died
on Friday, they knew that; and they also knew that he rose again on the third
day, on Sunday. So for Christians Sunday, not the Sabbath, not Saturday,
became worship day . . . the Lord's Day. Getting the time right.

So we're actually getting the time right when we sing "The Day of Resurrection, earth tell it out abroad, the [festival]of gladness, the [festival] of God." Every Sunday is the day of resurrection; every Sunday is festival.

II.

That business about "the third day" also helps me when I think about what the church means when we say Jesus is the Risen Lord.

There is a noncontroversial way to talk about resurrection that almost anybody can accept. We can just say that resurrection means "something happened."

Some wise theologians have thought that what happened was that the disciples, who were left behind, finally came to realize how important Jesus had been; great teacher, great healer, even great revelation of God's love. And they realized that his influence lived on and on and on, and the shorthand way they could talk about that was to say, "He is risen."

The most important New Testament scholar of the twentieth century was Rudolf Bultmann, and he was most impressed with the fact that after Jesus' death the church not only remembered him, it began to preach about him. Week after week in church and in the marketplace faithful people kept telling other people the good news of God's love in Jesus Christ. For Bultmann Christ rose again because he was the subject of Christian preaching. A shorthand way to talk about how we still confront people when we preach is to say: "Christ is Risen."

Something happened. But then there's that complicated business about "the third day." We can say resurrection is the way in which the church remembered Jesus . . . but we can't say that somehow that remembering happened "on the third day." We can say that Jesus is raised into our preaching and listening, but the development of preaching and listening happened over a long period of time—not on "the third day."

Paul's letter to the Corinthians is one of the earliest Christian writings we have, and he tells us that even before he wrote his letter, probably when he first became a follower of Jesus, people who had been believers before him passed on the word about the resurrection.

Here's what Paul tells the Corinthians:

> For I passed on to you, as of first importance, what I in turn had received: that Christ died for our sins, according to the scriptures, and that he was buried, and that he was raised on the third day in accordance with the scriptures.
>
> (1 Cor. 15:3–4, au. trans.)

When Mark writes the very earliest Gospel he tells his own version of the resurrection story, and what's clear is that he puts a specific date on the resurrection he proclaims: "Very early on the first day of the week" that is, the third day after the crucifixion, they went and found the empty tomb.

III.

John Updike, the novelist and poet, died a few months ago. Perhaps because he was a novelist and poet and not a theologian he did not worry so much about making the resurrection seem plausible. Of course something happened he said; it happened on the third day. Here are his words.

> Make no mistake: if He rose at all
> it was as His body;
> If the cells' dissolution did not reverse, the molecules
> reknit, the amino acids rekindle,
> the Church will fall.
>
> It was not as the flowers
> each soft Spring recurrent
> it was not as His Spirit in the mouths and fuddled
> eyes of the eleven apostles;
> it was as His flesh: ours. . . .
>
> Let us not mock God with metaphor,
> analogy, sidestepping, transcendence;
> making of the event a parable, a sign painted in the
> faded credulity of earlier ages:
> let us walk through the door. . . .
>
> Let us not seek to make it less monstrous,
> for our own convenience, our own sense of beauty,
> lest, awakened in one unthinkable hour,
> we are embarrassed by the miracle,
> and crushed by remonstrance.[1]

I wish I could believe that as clearly as Updike does. I don't want to be embarrassed by the miracle.

The Gospel of John believes pretty much what Updike believed and so does the Gospel of Luke and so does the Gospel of Matthew.

---

1. John Updike, "Seven Stanzas at Easter," in *Collected Poems, 1953–1993* (New York: Knopf, 1993), 20, 21.

Paul hedges a little bit. Or put another way, he does not tell us anything directly about amino acids or reknitting molecules. What he tells us is that resurrection didn't just happen over time; it happened on the third day.

What he tells us is what people saw. What people saw was Jesus. They did not just remember him fondly. They did not just preach him fervently. They saw him. Peter saw him first. Paul knew Peter pretty well and no doubt Peter was one of those who told Paul about the resurrection. Then the twelve saw Jesus. Then five hundred and more. Then Jesus appeared to more apostles, including James, Jesus' own brother, whose life got pretty much turned around.

And so did Paul's life get pretty much turned around, not when he heard about Jesus or remembered Jesus but when he heard—Jesus—and saw—Jesus. Not amino acids maybe, but blinding light and clear voice.

III.

What I think the church says about Jesus resurrected is what Paul says: It was really Jesus who rose again . . . not our memory of him and not our sermons about him. Jesus.

Resurrection is not first of all about what happens to us; it is first of all about what happened to him. He was dead; and then he was alive again. On the third day.

Had the church not believed that, there would be no church. At most we'd have the "Think kindly of Jesus remembrance society." Kind of the way the Daughters of the American Revolution remember Thomas Jefferson and John Adams. Weren't they great? Aren't we grateful?

That's why we have the ancient cry of Easter worship. "Christ is risen." "He is risen indeed." Not, He is risen, sort of. He is risen indeed.

IV.

Then Paul goes on to tell us what it means for us, for our lives and our hopes that Christ is risen indeed—and what it means for the future of all creation. We'll come back to that theme and maybe even to this chapter in a couple of months, but this morning I want to look at another witness to what it means to say that Christ is risen, not only what it means for Jesus, but what it means for us.

And that witness is not St. Paul but St. Mark.

Mark does not actually show us any appearances of the risen Lord. He tells us that Jesus will appear, but by the time the Gospel is over we have not seen those appearances yet.

What Mark does do is tell us something of what resurrection means. The women who have followed Jesus come to the tomb on the third day to anoint his body. The tomb is empty and a young man—maybe an angel, maybe not—preaches to them the Easter Gospel.

"Do not be alarmed; you are looking for Jesus of Nazareth. . . . He has been raised; he is not here. . . . He is going ahead of you to Galilee; there you will see him" (Mark 16:6).

He is going ahead of you.

The women come to the tomb thinking they will find Jesus where they last saw him. They come to the tomb because they want to hold on to their memories. They come to the tomb because they want to hold on to him.

They come to do a pious thing; to keep him in the past. The young man tells them that Jesus will not be contained: He is going before you.

The Risen Lord is always going before us; the risen Lord is always calling us on.

In the church of my childhood there was an elderly couple. (I thought they were elderly; probably I'd discover that they were younger than I am now.) Their names were Mr. Tourtelot and Mrs. "Tourtelo"—they spelled their last name exactly the same way, but Mrs. Tourtelot always insisted that Mr. Tourtelot mispronounced his own family name.

She was, you will note, a woman of strong opinions, strongly voiced. The one other opinion I remember reported of her had to do with the scope of her entire adult life. When Mr. Tourtelot married her, he brought her from her childhood home in Newton, Massachusetts, to their adult home in Evanston, Illinois, and Mrs. Tourtelot once opined: "I have lived for forty years in Evanston, but I left my heart in Newton Center."

In Mark's Gospel the women who come to anoint Jesus think they can leave their hearts in the tomb.

Each of us is tempted to fancy up a tomb; to find that moment back there when faith was real and earnest and God was close and things were simple: the Newton Centers of our soul.

Every church I know is tempted to sanctify some sacred moment in the past when dear old so-and-so preached so powerfully and we sang the old songs and the sun shone more brightly, too, as a matter of fact.

He's not there. He is risen. If you look back to find him, I promise you will miss him.

If you move forward in faith; I promise he will find you.

Christ is risen; he is risen indeed.

V.

Years after Evanston, I was at college, far from home at Eastertime. The local Presbyterian Church sponsored a retreat for students who weren't leaving for the holiday, and the Bible studies of course focused on the stories of the resurrection.

We talked away in our most college student way about probability and possibility and miracle and rationality until finally one woman, having heard all she cared to hear about resurrection, pulled back from the table.

"It can't be true," she said.

"Why not?" asked the pastor leading our discussion.

"Because if that is true, then everything is changed."

Here is what we believe.

It is true; and everything is changed.

Amen.

35

This We Believe:
What Do We Hope For?
New Heaven and New Earth

2 CORINTHIANS 5:1–11

REVELATION 21:1–5

This is the seventh sermon in the series "This We Believe" preached at The Congregational Church of New Canaan, Connecticut, on April 11, 2010. Skip, referred to in the text, was Harold Masbeck, the Senior Minister at the church and a former student of David's at Yale Divinity School. Jonah, also referred to in the text, is our son, Jonah Smith Bartlett, who then was the Associate Minister working with children and youth at the church.

I.

Christian hope comes in two sizes: There is the personal hope we have for ourselves. And there is the larger, cosmic hope; the hope we have for human history and indeed for the whole creation.

Forty years ago or more Krister Stendahl came to lecture to ministry students at Yale Divinity School. Stendahl was a distinguished New Testament scholar, dean of Harvard Divinity School, and soon thereafter became the bishop of Uppsala, Sweden.

He told us what to expect when we started our preaching ministry. "Don't make the mistake of thinking that people are worried about what happens to them when they die," he said. "People are worried about whether history has any meaning." To paraphrase: people's real question isn't "what happens to me" the real question is: "What's it all about?"

Now I've been preaching pretty regularly for forty years and my sense is that Stendahl's right about what he affirms and not quite right about what he denies.

Indeed people are worried about whether history has any meaning. Shakespeare's Scot King Macbeth was an ambitious and violent man but he spoke the suspicion of Shakespeare's time and ours: "Life . . . is a tale told by an idiot, full of sound and fury. Signifying nothing." That's our cosmic worry, and we'll return to that in a few minutes.

But I have also discovered that we have plenty of time and energy for personal worry, too. We do not worry so much about ourselves, what will happen to me when I die? But we do worry about those we love: "Is this it? Are they now simply nothing? Has God turned away?"

Jerry Irish has taught religion for many years at Pomona College. When he was still a young man, his older son Lee died, suddenly, of meningitis, at the age of thirteen. Jerry felt what any of us would feel—bereft. And Jerry's younger son felt the loss, too. He wrote a poem about his brother's death:

> He was my brother,
> my only brother . . .
> He died because he happened to breathe in some bacteria
> that probably can only be seen under some special microscope,
> I guess all I can say is I loved him and needed him
> and that I don't understand.[1]

The Apostle Paul wrestled with that kind of loss all through his ministry. As far as we can tell, when he started his ministry he believed that Jesus would return soon and gather all faithful people to be with God, so there was no point in worrying about illness or death.

Then Christians started dying; then Paul faced his own death. Then he discovered we all need personal hope. Then he did what he always did in those days: he turned to God. He remembered Jesus.

What he remembered was what Skip and Jonah proclaimed last week and I proclaimed last month and the church always proclaims. Jesus Christ is risen. And because he is risen he is Lord over life but also over death.

Now Paul talks about that personal hope in different ways. Sometimes he seems to believe that when we die we sleep until the last day when God will raise all faithful people as God raised Jesus. Sometimes he seems to believe

---

1. Jerry A. Irish, *A Boy Thirteen* (Louisville, KY: Westminster Press, 1975), 17.

that when one of our family or friends dies, God brings the one we love to God's self.

In this morning's passage from 2 Corinthians, Paul seems to believe in that more immediate hope: "For we know that if the earthly tent we live in is destroyed, we have a building from God, a house not made from hands, eternal in the heavens" (5:1).

Paul sounds like Jesus talking to his disciples in John's Gospel: "In my father's house are many rooms; I go there to prepare a place for you" (14:2, au. trans.).

Look, the New Testament has many ways to talk about the single hope. The single hope is that God is stronger than death, even the death of those we love. The single hope is that the creator will not bring to nothing any child God has created. The single hope is that by God's grace Jesus Christ died and rose again, so that he might be Lord both of the dead and of the living. He was raised for us, says Paul in this morning's passage. He was raised for you. He was raised for those you love.

Beyond that, I think, is mystery. In that, is hope.

Glenn Brown was the youth minister in the church where I grew up. After a time he left that congregation to become chaplain at a college in Colorado. While he was still very young he was diagnosed with terminal cancer, and faced his own death and anticipated the grief of his wife and four young children.

He kept hoping and he kept preaching, and in the last months this is part of what he preached:

> Some who face the possibility of their own imminent death are led to believe that God has deserted them. Some who grieve over the death of someone they love will sometimes say: "Why did God do this to me." Death is a fact of life. It does not separate us from the love of God. God's love overcomes death. And in these times when we lose our own faith, the whole church stands by supporting us with love and faith, to remind us, to assure us, of how profound God's love is.[2]

So he believed. So we believe.

2. Glenn Brown, "Who Shall Separate Us," in *Life Is a Gift* (Denver: Colorado Women's College, 1965), 31–32.

II.

Christian hope comes in two sizes. Personal hope but cosmic hope as well.

In our passage for this morning Paul focuses especially on personal hope; Revelation focuses especially on hope for history, hope for all creation.

Revelation is an odd book, full of cryptic sayings, insoluble puzzles, and images that defy our understanding. What helped me understand was when Allan Boesak, who had been a leader of the black South Africans in the fight against apartheid, said that the biblical book that most helped him was Revelation, because in Revelation God promises us that God is working good not just for us individually but for human history, and for the whole creation.

That's why Revelation comes to its astonishing conclusion in chapter 21. The writer, a poet named John, talks about his vision and as the vision comes to a close, here is what he says, hopes, prophesies: "I saw a new heaven and a new Earth" (v. 1).

That is the promise that kept Christians in South Africa struggling against apartheid even when the odds seemed hopeless and justice far away.

I've been talking a great deal during recent weeks. Lent is boom time for seminary professors, but someone either here or in a Georgia church asked me recently if I could point to any moment in my lifetime that looked like the Kingdom of God, and I said that one such moment was the moment when Nelson Mandela walked out of his jail cell into freedom.

Not perfect; not an entirely new heaven or an entirely new earth. But close enough to raise our faith and cheer our hearts.

The promise of the risen Christ is not only that death will have no dominion over those we love; the promise of the risen Christ is that death and evil will not finally thwart the loving purposes of God.

Life is not a tale told by an idiot, full of sound and fury, signifying nothing. It is a drama authored and directed by God, lived out according to the pattern God shows us in Jesus Christ, God's son, our Lord.

Thornton Wilder was a distinguished American playwright. I honor him as a playwright and I honor him because his brother was Krister Stendahl's fellow New Testament teacher at Harvard. What an honor for Thornton!

Thornton Wilder's most famous play is *Our Town*; early in that play the girl Rebecca tells her brother George about the letter that put their neighbor, Miss Jane Crofut, in her place.

> **Rebecca:** "I never told you about that letter Jane Crofut got from her minister when she was sick. He wrote Jane a letter and on the envelope the

address was like this: It said: Jane Crofut; The Crofut Farm; Grover's Corners; Sutton County; New Hampshire; United States of America."

George: "What's funny about that?"

Rebecca: "But listen, it's not finished: the United States of America; Continent of North America; Western Hemisphere; the Earth; the Solar System; the Universe; the Mind of God—that's what it said on the envelope."[3]

That's what it says in Revelation, too, what it says in the whole New Testament. Our lives are not insignificant because we have a place in God's great drama; God's universe, God's mind, really is our town.

And history is not insignificant because the drama is God's drama . . . God's mercy and power driving us and those we love toward a new heaven and a new earth.

III.

Martin Marty is a distinguished historian of American religion, now well into his eighties. Some years ago I was privileged to be his very junior colleague at the Divinity School at the University of Chicago.

The Divinity School had and has a splendid custom of students and faculty eating lunch together every Wednesday noon. One Wednesday noon I was sitting at the table with a student named Joe Price.

Professor Marty sat down with us, clearly distressed. When we asked what was wrong he told us that his college roommate had died that week, still a young man. Marty said that he had wondered what to do to share grief and sympathy with the widow and decided to take paper and pen and in beautiful calligraphy (one of Martin Marty's 611 talents) he wrote for her these words from another letter of St. Paul:

> For I am persuaded that neither death, nor life, nor angels, nor rulers, nor things present, nor things to come, nor powers, nor height, nor depth, nor anything else in all creation, will be able to separate us from the love of God in Christ Jesus our Lord.
>
> (Rom. 8:38–39, au. trans.)

---

3. Thornton Wilder, *Our Town*, act 1, part 2 (New York: Harper, 1960).

Sadly, sadly not many years later Professor Marty's beloved wife Elsa died of a brain tumor. Shortly after her death I was again spending time with Joe Price.

"Carol and I sent a note, of course," I said.

And Joe said, "I remembered our luncheon conversation and I took paper and pen and in calligraphy I wrote:

> For I am persuaded that neither death, nor life, nor angels, nor rulers, nor things present, nor things to come, nor powers, nor height, nor depth, nor anything else in all creation, will be able to separate us from the love of God in Christ Jesus our Lord.

Not one thing.
Amen.

36

This We Believe:
"Who Is the Holy Spirit?"

JOHN 14:18–31
GALATIANS 4:1–7

This is the eighth sermon in the series "This We Believe," preached at The Congregational Church of New Canaan, Connecticut. The series was one of two series David was asked to preach by the Adult Education Committee. This sermon was preached on May 9, 2010.

I.

In two ways, preparation for this morning's sermon got complicated.[1]

First, I knew that our theme for the day was the Holy Spirit so I went to an excellent book I own about major Christian theological themes for the twenty-first century. I turned to the Table of Contents to find the chapter on the Holy Spirit, and there was none. I have no doubt that the Holy Spirit is mentioned often in the book, but not one chapter dedicated to the third person of the Trinity alone. This is, I fear, indicative of the fact that while we as Christians believe in the Holy Spirit we don't think much about that article of our faith.

Second, I realized that this is Mother's Day. Our hymns and our prayers in worship have captured that theme, but in Baptist churches that is seldom

---

1. Thanks to Carol Bartlett and Mark Douglas for helping me get beyond the complications.

enough. We may slight Ash Wednesday and gloss over Pentecost, but Mother's Day counts.

Mother's Day counts, I think, not just because we want to honor our mothers, though many of us do honor them. Mother's Day counts not just because some have taken on the privilege and duties of motherhood; that in fact is always a little tricky when we seem to ignore women who do not happen to be mothers, too.

Mother's Day counts because it speaks to a need that is deep and strong in every human being, whatever gender, whatever marital status, whatever age: we need to belong. Mother's Day brings us back to family, the one we have or the one we wished for. And with Iris's death this past week and our prayers for Skip and Amy and their family, we have been reminded how essential it is for all of us to belong.

In that great paraphrase of the twenty-third Psalm the hymn writer catches our longing in the last stanza of the song.

> There would I find a settled rest,
> while others go and come;
> no more a stranger, or a guest,
> but like a child at home.[2]

Now here is the theme of this sermon in one sentence: the rest will be elaboration. By the Holy Spirit God claims us as God's own children; by the power of the Holy Spirit, God brings us home.

God the Father creates us; God the Son redeems us; God the Spirit welcomes us.

II.

Here is what I mean. By the Holy Spirit God reaches out to us as God's children; by the Holy Spirit we reach out and claim God.

Look at our passage from John. Jesus speaks to the disciples a word of comfort because they are entirely afraid. They are not afraid of danger that will come later. They are not afraid of death; most of them will learn to live with that. They are afraid of loneliness. Jesus, who has been more than father and mother to them is about to die, and they are filled with fear.

---

2. Isaac Watts, "My Shepherd Will Supply My Need," in *Glory to God* (Louisville, KY: Westminster John Knox Press, 2013), 803.

Here is what Jesus says before he promises to give them the gift of the Holy Spirit: "I will not leave you orphaned" (14:18).

"I will not leave you orphaned." I will not leave you bereft.

And then Jesus tells the disciples why they will not be orphaned. He is sending them the Holy Spirit.

Now in John's Gospel only in the whole New Testament the Holy Spirit has another name as well: the Paraclete. Jesus says, "The [Paraclete], the Holy Spirit, . . . will teach you everything." That word "Paraclete" is a name so full of meaning that no English translation has ever captured it. The New Revised Standard translates the term as "Advocate," the Revised Standard translates the term as "Counselor," the Gideon, whose Bible seems to be on my shelf in Georgia rather than in the hotel room where it belongs, says "Helper." When I teach courses on the Gospel of John I just give up and use the English version of the Greek word: The Paraclete . . . when I type it into my sermon, Spellchecker sends up a red line and says, "You must be kidding."

For John the Holy Spirit is all those things: advocate, counselor, helper, but most of all for John the Paraclete is God's welcome, God's acceptance, God bringing us home.

III.

God brings us home by guiding us, of course. When the good-hearted Christians with their brochures come and knock at my door and say: "Are you lost?" I'm always torn.

Am I bound for eternal damnation? I hope not.

Am I sure where I'm going? No, not always, not altogether. Maybe I am kind of lost.

The great hymn about the Holy Spirit captures something of the promise:

I ask no dream, no prophet ecstasies,
no sudden rending of the veil of clay;
no angel visitant, no opening skies;
but take the dimness of my soul away.[3]

When Jesus gets ready to leave the disciples in John's Gospel, they are afraid that no one will show them the way. No light will lighten the dimness of their souls.

3. George Croly, "Spirit of God, Descend upon My Heart," *Chalice Hymnal* (St. Louis: Chalice Press, 1995), 265.

But Jesus says: "the Holy Spirit . . . will teach you everything and remind you of all that I have taught you" (John 14:26, au. trans.).

I told my seminary classes, somewhat to their dismay, that for John the Holy Spirit is a kind of substitute teacher. Jesus, the original teacher, has taken leave at least for the time, and here is the substitute in the teacher's place.

But Jesus, like a good teacher, has prepared a lesson plan. The Spirit teaches what the Lord has commanded: Love God, love your neighbor; follow these instructions; don't get lost.

And of course, unlike many substitute teachers of my childhood this substitute teacher is like the first teacher, loving, kind, and wise.

"I will not leave you orphaned."

IV.

The Holy Spirit brings us home by instructing us. And the Holy Spirit brings us home by comforting us. When Jesus says, "I leave the Holy Spirit with you," he goes on to say pretty much the same thing with other words: "Peace I leave with you; my peace I give to you" (v. 27).

We return to Mother's Day—we return to the mothers we had or the mothers we wish we had—as a reminder of that acceptance, that love, that kindness which is really God's peace.

The Spirit is God's peace.

For our children, in remarkable ways Fred Rogers, Mr. Rogers of TV fame, was a striking symbol of the Holy Spirit.

Some years ago, in his last years, Fred Rogers came to New Haven to speak at Yale University. Graduate students and faculty came from all over the New Haven area bringing their children to see Mr. Rogers.

But by the time the parents and children got to the auditorium, the seats were all taken—by undergraduates. By students who day by day and hour by hour lived by the Yale Creed which is not really Lux et Veritas but "Succeed and Compete."

And for just one moment in the midst of that rush and that loss and that longing for the people or the places that made them feel entirely at home, they stopped to greet the man who day by day looked each of them straight in the eye and said: "I like you just the way you are."

> Pretty much like the Holy Spirit. I will not leave you orphaned. Peace I give you.
> All of us are bereft; every one of us.
> All of us mourn; every day, every one.

Peace I give you; my peace I leave with you.
I will not leave you orphaned.

V.

By the Holy Spirit God reaches out to us as God's children; by the Holy Spirit we reach out and claim God.

And now we turn for a minute from the Gospel of John to Paul's letter to the Galatians where Paul talks about the Holy Spirit, too, and says this surprising thing: "Of course you used to feel orphaned, we all do" (that's a paraphrase—the next part is straight Paul). "God has sent the Spirit of his Son into our hearts, crying 'Abba! Father'" (Gal. 4:6).

How do we know that God welcomes us? Because God sends the Spirit into our hearts, and when the Spirit comes to abide in our hearts we cry out: "Abba! Father."

Paul is talking about what happens when Christians pray. When early Christians prayed they started with an Aramaic word: "Abba!" which is the word Jesus used when he claimed us as his family, as God's family. The word means "Father" and whenever we say "Father" or "Our Father" or "our Father Mother God" in worship, we claim our own place in God's own family.

In Paul's churches, which were probably less formal than The Congregational Church of New Canaan, people probably cried out "Abba!" and "Hallelujah" and "Amen" at places where we just nod appreciatively or smile slightly.

But even in our church we say our own version of "Abba! Father." Every time we say "Our Father who art in heaven" we are claiming God as our parent; we are saying, "We are no longer orphans." And that's not just us crying out our prayer.

That is God's Spirit crying out in us, crying out through us: "Our Father, Our Mother, Holy God, thank God. We're home."

VI.

John Cheever was the twentieth-century novelist and short story writer who especially captured what life was like for suburban New York Protestants.

His daughter, Susan, wrote a memoir of growing up in the Cheever family called *Home Before Dark*.

Here is the story from which the book takes its name.

My father liked to tell a story about my younger brother Fred. When Fred was a little boy we lived in a small house on a big estate . . . in Scarborough. Once, at twilight, after a long summer day, my father was standing outside the house under the big elm tree that shaded the flagstones in front of the door. Fred came back from playing with some friends, worn out and tired too, and when he saw Daddy standing there he ran across the grass and threw his little boy's body into his father's arms. "I want to go home, Daddy," he said, "I want to go home." Of course he was home, just a few feet from the front door in fact. But that didn't make any difference as my father well understood. We all want to go home, he would say when he told this story, we all do.[4]

"I will not leave you orphaned," Jesus tells us, "but I send the Holy Spirit to comfort you."

Welcome home. Amen.

---

4. Susan Cheever, *Home before Dark* (Boston, Houghton Mifflin, 1984) 10–11.

37

This We Believe:
Who Are We, the Church?

ACTS 2:1–17

I CORINTHIANS 12:12–31

"Who Are We, the Church?" is the ninth sermon in the series, "This We Believe," preached on May 23, 2010, at The Congregational Church of New Canaan, Connecticut.

I.

In the years when I was a pastor, we always had a hard time figuring out how best to celebrate Pentecost. We knew well enough how to celebrate Christmas and how to celebrate Easter, and the traditions were both well-established and always fresh and alive.

But when it came to Pentecost, the third great festival of the Christian year, of the Christian life, we never quite got it right.

This is the birthday of the church of course, so sometimes we sang: "Happy Birthday Dear Church" and had a cake.

Those who help us think about worship tell us that the appropriate color for Pentecost is red, so sometimes we suggested that everyone dress in red, or at least wear a red ribbon or a red tie.

There was one year with balloons and another year with noisemakers, but none of these rituals seemed rich enough to warrant repeating the next year. We kind of muddled on.

One great tradition did remain through all those years; the children in the children's church school would stand at the front of the sanctuary and sing what has become the unofficial anthem of Pentecost.

> The church is not a building
> The church is not a steeple
> The church is not a resting place
> The church is people.[1]

And then children and adults alike would join in the refrain: "I am the church! You are the church! We are the church together!"

As Congregationalists you know perfectly well that the church is not a building; we meet in the meeting house as the church, not in the church. And nobody ever thought the church was a steeple, that one's clearly in there to give the lyricist a word to rhyme with "people." And no one who has paid the slightest attention to the program of this congregation thinks that the church is a resting place. Sometimes I think you need to rest from church, not at church.

We know the song is right enough: We are the church. But what kind of "we" makes up a church? What is it that makes church different from any other social gathering, or educational institution, or nonprofit charity?

Two claims for this morning; one from each text, from Acts and from 1 Corinthians.

II.

The first claim: We are the community of the Spirit. Now some of you may remember that two weeks ago I talked about the Holy Spirit and I suggested that in the Holy Spirit God welcomes us home, and in the Holy Spirit God leads us home.

What I did not say is what our text says this morning: The Holy Spirit brings us home together. The Holy Spirit brings us home as community . . . as the Spirit's own community.

Because we are the Spirit's community, and not our own community, we are always glad to be different one from another.

Until Pentecost all the people who followed Jesus, all the disciples, were Galileans. At Pentecost, look who else gets brought home by the Spirit: Parthians, Medes, Elamites and residents of Mesopotamia, Judea and Cappadocia, Pontus and Asia . . . and the list goes on and on.

---

1. Richard K. Avery and Donald Marsh, "We Are the Church," in *United Methodist Hymnal* (Nashville: Methodist Publishing House, 1998), 558. "We Are the Church," by Richard K. Avery and Donald Marsh, © 1972 Hope Publishing Company, Carol Stream, IL 60188. All rights reserved. Used by permission.

The churches that we call "Pentecostal" in some ways aren't very much like Pentecost. At Pentecost people who were seized by the Spirit were not "speaking in tongues" they were speaking Galilean, or Aramaic, so when Pentecostal churches speak in tongues, in special spiritual languages, they are following an early Christian practice but not a Pentecostal practice.

But here's where Pentecostal churches do look like Pentecost. Have you noticed how often churches called things like "The Rock" or "The Assembly of God" have a greater diversity of races and backgrounds and social class than those of us who are called The Congregational Church of New Canaan or the Friendship Baptist Church of Atlanta?

Here in New Canaan you have wonderful ways of being part of the larger church, the diverse church, through your ministries and your partnerships. But Sunday after Sunday we mostly see white, upper-middle-class folk. And at the Friendship Baptist Church of Atlanta Sunday after Sunday we mostly see African American lower-middle-class folk.

On Pentecost, the Spirit nags us a little; urges us to reach out; urges us to welcome in. It's homecoming, and we have room for a few more kinds of people at our home.

III.

But here's the other thing, at Pentecost the Spirit allows all those diverse people to understand each other. And whoever you may be racially or ethnically or economically, you are a wonderfully diverse people theologically. Just check out any conversation after one of these sermons on What We Believe.

Theologically, we are just where Pentecost was: all over the map.

But the gift of the Holy Spirit is that we listen to each other, and by God's grace we even understand each other.

Four years ago on Pentecost Sunday, Carol Bartlett and I were sitting with some of our Columbia Seminary students in the United Church of Shanghai.

As the preacher began to speak in Mandarin Chinese I tried to look interested but of course I was primarily puzzled. Then in my ear came a voice translating what the pastor was saying so that words that were spoken to the Chinese congregation were also now addressed to me.

The Holy Spirit came that morning in the person of a Chinese student who spoke English beautifully. But she became to me and to those of us in our pew a sign of the way in which Church is always a community of conversation: not of agreement, but of conversation. All of us, from our different perspectives, and with our different ways of talking and thinking, all of us joined in the praise of God.

The community of the Spirit.

IV.

But then the other claim that our text makes. "We are the Body of Christ."

According to Paul's understanding of church, the familiar song has it right but not entirely right: "The church is people." True but not the whole truth. Here's the other part of the truth: "The Church is Jesus Christ."

Now we like to think that that is kind of a wonderful metaphor: "Like Jesus Christ the church is one body." Or "the church is that one community that honors Jesus Christ."

But Paul didn't think that the church was like the body of Christ, he thought the church was the Body of Christ. Paul is writing to the church at Corinth; a few chapters earlier he has been showing his exasperation at some of the men in the Corinthian church.

He says that they have been engaged in immoral behavior, and that when they act immorally, the Corinthian Christians are members of the Body of Christ, and when they go astray they take the Body of Christ astray. And that is not just immorality; it is blasphemy.

V.

But now in 1 Corinthians 12 Paul is making the same claim much more positively and much more happily.

Here is the good news. You are not just the congregational church of Corinth; you are the Body of Christ.

And here's what that means.

It means that every one of you, every one of you, is a part of Christ. Every one of you is Christ to each other and every one of you is Christ to the world.

The church council is no more Christ than those who vote them into office, the choir no more—and no less—Christ than those of us who listen to them appreciatively. And perhaps most important, the clergy are no more Christ than the laity.

As a Protestant I long ago read a book by the distinguished Catholic Avery Dulles who said that one of the problems with traditional Catholicism is that it has tended to identify the church with the clergy. They are the church, and the rest of the believers are the spectators who cheer them on.

That has changed a good deal in Catholicism since Vatican II in the 1960s, but I think we've seen the issue arise again in just the last few months.

Too often the hierarchy has thought that any criticism of the clergy is a condemnation of the church. They have protected priests as if they had to do so in order to protect Christ himself.

If we are all the Body of Christ then the failure of priests is a matter of deep concern and the Body may need radical surgery. But the Body is richer, stronger, and far more larger than that little group of us who are paid to be professionally Christian.

And Protestant churches, too, it need hardly be said, are richer and stronger and more supportive than even the most gifted of our clergy.

Sometimes our tendency as Protestants is to think that the clergy are our designated Body of Christ. If we need some new service or envision some new mission—we too often simply ask our ministers to put it on their plate.

We are the Body of Christ, all of us.

VI.

"You are the body of Christ," says Paul (1 Cor. 12:27). And here's what it means: not just that every one of you—every one of you—is a member of Christ, it means that every one of you, every one of us, is a member of each other.

Here is how Paul summarizes it: "(in the Body of Christ all) the members . . . have the same care for one another. If one member suffers, all suffer together with it; if one member is honored, all rejoice together with it" (vv. 25–26).

A sobering moment some years ago: A group of friends who had been together at the University of Chicago Divinity School met on occasion in California, where we now lived, for lunch.

One of our group was just undergoing a difficult divorce. She joined us one noon, her eyes slightly chlorinated and her hair slightly damp. "I've just come from my swim club," she said. "You know I get more support and understanding there than I do in my own church."

Not here; not among you.

You know what moment Paul would love best in your worship service? It's that moment when the ushers come forward carrying those little folded notes for the minister so that when the time comes to pray we can share our celebrations and our concerns. . . . It is the moment when we bring before God and to one another the deepest longings and the strongest rejoicings of our hearts.

"Almighty God," says the old Anglican prayer, "Unto whom all hearts are open and all desires known."

As Christ's Body we are bold to open our hearts and confess our desires. In the light of those hearts and desires we seek to serve one another, and we serve one another first of all by doing what we are always called to do: Praying for the other members of the Body.

VII.

I am the church!
You are the church!
We are the church together!
All who follow Jesus all around the world,
yes, we're the church together."[2]

We are the church together.
The Spirit's Home.
Christ's Body.
Us.

Happy Pentecost. Amen.

38

This We Believe:
What Shall We Do?

MATTHEW 5:1–13
ROMANS 12:1–2, 14–21

This is the tenth and last sermon in the series "This We Believe," preached on June 6, 2010, at The Congregational Church of New Canaan, Connecticut.

I.

Paul Tillich was a German theologian who came to the United States in time to escape the ravages of the Third Reich and taught for many years at Union Theological Seminary in Morningside Heights, New York, New York.

In 1955 he wrote a sermon that had an enormous influence on seminary students for many years to come. He was preaching on the great Protestant theme that we are saved by grace and not through good works, and he was seeking to explain the meaning of the word "Grace."

The title of the sermon catches the heart of his theme: "You are accepted." Here are the lines that have stuck with many of us through the years.

(Grace) strikes us when year after year the longed-for perfection of life does not appear, when the old compulsions reign within us as they have for decades, when despair destroys all joy and courage. Sometimes at that moment a wave of light breaks into our darkness, and it is as though a voice were saying: "You are accepted, . . . accepted by that which is greater than you. . . . Do not try to do anything now;

perhaps later you will do much. . . . Simply accept the fact that you
are accepted."[1]

I was profoundly impressed by that sermon and not long after I first read
it, I returned to my home church, the First Baptist Church of Los Angeles, to preach the morning sermon. I preached on the familiar parable of the
Prodigal Son, and I said something like this: "In this story the son who runs
away gets it right because all he needs to do is accept the father's forgiveness;
the son who stays at home gets it wrong because he's still trying to earn his
father's favor." By grace are we saved, through faith.

Afterward, one of the pillars of the church, Milton Mackaig, took me to
lunch. "I wish somebody would give credit to the older brother," said Milton.
"He stayed at home; he cared for the flocks and the fields; he took care of his
aging father, surely the Bible ought to give him a break."

I suspected then and know now that Milton had a point. He had himself
been a faithful and loving husband, a good father, an honest business person,
and as I said, an absolute pillar of the church.

"Surely," said Milton, "that counts for something."

Surely it does.

II.

Here is what I have come to understand through the years. We are accepted,
but we are also responsible. We are saved by God's grace but what we do in
the light of that grace makes a huge difference.

Notice the series of blessings we read from Matthew's Gospel, the beatitudes. They don't say: "You've got to be poor in spirit. You've got to hunger
and thirst after righteousness. You've got to make peace."

What Jesus says is: This is what life looks like for a member of the Kingdom of Heaven. This is what your life will look like as a member of the family
of God. And Paul doesn't say: "Shape up so that God will love you." He says,
"In Jesus Christ God loves you so much that you are transformed."

To say that we are responsible is to say what Milton Mackaig said: What
we do matters. But to say that we are "response-able" is also to say that we
live our lives in obedience as a response to the love we have received in Jesus
Christ. We do not obey in order to get into the family; we obey in gratitude

---

1. Paul Tillich, *The Shaking of the Foundations* (New York: Scribner's Sons, 1948),
161, 162.

for the fact that we have been welcomed already. This is what we do as members of this family, this Christian church.

III.

Both Jesus, in Matthew's gospel, and Paul, in the letter to the Romans, are talking about how we respond to the unswerving goodness of God. What does it look like to be a member of God's Kingdom, asks Matthew. It looks like blessedness and blessedness is not just a warm feeling, it's a way of being, a way of acting, a way of relating.

What does it look like to live in God's family, asks Paul. It means grateful belonging, but also grateful response.

There is a whole rich field of studies that talks about what faithful response might look like and I want to choose from the blessings, from the beatitudes, three examples of what that faithfulness might look like, will look like, in our own lives.

"Blessed are those who hunger and thirst for righteousness, for they will be filled" (Matt. 5:6).
"Blessed are the merciful, for they will receive mercy" (v. 7).
"Blessed are the peacemakers, for they will be called children of God" (v. 9).

"Blessed are those who hunger and thirst for righteousness . . ."
Notice that Christian responsibility isn't just about being in favor of righteousness; we are called to hunger for it. Right relationships to God and right relationships to people. We have to long for a world more just and kind.

When Milton Mackaig reminded me that what we do as Christians makes a difference I had to listen because I remembered a time not that many years before when the first African Americans tried to join the church Milton and I shared.

Milton was pretty sure that was a bad idea; it made him uncomfortable, but the issue would not go away. Through prayer and Bible study and his pastor's preaching God kept nagging Milton.

After a time an African American man joined the church and joined the choir. One of the choir members was so upset that he tried to beat up the man one Sunday in the robing room.

Milton heard about this sad incident and the next Sunday as we sat in our pews and watched the choir process we heard a not very distinguished baritone but saw a very distinguished Christian. Milton had joined the choir and marched down the aisle beside his African American brother in Christ. Hunger and thirst for righteousness.

IV.

And then, "Blessed are the merciful, for they shall receive mercy." Mercy is profoundly countercultural in our society. We specialize in holding on. Here's the problem, though, when I tell you I've got a grudge—the truth is the grudge has got me. The merciful receive one of the greatest mercies God can give: they move on.

And here I defend my early reading of the Prodigal Son. The problem with the older brother is not that he has done what's right; that's great. The problem is that he's not yet willing to have mercy on his brother who hasn't done so well. The Father doesn't want the son to be any less responsible; he just wants him to be more merciful.

Blessed are the merciful.

V.

And "blessed are the peacemakers, for they will be called children of God." Not just the passive, not just the nonaggressive, not just those who applaud peace: those who make peace.

In the time of the Sermon on the Mount and in the time of the Letter to the Romans it was fairly clear how to make peace. Christians acted one by one not to be vengeful, not to return injury with injury, to turn the other cheek. One by one Christians were called to make peace.

That is of course an essential part of peacemaking but for us as twenty-first century Christians in the United States it's not yet responsibility enough. In ways that neither Matthew nor Paul would have imagined we have at our disposal power, influence, resources.

We can help build peace beyond our own families, beyond our own churches, in our larger context as citizens.

I want to go back to Paul Tillich again. Not too long after he came to the United States the Third Reich did take over Germany and he knew that it was his Christian responsibility to respond. So he recorded a series of urgent messages to be sent to the German people urging them in the name of God to resist Hitler's oppression and the lust for war.

One of Tillich's students at Union Seminary was Dietrich Bonhoeffer. Bonhoeffer never heard Tillich's sermon "You are accepted," but he wrote eloquently about the fact that grace does not diminish our responsibility, it encourages it.

He worried about something he called "cheap grace."

> Cheap grace is the preaching of forgiveness without requiring repentance, baptism without church discipline, Communion without confession . . . Cheap grace is grace without discipleship, grace without the cross, grace without Jesus Christ, living and incarnate.[2]

For Bonhoeffer God's grace required even more than it did for Tillich. He felt called to return to Germany, though he could have stayed in the United States for the duration of the war. He joined the opposition to Hitler, finally even joining a failed conspiracy to assassinate the Fuhrer.

Making peace isn't always just making nice; you know that.

Just days before the war ended, Bonheoffer was hanged in the prison where he had stayed. He said he lived his final days with much fear; his fellow prisoners said he lived his final days with astonishing grace.

VI.

Listen, beloved, this Christian thing is a big deal. We are given gifts beyond our measuring and sometimes we are given responsibilities that seem beyond our capacities.

Paul talks about how the Holy Spirit helps us in our weakness. Matthew talks about the living Christ who is always present to nurture and sustain—Immanuel, God with us.

Years ago we took our sons to a campground for vacation and before dinner I took the boys to the men's room to wash our hands. After we had washed our hands, I reached up to the towel dispenser to get a towel for each of the boys. But Jonah protested loudly: "Let me do it myself."

Now it's hard to believe but in those days he was rather short and the towel dispenser was rather high, and I had no idea what to do until he made it clear: "Come on, Daddy, lift me up so that I can do it myself."

In the Gospel Christ gives us astonishing grace and demands of us astonishing responsibility.

But then he lifts us to obey.

To Christ be thanks and praise. Amen.

---

2. Dietrich Bonhoeffer, *The Cost of Discipleship*, trans. Reginald Fuller (New York: Macmillan, 1949), 47.

39

Great Words of the Faith: Love

I JOHN 4:7–11

I CORINTHIANS 13

This sermon is the first sermon in a series preached at The Congregational Church of New Canaan, New Canaan, Connecticut, titled "Great Words of the Faith." The sermon was preached on September 19, 2010.

I.

When we began to talk last spring about a series of sermons for this year, Skip told me that there had been a request for a series of sermons on the great words of Christian faith.

I think there are at least two problems for us with the use of traditional Christian language.

The first problem is that sometimes the words of the faith that seemed historically so important now sometimes seem obscure, old-fashioned, confusing: words like "justification" and "sanctification" seem left over from another era, more puzzling to us than helpful. And we'll look at some of those words in the months ahead and hope we can find renewed meaning in old phrases.

The second problem is that sometimes the words of the faith are used so often that they seem almost like a cliché. "Heaven" is one of those words. We turn heaven as the realm of God into movie titles like *All Dogs Go to Heaven* and trite phrases like, "That dessert was just heavenly." We use the words so often and so loosely that they seem to lose all their punch, all their power.

Today's word of the faith, "Love," is just such a word. We love our spouses or companions, our children, our best friends; we love God or try to love God. But we also love our new car and the Yankees, Mets, or Red Sox, depending on our allegiance, and the new restaurant that just opened at the center of town.

So my goal today is clear, if not simple. I want to revive the word "love" as a central term for understanding Christian faith. That doesn't mean we can't still love our favorite book or TV show, but it does mean that in the context of Christian faith love is stronger, deeper, and stranger than that.

II.

I begin by citing the model of preaching I learned in my early years, and for once I'm going to follow it exactly.

The shorthand for the structure of the typical sermon, as I learned in my youth, was that a sermon has three points and a poem. Three points because that's all we can expect anybody to remember, and a poem because we want to end on a note of inspiration and not just information.

So here we go, three points and a poem—all concerning Christian love.

III.

The first point: When Christians talk about love we mean both the love that God shows for us, and the love that we show for one another. And the two loves are so interrelated that they are very nearly one.

The writer of the first letter of John puts it this way: "Beloved, let us love one another, because love is from God; everyone who loves is born of God and knows God. . . . For God is love."

The poet E. E. Cummings begins a poem with these words:

love is the ever only god

who spoke this earth all glad and big
even a thing all small and sad
man, may his mighty briefness dig[1]

The letter of John and E. E. Cummings do not say everything that needs to be said about God, but they say the first thing: God loves the world. Out

1. e.e. Cummings, "Love Is the Every Only God," in *Complete Poems 1904–1962*, ed. George J. Firmage (New York: Liveright Publishing Corp., 2013).

of God's love, God created the world; out of God's love, God sent Christ into the world; out of God's love, God created us; and out of God's love, Christ brings each of us into the family of God.

And because we are loved, we can love.

Years ago when I was in seminary there was a young boy in our youth group named Roger. Roger had a tough time. His mother loved him but couldn't really afford to support him. The people he hung around with joined him in a variety of troublemaking that was moving quickly toward lawbreaking.

Roger and those of us who cared for him were faced with a choice. Either he would move to a new environment or he would move to a facility for juvenile offenders.

I did a truly sneaky thing for which I continue to repent before God and my family. I brought Roger home to our family home for the holidays—suspecting, yea, trusting that once my parents saw his dilemma, they would take him in.

And they saw his dilemma, and they took him in. For some years.

Roger wasn't always easy to love. Listen, no one is always easy to love. He was often surly, feisty, and more than a little ill-at-ease in his new environment.

But over the years I watched the love that he received turn into the love that he could share. One Christmas he'd come home to New Haven to visit his family and I went to pick him up to take him to the airport to return to Rochester and my family.

When I got to his house he showed me with great pride the gifts he had chosen carefully and wrapped lovingly for each member of my family. He began to love because he was loved.

Listen, we begin to love each other when we discover that in Jesus Christ God loves each of us—absolutely, unconditionally.

When we doubt that we are loved we spend all our energy taking care of ourselves; when we know that we are loved we turn much of our energy to caring for others.

We love because God first loved us; human love and divine love, woven together. The first point of this three-point sermon.

IV.

And the second point is this: Love is both a gift and a responsibility.

In 1 John the author tells us that God's love for us in Jesus Christ is the great, immeasurable gift; because of that love we are able to love. And the fact that we are able to love is also a great, immeasurable gift.

In 1 Corinthians Paul is trying to chasten members of the Corinthian church who are boasting about how gifted they are, and to encourage members of the Corinthian church who think that they're not so blessed in the business of being gifted.

Listen, Paul says, you all have one gift in common; you have the gift of love. God has given to each of you, wonderfully, powerfully, the gift of loving God and the gift of loving one another. And that gift is poured out equally, graciously, available to all.

And then Paul makes an odd but powerful claim. He says: "Since you can love, you should love."

And then he shows what love looks like: "Love is patient; love is kind; love is not envious or boastful or arrogant" (13:4). To paraphrase what Paul is saying to that congregation:

> Love doesn't get jealous about another person's gifts.
> And love doesn't brag about one's own gifts.
> Love IS a gift. But love is also a responsibility.

A good friend of mine and I are sitting at supper with the friend's daughter, who is about to give up on a relationship.

"Listen," says her mother. "Love is hard work."

Or another story: In my high school days I went to a very middle class school in a comfortable neighborhood in our city, Los Angeles. Through city-wide student government gatherings I became friends with a young man named Stan Sanders who lived on the south side of our city. We occasionally went to sports events together, and sometimes church together, and he even showed up for one of my birthday parties.

No respectable seventeen-year-old will talk about "love" when it comes to friendship, but I would have said it was a strong relationship; we knew each other pretty well.

Move forward a few years; I've moved away from Los Angeles when the so-called Watts Riots break out. Mostly poor African Americans demonstrating and telling their anger at the way in which our society had excluded them.

In *Life Magazine* an interview with one of the most articulate citizens of Watts: My friend Stan Sanders. I'd missed the passion; I'd missed the anger; I'd even missed the fact that his neighborhood was called "Watts."

Our friendship was a gift; but it was a gift that required a lot more work than I had known how to show. Love is a gift; love is a responsibility. "(Love) does not rejoice in wrongdoing, but rejoices in the truth" (v. 6). And that surely means taking the time to find out what the truth is, and rejoicing when wrongdoing ends.

V.

For Christians, love is both the love God shows to us and the love that we show to each other.

For Christians love is both a great gift and a great responsibility.

And now the third point—soon the poem—as Christians we believe that love endures.

Paul ends his own poem on love with these words to the Corinthian Christians. "Love never ends" (v. 8a). As for sermons, they will come to an end, as to speaking in tongues, they will cease. As for human knowledge, that will end, too.

"Three things abide: Faith, hope and love. And the greatest of these is love" (v. 13, au. trans.).

That's a promise, of course; not a proof. It's the promise on which the Christian faith is based. God's love for us in Jesus Christ, our love for each other—that never ends, not ever.

I want somewhat hesitantly to return to the story of Roger again . . . the boy who stayed with my family. If I were writing up his story as a fictional drama for movies or TV I'd tell you that he graduated from high school and went on to a successful life in some productive and worthwhile endeavor.

But it didn't happen that way. After the tough years with my parents, he went to live with an older sister, now grown enough to care for him, and then into the service. And then he pretty much drifted away.

Years later when I returned to New Haven to teach I tracked down the sister and through her tracked down Roger. He didn't have much, and he wasn't very well. We had a pleasant lunch, and he told me of his illness. (He had a couple of investment schemes where he thought surely I could help him and help myself as well. I cautiously declined.) Then a couple more phone calls over the next couple of years; and then silence.

Almost surely he is gone; almost surely his life in this world, its striving, its anxieties, his dreams and his schemes, the long last illness—all have passed away.

But here's what I believe. The love endures. The love my parents shared for him endures. The love he learned to show to others endures. God's love for him in Jesus Christ endures.

Those moments of genuine loving were not just shadows fated to disappear into the darkness forever. They were and are and shall be held and cherished in the very heart of God.

Love never ends.

VI.

That's three points. Now the poem. Though 1 Corinthians 13 is itself an even better poem than the one I'll quote.

It's Robert Browning's poem called "Love Among the Ruins" and it tells how a shepherd, coming home from watching the flock, returning to the woman he loves, journeys each day past the ruins of a great empire; all the stuff and pomp this world most cherishes, gone to dust.

What lasts, of course, is the relationship; lover to lover, parents and children, friend to friend, among the members of this church.

Here's the shepherd, coming home:

> (When the king looked on the city) every side,
> Far and wide,
> All the mountains topped with temples, all the glades'
> Colonnades,
> All the causeys, bridges, aqueducts,—and then,
> All the men!
> When I do come, she will speak not, she will stand,
> Either hand
> On my shoulder, give her eyes the first embrace
> Of my face,
> Ere we rush, ere we extinguish sight and speech
> Each on each.
>
> In one year they sent a million fighters forth
> South and North,
> And they built their gods a brazen pillar high
> As the sky
> Yet reserved a thousand chariots in full force—
> Gold, of course.
> Oh heart! oh blood that freezes, blood that burns!
> Earth's returns
> For whole centuries of folly, noise and sin!
> Shut them in,
> With their triumphs and their glories and the rest.
> Love is best.[2]

Amen.

---

2. Robert Browning, "Love among the Ruins," https://www.poetryfoundation.org /poems/43763/love-among-the-ruins.

40

Great Words of the Faith: Grace

ROMANS 3:21–28
2 CORINTHIANS 12:1–10

This sermon is one in a series on the "Great Words of the Faith," preached once a month at The Congregational Church in New Canaan, Connecticut. David preached this sermon on October 31, 2010. The two church people mentioned in the sermon are Tyler Simpson, who was a soloist in the church choir, and Jody Davis, who was the Director of Music Ministries at the church.

I.

Toward the end of the 1960s our country was angry, depressed, and polarized. An unpopular war and an uncertain economy divided us into feuding camps, and the popular music of the day showed the division. Pick one radio station and you'd hear variations on "God Bless America"; pick another and you could hear nothing but protest songs, usually to the accompaniment of a guitar.

Astonishingly in the midst of all that dissonance someone revived an old Gospel song. In my memory the reviver was Joan Baez, but she may just be the first voice I heard. And astonishingly across the dial you could hear, sung by different voices to somewhat different beats:

Amazing grace, how sweet the sound
That saved a wretch like me!

I once was lost, but now am found,
Was blind, but now I see.[1]

We had an alternative anthem to the songs that assured us that patriotism would save us or that protest would save us. What would save us, said Ms. Baez and countless others, was amazing grace.

The hymn that Tyler sang so beautifully at the beginning of our service, we soon discovered had been written by John Newton and published in 1779. John Newton had been the captain of a ship engaged in the slave trade. A huge storm arose and swamped the ship. Newton prayed with a faith he barely knew he had, and when the storm abated he was still, almost miraculously, alive. And so the song: "Amazing grace, how sweet the sound that saved a wretch like me."

II.

Of course as Newton knew full well it wasn't the word grace that saved him; it was the God of grace who saved him. But his hymn revived for the American audience of the late twentieth century a great reminder. Through grace, God saves us. (We'll have another reminder later in the sermon. Through grace God sustains us.)

But when Newton celebrated the grace that saved he wasn't only celebrating the fact that he'd been saved from the waves. Far more important he'd been saved from his sins. Sometimes we wonder what "sin" looks like, but in Newton's case it was pretty clear to him and is pretty clear to us. He'd been making a living by slavery, by a practice that owned, exploited, and disposed of his fellow human beings.

So he didn't just sing about grace; he lived it. As a man forgiven he gave up his work for the slave owners and became one of the leaders of the abolition movement in Great Britain.

And here's what he knew. He hadn't been saved because he was such a good man, because he wasn't all that good. He hadn't been saved because he was a pious man. He had been saved by God's amazing grace.

Another way to translate the New Testament word for "grace" is to say "gift." Newton had been saved, forgiven, set on the right path by the sheer gift of God.

1. John Newton, "Amazing Grace, How Sweet the Sound," *The Presbyterian Hymnal* (Louisville, KY: Westminster/John Knox Press, 1990), 280.

III.

Speaking of gifts, I was marching along with the preparation of this sermon when Jodie reminded me that today is Reformation Sunday, the day when we celebrate the gifts God gave the church through Martin Luther and the Protestant Reformation.

When Luther learned about God's grace he wasn't a slave ship owner, he was a monk. He had given his life to God and he had striven night and day to be good enough for God to favor him. But the more he strove the more he feared that God's righteousness was so great that nobody had a chance of getting God's favor, not even a pious monk.

Here's what Luther said about the great reformation in his soul:

> Though I lived as a monk without reproach, I felt that I was a sinner before God with an extremely disturbed conscience. I could not believe that God was placated (by my piety.) I did not love; indeed I hated the righteous God who punishes sinners.[2]

But of course, eager as he was to please God, Luther kept studying scripture and what he found in scripture was Paul's letter to the Romans and what he found in Romans were the verses that we read this morning: "Since all have sinned and fall short of the glory of God; they are now justified by his grace as a gift" (3:23–24a). Grace. Gift.

Not in striving but in receiving; not in accomplishment but in gratitude.

Luther could have sung Newton's song if he'd had Newton's song to sing: "Amazing grace, how sweet the sound that saved a wretch like me."

Instead he wrote his own song, not about God the terrible judge, but about the God who saves, and forgives.

> A mighty fortress is our God,
> A bulwark never failing;
> Our helper He amid the flood
> Of mortal ills prevailing.[3]

---

2. Martin Luther, *Selections from His Writings*, ed. John Dillenberger (New York: Anchor, 1958), 1.

3. Martin Luther, "A Mighty Fortress Is Our God," *The Presbyterian Hymnal* (Louisville, KY: Westminster/John Knox Press, 1990), 260.

IV.

Listen, beloved, this is the real protest song: Against the claims that we must save ourselves by our effort; or by our energy, or by our intelligence, or our success.

Against the sure and certain knowledge: That when we have knocked as hard as we can against heaven's door, we will not feel that we have done enough.

Against the great American claim that God's main job is to award our achievements and then get out of the way.

> Amazing grace, how sweet the sound
> That saved a wretch like me.

> A mighty fortress is our God,
> A bulwark never failing.

V.

Of course John Newton and Martin Luther and especially the Apostle Paul, who gave them the idea of relying on grace, all of them knew that grace didn't just happen.

Grace was a gift, and it was a gift given through the life and death and resurrection of Jesus Christ: An expensive gift; a priceless gift. We'll talk more about the meaning of that gift when we talk about "atonement" in a couple of months, but let me sketch just a beginning of what it means to say that the grace of God is given us in Jesus Christ.

Now in our journey through famous lyrics we move from John Newton and Martin Luther to Alan Jay Lerner and *My Fair Lady*.

Eliza Doolittle is complaining to her boyfriend Freddy that he talks a good line but that talking about love is never enough.

"Words! Words! Words!" she sings. "I'm so sick of words! Don't waste my time, show me! Don't talk at all! Show me!"

I know this is much too simple, but for this morning simply will have to do. From Moses through the prophets, through David and the Psalmists up through John the Baptist, God had been using all the right words: By grace you are saved. By my love you are redeemed.

But like Eliza we still didn't get it. Show us! We pleaded. And God did. Hands outstretched upon a cross. The gift of forgiveness and love, that none of us could ever achieve, and none of us could ever deserve.

So the Apostle Paul: "[All] are . . . justified by [God's] grace as a gift, through the redemption that is in Christ Jesus" (Rom. 3:24).

So Martin Luther,

> [God's grace] above earthly powers,
> No thanks to them, abideth
> The Spirit and the gifts are ours
> Through him who with us sideth; . . .
> Dost ask who that may be?
> Christ Jesus, it is He.[4]

VI.

Grace saves: God's grace through Jesus Christ our Lord.

And grace sustains. Paul discovered that God's grace saved him, forgave him, and drove him on.

But what would sustain him when times grew hard? Why of course, God's grace. Not what he achieved but what he received. Not just grace for all time but grace for the day.

The great story we read from 2 Corinthians. Not the beginning of Paul's faith but the gift that sustained that faith. Something has gone wrong; he doesn't say what: a thorn in the flesh.

Three times he prays that it will go away, and three times God's word is no.

Until God's word is an even greater yes. "'My grace is sufficient for you, for my power is made perfect in weakness'" (2 Cor. 12:9).

Grace. Now not the grace that saves us but the grace that sustains us; not the grace that makes us strong but the grace that uses even our weakness.

> Amazing grace, how sweet the sound
> That saved a wretch like me.

And oh yes, amazing grace, how sweet the sound that gets me through the day.

VII.

A personal word and then we're done. Early in my adulthood I was told by a friend that I was a classic overachiever. I've never been quite sure whether

---

4. Martin Luther, "A Mighty Fortress Is Our God," in *The Presbyterian Hymnal* (Louisville, KY: Westminster/John Knox Press, 1990), 260, stanzas 4 and 2.

that means that I was pushing myself amazingly hard or that it was amazing that I'd achieved anything at all, given my basic limitations.

But at least my sense of myself was that I had to prove myself, pretty much all the time. Pretty much to everyone.

College was a great gift and a great pain. Somewhere in the middle of sophomore year it all came crashing down on me. However good I wanted to be, somebody would be better; if I graduated someone would graduate cum laude, if I made cum laude, someone else would be magna cum . . . and on and on until that darned classmate of mine won the Nobel Prize. I didn't just feel disappointed I felt pretty much helpless.

I was reading a small book on what it means to be Christian and I heard between the lines of that book an assurance that I'm not sure is actually found on the page but that has sustained me ever since.

"You are not asked to be sufficient."

There it is. My byword. My testimony. God's word to Paul translated for me, and translated for you as well. "My grace is sufficient for you, for my power is made perfect in weakness."

Grace that saves. Grace that sustains.

Amazing grace.

To Christ be thanks and praise.

Amen.

41

Great Words of the Faith: Incarnation

JOHN 1:1–18

This sermon was preached on December 12, 2010, at The Congregational Church of New Canaan, Connecticut. It is the third sermon in the series "Great Words of the Faith."

I.

In the beginning was the Word, and the Word was with God, and the Word was God. . . . And the Word became flesh and dwelt among us.
(John 1:1, 14)

John William Bailey was a distinguished New Testament scholar. I never knew John William Bailey, but I knew his wife, Louise. Louise, at least in the halo-like glaze of memory, was sure that John William could have done no wrong. And each year Louise could hardly wait for Christmastime to announce: "John William Bailey hated all this talk about the baby Jesus. Sweet little baby boy, you've got to be kidding. What about the strong Jesus, the prophet, the master."

I suspect that the reason Louise Bailey always got so exercised at Christmas was that John William Bailey not only didn't much like the Baby Jesus; he didn't much like incarnation.

"Incarnation" is the traditional word for the traditional claim that in the man Jesus of Nazareth, the great God, creator of the universe and judge of the nations, came to dwell among us . . . "in carne" . . . "In the flesh" . . . "incarnation."

And that's a little embarrassing because if in Jesus Christ God came to dwell among us then we have to talk about God starting out in a manger and ending up on the cross.

If we don't have incarnation we can keep God safely powerful and in charge—fully God; and we can keep Jesus as a great prophet and religious leader—fully human: God's in his heaven; all's right with the world. Jesus is on earth, talking about God.

And while it's not exactly that never the twain shall meet, it is quite clear that we'll never have to worry about confusing questions about how one person can be really God and really human, which is what the classical doctrine of incarnation has claimed.

II.

When the Gospel of John talks about Jesus being fully God and fully human, it talks in poetry. The Word that was with God and that was God became flesh and dwelt among us.

In the years that followed, some of the best minds of the church tried to figure out how Jesus could be both fully divine and fully human, and they used the best philosophical language of the day to make the point . . . talk about substances and hypostases and unconfused intermingling.

While it's hard for me always to understand what these early Christian theologians were saying, I'm pretty clear what they were not saying. They were not saying that Jesus had these two personalities—a trimmed down version of the *Three Faces of Eve*, for those of you who remember that book by Corbett H. Thigpen and Hervey M. Cleckley.

Sometimes first year students at seminary read the biblical texts and try to assign different personalities to different sentences in the stories about Jesus. In this same Gospel, for instance, the Gospel of John, students suggest that when Lazarus dies the human part of Jesus weeps and then the God part of Jesus raises Lazarus, presumably making the human part of Jesus feel better.

But the faith in incarnation is that Jesus is both God and human all the time. An inadequate but helpful way that I think about it is to say that in Jesus Christ we see what it really means for God to be God and what it really means for us to be human.

Again in John's Gospel the disciple Philip says: "Lord, show us the Father and we shall be satisfied." And Jesus says: "If you've seen me you've seen the Father" (14:8–9 RSV and au. trans.).

III.

And especially when it comes to the claim that in Jesus we see what God is like, the doctrine of incarnation gets really tricky.

Is that baby in the manger a picture of what God looks like? Vulnerable? Counting on people like Mary and Joseph? Not so high and lifted up above us, but humble and serving among us. Is that who God is?

Is that outlaw on the cross a picture of what God looks like? Suffering for us; suffering with us; caught between terrible pain and unquenchable hope.

Is God most God not when God rules over us but when God rejoices and suffers and rejoices again—with us? I think so. I think incarnation binds us irrevocably to the God of the manger and the God of the cross.

For years I've been waiting to tell this story and as Jonah pointed out when we talked about this sermon last week the time at last has come.

In our family we collect crèches, scenes of the holy family at the manger for the nativity. And at one shop that sold crèches I long ago noticed a sign that simply informed shoppers with the following words: "the price is under the Baby Jesus."

Of course that meant that if you lifted up the babe in the manger and looked closely you could see what the crèche cost, the manger, the family, the whole business.

Even at Christmas if we look closely at the baby Jesus, all that vulnerability, all that weakness, all that hope—we begin to realize the price. The price of incarnation is crucifixion. God born for us is bound to be God dying for us, too.

Oddly, God is most God when God is most God for us; oddly God is most God just when God is most vulnerable, most human.

IV.

And incarnation still goes on. When Matthew begins his Gospel, he tells the story of the magi, the wise men; he says that the best name for Jesus is "Immanuel," which means "God with us." Not God used to be with us, but God, with us. Incarnation.

And John's Gospel that we read this morning starts not with a manger but with a hymn, and after the hymn has sung about the Word made flesh it says this about Jesus, the incarnate Word. "The light shines in the darkness, and the darkness has not overcome it" (1:5 RSV).

Not "the light shone at Bethlehem" or at Calvary or at the empty tomb, but now; the light shining now.

God incarnate, God with us, isn't always as flashy as we might like. More like the light that lighted the manger, but stronger than the darkness, surer than the night.

Still today the faith by which we live the light shines in the darkness and the darkness has not overcome it.

A friend told the story of her childhood in Sweden. In Sweden the days are short and the nights are long and night can fall quick and harsh.

One afternoon my friend and her brothers and sisters had been playing on the lawn, and when night fell they dashed into the house leaving the toys unattended on the yard. After supper and before they could go to bed their mother sent them out to gather the toys. Of course, said my friend, they were a little, maybe more than a little afraid of the dark. But there on the front stoop their mother stood with a lighted candle, and for as long as it took them to do what they had to do, she repeated again and again: "I am here; I am here."

The Word became flesh; and now God dwells among us.

The light shines in the darkness, and the darkness has not overcome it. Will not overcome it.

Incarnation.

Merry Christmas.

Amen.

42

Great Words of the Faith: Heaven and Hell

This sermon was one of a series of sermons preached on the "Great Words of the Faith" at The Congregational Church in New Canaan, Connecticut, May 22, 2011. The people referred to in this sermon are: Harold "Skip" Masback, Senior Minister of the church; Jonah Smith Bartlett, who was on the ministerial staff and is our son; Jody David, Director of Music Ministries; and David Winkworth, who sang in the choir and worked in the office and prepared bulletins for Sunday worship.

I.

In case you haven't been counting, this is sermon number twenty in the two series of sermons I have preached in this pulpit over the past two years.

It has been an enormous gift and privilege to preach here month after month, and I'm deeply grateful to those who made this financially possible and to the adult education committee and to Skip and Jonah and the ministerial staff for doing the hard work of coordinating the series and to Jodie for her unfailing attention to the correlation between sermon and music—its own kind of sacrament.

The very first sermon, nineteen back, was based on the first words of the Bible: "In the beginning God created the heavens and the earth" (Gen. 1:1), so it seemed appropriate in addressing the topic of heaven and hell that I turn to the last words of the Bible in the book of Revelation.

Or, almost the last words. It was chapter twenty-one and not chapter twenty-two that gave me the verses I wanted to explore together, and I looked quickly at the first paragraph of Revelation 21 and sent word to David Winkworth that I'd be preaching on Revelation 21:1–8. What better way to end the series than with John of Patmos' familiar promise that God himself will be with us and will wipe away every tear.

Unfortunately, when the time came to pay closer attention to the text I discovered that John goes on in the last verse of our paragraph. "As for the cowardly, the faithless, the polluted, the murderers, the fornicators, the sorcerers, the idolaters, and all liars, their place will be in the lake that burns with fire and sulfur" (v. 8).

II.

The truth is, of course, that the lake that burns with fire and sulfur doesn't get much attention in the so-called mainline Protestant churches of America, like this church and the church we belong to in Georgia.

Among our fellow Americans in general I would have said that hell has pretty much faded from consciousness while heaven continues to draw more attention.

For some weeks the most popular book on the New York Times Best Sellers list has been a father's report of his son's near-death experience including information about heaven. Among evangelical Christians, the preacher Rob Bell has stirred up a storm by suggesting that heaven is a lot bigger than many more conservative Christians would have dreamed.

But just when I thought hell had dropped off the charts forever, Osama bin Laden was killed and CNN did a survey of the American people and it turns out that 63 percent of us are pretty sure that bin Laden is in hell.

In important ways, this makes sense. John of Patmos is deeply concerned with the lake of fire and the burning sulfur as a final resting place for those powers of the Roman Empire who had been imprisoning and killing John and his fellow Christians. Surely there would be a price to pay.

And when we think back on the horror that Osama bin Laden wreaked on our country and on people we love . . . surely, we think, there is a price to pay.

Now let me wander into my professor mode for just a minute and say a word about heaven and hell in the Bible. The words "heaven" and "hell" don't occur nearly as much as you might think.

It's Matthew's Gospel that speaks most often of the Kingdom of Heaven, but that's Matthew's way of trying to speak reverentially of the Kingdom of God. He doesn't care about where heaven is, he just cares that God is in charge. It's Matthew who gives us the familiar prayer: "Thy will be done on earth as in heaven," which means, "Thy will be done among humans as it is among the blessed, among the saints."

And "hell" is usually the translation of a Hebrew word Gehenna, which was the garbage dump outside Jerusalem where the trash was burned.

Mostly, as someone famously said, the Bible doesn't care much about the furniture of heaven or the temperature of hell.

What the Bible does care about is two things.

> God is in charge.
> There are consequences for what we do.

III.

Let's start with the consequences. The doctrine of hell is mostly a dramatic way of insisting that there are consequences for what we do. I may have a hard time with Revelation's claim that liars and murderers are in hell, but as Christians we do believe that lying matters not just to us but to God and that in the economy of God you can't get away with murder—not forever, not eternally.

In Christopher Marlowe's play *Doctor Faustus*, Faust has sold himself to the devil for the sake of his own sordid ambitions and finally discovers that he doesn't have to wait for death to know the reality of judgment:

"Why this is hell, nor am I out of it."

Faust discovers what the church at its clearest has affirmed. Hell is not so much about fires or eternal tortures; it would be a bizarre God who took it as God's job to torture the torturers. Hell is about separation from God. To be apart from God, why that is hell, and when we're apart from God, we are not out of it.

IV.

And heaven, by this understanding, is not so much a place—heaven is the presence of God. To be with God, that is heaven, and when we are with God, we are heaven's citizens.

And that is true in life and it is true in death, which is why we have the great affirmation of the book of Revelation: "See the home of God is among mortals. He will dwell with them as their God. They will be his people, and God himself will be with them and will wipe away every tear" (vv. 3–4 au. trans.).

I think that in about half the sermons this year I've turned again to the story of the prodigal son, and it seems to me now that that story also gives us a kind of parable of heaven and hell as the Bible understands them.

When the younger son is in the far country he is in hell because he is separated from his family. He's in hell whether he knows it or not. He's in hell when he's suffering famine and torment, of course. But he's also in hell when he's partying away everything he owns, having wasted his substance the King James says: Far from home.

And the return, not so much the party and the fatted calf, but the welcoming Father and the outstretched arms: that's heaven. Like the great paraphrase of Psalm 23 when the wanderer comes back to his house: "No more a stranger or a guest but as a child at home."

V.

You know that in movie reviews the movie critic will sometimes give the reader a spoiler alert. If you read on, you're going to find out more about the movie than you may want to know before you've actually seen the film.

I'm now providing a heresy alert. These next few minutes will represent a minority opinion in the history of Christian theology. The patron saint of this minority opinion is a great early African theologian named Origen, but I suspect the blessed St. Paul came close to this sometimes.

Look at the Prodigal Son. Hell is being apart from God; heaven is repenting and turning and coming home.

Now traditional theology has said that there's a time limit on the invitation to come home. When we die, if we're still in the far country, the door slams shut. The loving father rescinds the invitation, and we are doomed to eternal separation.

Origen believed so strongly in the strength and mercy of God that he imagined that the loving father never cancelled the invitation, never stopped looking for the prodigal, and never turned his back in disgust.

Maybe someone is in hell for all eternity. That's God business and not ours. What we know of God, what we see in Jesus Christ, is the love that will not let us go.

Not now. Not ever.

VI.

I said a few minutes ago that there are two great claims when it comes to talking about heaven and hell.

> The first claim is that God is in charge.
> The second claim is that there are consequences for what we do.

The book of Revelation is partly concerned with the second claim: there are consequences for what we do. That's why our passage ends with the fornicators and the sorcerers in the lake that burns with fire and sulfur—far from God, far from home.

But the book of Revelation is much more concerned with the first claim—that God is in charge.

At the beginning of my time with you we looked at that beginning claim: God is the maker of heaven and earth. Alpha.

Now as our time together closes, we look to the claim that closes our story. In Jesus Christ God redeems the heaven and the earth that God has made. Omega.

I want to end our chapter from the book of Revelation as John of Patmos should have done, not with the fire, but with the faith.

> Then I saw a new heaven and a new earth, and I heard a loud voice from
>> the throne, saying:
> "See the home of God is among mortals.
> He will dwell with them;
> they will be his peoples,
> and God himself will be with them;
>
> he will wipe every tear from their eyes.
> Death will be no more."

In the name of the Father; and of the Son; and of the Holy Spirit. Amen.

43

Great Words of the Faith: Justification

ROMANS 5:1–11
LUKE 15:11–32

This sermon is the sixth sermon in the series "Great Words of the Faith." The sermon was preached on January 2, 2011, at The Congregational Church of New Canaan, Connecticut.

I.

Okay, here is the assignment the adult education committee gave me. Preach a series of sermons about the great words of the Christian faith. Most of the great words aren't words we toss around very much, but at least they make some connection with our everyday language.

"Providence" is so important that Rhode Island named a town for it. "Grace" is a popular girl's name and it's part of the title of the one Christian song pretty much everyone, believer or non-believer or just curious, knows how to sing: "Amazing Grace." "Incarnation," which was last month's word, isn't very commonly used either, but that Sunday we had the great advantage of the Christmas pageant with real live babies and it was hard to miss the great claim of incarnation, that in the baby Jesus, God comes to dwell among us.

But "Justification," I dare say doesn't pop up very often in our conversations or in our ponderings. Yet that word "Justification" split the Roman Catholic Church in 1517 into Catholics and Protestants. For better or for worse the debate about justification was used to justify—see, I can sneak the word in—was used to justify the Thirty Years War which tore Europe apart.

To this day theologians from the Vatican on the one side and from the World Council of Churches on the other continue to debate about justification and to wonder whether we can ever all just get along when it comes to that issue.

Our attempt to understand "justification" is complicated by the fact that the Greek word that is translated as justification can mean so many slightly different things. It can mean "justice" or "righteousness" or "uprightness" or, believe it or not, "rectification," and when the translations try to translate texts like Romans 5 they keep using different English words to translate the same Greek root because we haven't got any English word that even begins to catch it all.

So let me rush in where angels and great theologians tread very gently and then of course I'll elaborate. "Justification" is the word the Bible and the church use to talk about being right with God.

In the part of the country where we live you can still see billboards that often cite the passage from Romans we read this morning, and the billboard's designers make the simple plea: "Get right with God." Rightness with God: that's justification.

II.

The Reformation came to pass, the church split up, because Martin Luther thought that the Catholic Church was preaching justification by good works. That is, he thought that priests were telling the people that if they were good enough God would accept them. Being good enough meant doing good works, including giving generously to help build St. Peter's in Rome, and that annoyed Luther, but what really annoyed him was the idea that we could win our way to God's favor. He thought the main word of the Catholic Church was: "Get right with God, and we'll tell you how to do so."

Luther said, on the contrary, that justification doesn't come by works it comes by faith. Getting right with God isn't something we can do, it is what God has done for us; when we accept that God made us right with God, we have faith. We are justified—made right—by faith.

Paul Tillich was a great theologian of the twentieth century who taught at Union Theological Seminary and then at Harvard and then at Chicago. He tried to explain justification by faith in language that twentieth-century people could understand, and for me as a college student and for Skip who came to Tillich some years later, he helped.

Tillich said that one way to understand being justified, being right with God, is to know that we are accepted. But in order fully to be justified we have to accept that we are accepted; we hear the word: "In Jesus Christ you are accepted" if we say: "I accept that," that's faith; and by that faith we are justified; brought into right relationship with God.

III.

Let me try to make this business of justification more concrete and maybe even clear by telling two stories and talking about one supper.

"Justification" is Paul's great word, so I think we should start with Paul's story. Paul gets a bad press because he can be kind of authoritarian, which is true, and because it's thought that he was against women's leadership in the church, which is not true. But with no Paul we'd probably have no Christian church, and we'd certainly have no reformation and no congregational churches sitting in New Canaan or Baptist preachers, either. No Paul . . . no recognizable us.

So here's his story. Paul wasn't just interested in justification, he wasn't just interested in getting right with God, he was obsessed by getting right with God. Think of the most overwrought student from your school days, especially if you're still in school. The one so determined to be a physician that she basically camps out in the bio lab. The one so determined to be an author that at the age of sixteen he's written two 640-page novels.

That's how determined Paul was to get right with God. Lots of study. Lots of prayer. Endless synagogue attendance. Even a little persecuting of heretics to see if that would help.

Maybe all the time Paul was obsessing about getting right with God he realized that he hadn't really made it. Maybe it was only afterward, looking back from the Biggest Day in his life that he realized he hadn't really made it.

But in any case, he hadn't really made it as he discovered on the Biggest Day of his life. He was in a particularly Get Right with God mood that day and had gotten up early to go chase down a few heretics—followers of the crucified Jesus of Nazareth.

And then in some mysterious way—maybe with lights and voices—he was found by the very Jesus he thought he hated. He discovered that all the stuff he'd done to commend himself to God, to get right with God, couldn't do it, because getting right with God isn't something we do, it's what God does for us.

It literally knocked him off his high horse, you know. And looking back he could see that no matter how good he tried to be he wasn't good enough. The way he talked about justification was no longer: "See how good I am."

It was this: "While we were still sinners, Christ died for us" (Rom. 5:8b NIV).

That dying for us; that loving us; that was God's justifying us: justification. And when Paul accepted that acceptance, he was justified through faith.

IV.

The second story is a story Jesus told, the story of the Prodigal Son. I know it's a story about the older brother, too, but for today let's focus on the Prodigal.

The problem for the Prodigal is how to get right with his father. He starts out very badly by essentially telling his father that he wishes Dad were dead, but since that wasn't about to happen, how about at least giving me my share of the inheritance right now.

He goes from bad to worse because, as the King James Version says, "[He] wasted his substance with riotous living" (Luke 15:13). And then like Paul he had his great day and on his great day he came to himself and said, basically: "I miss my father."

Now maybe he came to that realization because he discovered that he was more pious than he thought. Or maybe he came to that realization because he was hungry.

But either way what he realized was that he desperately wanted justification; he desperately wanted the separation from his father to end; he wanted to get right with the father who had loved him.

He does get right, of course, you know how the story goes. He turns around and heads for home and he memorizes the little speech he's going to recite. For any of us who occasionally get in trouble and work hard on our "I'm sorry" speeches, the scene will be familiar. "Father, I have sinned against heaven and before you; I am no longer worthy to be called your son" (vv. 18–19).

And of course there's the welcome; and of course there's the party. And it would be easy to think that the prodigal was justified by repentance, by what he did.

But notice how Jesus tells the story. Before the Prodigal can get out one word of his speech, his father has already come running down the road to meet him. Before he knew how to repent, he was welcomed; before he could justify himself, he was justified by the Father's love.

And here's something I got only when I became a parent. All the weeks or the months or the years that the son was away, in his heart the father was stumbling down the stairs and running down the road. It wasn't that at the last minute the son was welcomed home; he was always welcome, but at the end he knew it. Justified. Made right.

While we were still sinners Christ died for the ungodly. Jesus Christ on the cross is God running down the road to throw God's arms around us, to bring us home.

V.

Two stories and a supper, this meal we are about to take. This is justification meal, dear brothers and sisters. This is "get right with God" table.

> Which of us earned this meal? Not one.
> This is his body; given for you. This is his blood shed for you.
> Which of us deserved this meal? Not one.
> Which of us is refused this meal? Whose faith is too small to receive this gift or whose repentance is too weak to find nurture here? Not one.

This is the Prodigal's Feast and long before we thought to turn toward home, in Jesus Christ the Father came running down the road to welcome us. Open arms. Open heart.

Justification.

To Christ be thanks and praise.

Amen.

44

Great Words of the Faith: Atonement

2 CORINTHIANS 5:1–11

This is the seventh sermon on "Great Words of the Faith" preached on February 20, 2011, at The Congregational Church of New Canaan.

I.

I think this may be the toughest of the great words of the faith to understand. I've been trying to understand it for years. I had lunch with two of my colleagues in the theology department at Columbia Seminary on Wednesday; they had just finished the annual class session on Atonement, and they were still not quite sure what to say about atonement to their students.

I looked through a number of books on the Doctrine of the Atonement in the New Testament and discovered what I had always suspected: There isn't a doctrine of atonement in the New Testament. There isn't even a clear definition of atonement in the New Testament. There are images and snatches and stories and hints, but nobody put all those images, snatches, stories and hints together systematically.

There are two claims we can make about the word "atonement" that may help to get us started.

The first claim is that the familiar play on words actually works pretty well. If you take the word "atonement" apart you find that it spells "At One Ment." And atonement in the New Testament is all about being at one—with God

230

first of all but also with our brothers and sisters. When we have been separated and are brought together, joyfully, that's atonement.

The other claim is that for Christians atonement is always centered on the cross of Jesus Christ. Jesus' parables are wonderfully illuminating, the miracles are, well, miraculous, the birth stories give us the peace of Christmas and the Easter stories give us the promise of resurrection. But atonement, for all the biblical writers and for most Christians ever since, has focused on the cross.

II.

I have known how difficult it is to hold together "at-one-ment" and the cross of Jesus Christ from the time that I preached my first sermon on the atonement in the first parish I served in Minneapolis. It was one of the summer services that the Baptists shared with the UCC and safe to say I didn't make either group happy.

I started with the very difficult story of Abraham and Isaac in Genesis 22. You'll remember the story, God tells Abraham to take his son, his only son, Isaac, to the mountain and there to sacrifice Isaac to God. Abraham obeys, brings the boy up the mountain, places him on the altar and is rescued only at the last minute when an angel tells him to stop and points to a ram caught in the thicket that becomes the sacrifice instead.

I pointed out that what God asked of Abraham seemed overwhelming and that had Abraham gone ahead with the sacrifice he would have left us a terrible example of child abuse.

Fortunately, I said, Abraham did not make that sacrifice and neither did we because God had made that sacrifice for us. Then I read the scripture that we all memorized in church school, John 3:16, which I'm sure is an echo of the story of Abraham and Isaac: "God so loved the world that he gave his only begotten son" (KJV).

"There," I thought, "that takes care of that."

But that didn't take care of that. Members of the congregation rushed up to tell me what was wrong with my story, with my theology. In my sermon, didn't God turn out to be just as bad as Abraham in Genesis 22? Wasn't he willingly handing up his own son to arrest, torture, and death? Wasn't that simply a case of divine child abuse?

I started pondering the issue then and not surprisingly pondered it even more when I became a father. I devoutly hoped that if I were ever in Abraham's position and God asked me to sacrifice my child, I'd just say no and suffer the consequences.

I devoutly hoped that if I were ever in God's position—I know this is a little blasphemous but bear with me—if ever I was in God's position I would find a better atonement plan than giving my only son up for sacrifice.

III.

So in my preaching and writing I returned to a description of the atonement which I had loved before I went to seminary and got waylaid by having to think hard theologically.

Now my more accessible doctrine of the atonement goes something like this. The man Jesus was so filled with his own awareness of God that God chose him to show God's love and goodness to people. But as is so often the case, love and goodness aroused hostility on every side. (I could point to Gandhi; I could point to John Lewis or Martin Luther King Jr).

In the garden of Gethsemane, went my version of atonement, in the garden of Gethsemane Jesus had to decide whether or not to remain faithful to his mission or to back down, return to Nazareth and never be heard from again. Jesus did not back down, even though the cost of his courage was death. Because he didn't back down he revealed to humankind the love of God.

IV.

I still think that sense of Jesus showing us God's love is an important part of our understanding of atonement but what it tends to leave out is that for the New Testament Jesus didn't just show us God's love on the cross, Jesus did God's love on the cross. Jesus didn't just die to show us something; Jesus died to accomplish something.

Paul, though he does not give us a doctrine of atonement, still preaches that atonement theme in the passage we read a few minutes ago:

> God . . . reconciled us to himself through Christ, and has given us the ministry of reconciliation; that is, in Christ God was reconciling the world to himself, not counting their trespasses against them, and entrusting the message of reconciliation to us.
>
> (2 Cor. 5:18–19)

I know "reconciliation" is almost as unlikely a word as "atonement." But think of what happens when you reconcile your checkbook with the bank statement; however painfully, you bring together what has been apart.

Or think of the great stories from Jacob and Esau to the Prodigal and his Father to the latest marital separation you know that blessedly ended, not in divorce, but in reconciliation.

God is in the bringing together business. God is all about bringing people back to God's own self. God is all about bringing people together with one another.

And here's what the Bible says, God doesn't just bring people together to God's self and God doesn't just bring people together by talking about love or by showing examples of love. God loves us into love.

In the cross it's not that God the Father sent his poor helpless Son to suffer for us. It is that God who is Father, Son, and Holy Spirit suffered for us, and with us.

Karl Barth, the great Swiss theologian of the twentieth century, says it this way:

> It was first of all in [God] Himself that the . . . affliction which threatened [Jesus was] experienced and borne. What are all the sufferings of the world, even those of Job, compared with this fellow-suffering of God Himself, which is the meaning of the event of Gethsemane and Golgotha.[1]

V.

Let me try two stories. Neither of these says everything we need to say, but stories are what we have and what the New Testament has—images, glimpses.

John Buchanan was a long-time congressperson from Alabama and an active layperson. I heard him tell the story of his time serving in Asia in World War II. A lieutenant was leading Buchanan and his fellow soldiers into battle; as they crossed a clearing in the jungle a grenade flew out from the trees on the other side, right in front of the men.

And the lieutenant, unhesitatingly, fell on the grenade. Absorbed the explosion. Died so that his men might live.

That story drew Buchanan to an even larger story. Not the story of God the Father forcing his reluctant son to take on some long-planned punishment. The story of God the loving Father and the obedient son, caught, hurt, helping all of humankind in the hour of our need.

---

1. Eberhard Busch, *The Great Passion: An Introduction to Karl Barth's Theology* (Grand Rapids: Wm. B. Eerdmans, 2004), 205.

VI.

The other story my wife heard a few weeks ago. Not a doctrine, remember, more like a parable, a story: atonement is something like this.

James Forbes, now pastor Emeritus of Riverside Church, was speaking to a group at Columbia Seminary. He told of a recent reunion at the Edmund Pettus Bridge outside of Selma, Alabama.

In March of 1965, some of us remember the Southern Christian Leadership Conference and the Southern Nonviolent Coordinating Committee led by John Lewis and Hosea Williams organized a march supporting Negro voter registration. The march started on the road from Montgomery to Selma over the Alabama River, across the Edmund Pettus Bridge.

Let the historian Taylor Branch tell some of what happened:

> After one minute and five seconds Major Cloud addressed his front unit without the bullhorn: "Troopers advance" . . . with night sticks held chest high, parallel to the ground, the troopers pushed into the well-dressed formation . . . then toppled marchers with accelerating speed as troopers hurdled over and through them. Almost instantly silence gave way to a high-pitched shriek . . . as the march line shriveled and white spectators thrilled, some waving encouragement alongside the charge. . . . John Lewis shot out of the mass at an angle, leaning oddly as he sank to the ground in five steps, followed by a truncheon blow to the head. . . . The sharp report of guns sounded on the launch of tear gas. . . . From the tangle in the foreground, a Negro woman came spilling out to the side, pursued by one masked trooper and struck by two others as she passed.[2]

In March of 2005 there was a reunion on the Edmund Pettus Bridge, remembering the march, remembering the hurt, celebrating progress, praying for more progress.

James Forbes says that Jesse Jackson was there and as the celebration came to an end an older white man came up to shake his hand. "I was at the Bridge for Bloody Sunday, too," said the white man.

"And we're grateful for your help," said Jackson.

"No, you don't understand," said the man. "I was there with the Ku Klux Klan, jeering at you, cheering the troopers."

"But now," he continued, "Now I know you were right. Can these people take a picture of you and me together so that I can show my grandson how far we've come?"

---

2. Taylor Branch, *At Canaan's Edge* (New York: Simon & Schuster, 2006), 51.

Reconciliation: finally crossing the bridge; not without suffering, not without loss, not without human hurt, not without hurting God.

"In [the cross of] Christ God was reconciling the [whole] world to himself, not counting their trespasses against them and giving us the ministry of reconciliation" (2 Cor. 5:19, au. trans.).

Atonement.

45

Great Words of the Faith: Forgiveness

LUKE 15:11–32
GENESIS 50:7–21

This sermon is the eighth sermon in the series "Great Words of the Faith" preached at The Congregational Church of New Canaan, Connecticut, on March 20, 2011.

I.

For those of you who are joining us this morning, not really as guests but as members of the extended family, as brothers and sisters in Christ, let me just say a word about what's going on in this Meeting House once a month.

We have been having a series on Great Words of the Faith, and the list of words was assigned to me by the adult education committee. Now we've come from a string of not too familiar words, "justification" and "atonement," to a far more familiar word: "Forgiveness."

And I'm turning to a familiar text, usually called the story of the Prodigal Son but really the story of the father and the two brothers. I realized that I've actually used this story as part of several sermons this year and probably as the heart of dozens of sermons over the dozens of years that I've been preaching. But here it comes again, because I love this story and because it helps us understand what "forgiveness" means in our faith.

Usually when I preach the text, I have to decide whether I want the congregation to focus on the younger brother or the older brother, to identify with the wandering brother or with the one who stayed at home.

Today I want to look at both brothers, briefly, because if you're like me you can see yourself in both brothers. And I want to suggest that the text really has two parts: Part one is about "being forgiven." Part two is about "being forgiving."

II.

"Being forgiven."

Of course this story that Jesus told is not just a story about us and God, but it is a story about us and God and that's how we'll think about it this morning.

The story begins by talking about the younger brother's sin. Jesus never uses the word "sin" in this story, but it's pretty clear that's what he's talking about.[1]

The first mistake the younger son makes is that he treats his father as dead. He knows full well that when the time comes he will receive his share of the family inheritance, but he can't wait, so he says to his father, "You might as well be dead. I'll take the money and run."

If the father is like God and the son is like us, then this isn't a story about atheism. It's a story about practical atheism. It's not that the son doesn't believe in his father's existence, he just doesn't pay any attention to it. The Father doesn't function in his life anymore.

All the polls show us that Americans overwhelmingly believe in God. What the polls can't show is whether we overwhelmingly pay attention to God. Sometimes I think, for instance, that when we look at the way America seems to ignore poor people, or how anxious we get when those poor people mostly speak Spanish, I suspect that the way we get along is not to deny God, it's just to deny God's importance. Treat God as dead.

III.

The second mistake that the younger son makes is that he treats himself as trash. The NRSV pretties up the language a bit: "he squandered his property in dissolute living" (Luke 15:13). The old King James is better: "[he] wasted his substance in riotous living." He wasted his substance; he took his very self and tossed it out like so much garbage.

---

1. And Luke uses the word in 15:1–2 to give the context for this parable, so he obviously thinks it's about sin and sinners.

We have no idea what the riotous living looked like; his older brother claims he wasted his money and himself on prostitutes, but his older brother is not the most reliable source. What Jesus tells us is just that the brother took his own self and tossed it away.

IV.

And at that point the younger son has gone about as far as he can go, and thank God our story becomes not a story about sinning but a story about forgiving.

From the younger son's side the forgiving begins with repentance. We'll talk about what forgiving looks like from the father's side in a few minutes. From the son's side being forgiven begins with repentance.

Repentance in its biblical root just means turning around. And we can actually watch the younger brother turn around when he's gone as far as he can go.

Here's how he repents: he repents when he "comes to himself." That's Jesus' phrase for what happens to this young man. "Comes to himself." Sees himself for who he is.

I regret to say that there's a kind of cottage industry at Columbia Theological Seminary in doing impersonations of faculty. Rumor is that there are students who are very good at catching the nuances of our behavior, if not the state of our souls.

And in fact, one year when I learned who the most notorious Bartlett imitator was, I actually prevailed upon him to do his act for me. Who knew that I tugged my beard, rubbed my head, or said "Nice idea" so often? In a somewhat friendly and fairly amusing way I had come to myself.

Repentance is like that, only more so. We discover not just the quirks and the habits that mark us, but the shortfalls and the obsessions that mar us. Repentance begins when we look ourselves pretty much straight in the eye and don't like what we see.

Now I know, because some of you have pointed it out to me, that this isn't actually a purely religious repentance on the part of the younger brother. He comes to himself only when he realizes that he's hungry and that the servants at his father's home eat better than he. Not exactly a refined spiritual moment.

My friend James Nelson, a distinguished Christian ethicist, has written a book called *Thirst* about his struggle with alcoholism. He came to himself one night in a hotel room a mile from his home when the vodka had run out and the liquor stores were closed for the evening. There's no way of knowing how much his spirit recanted, or how much his body simply burned out. Either way, he turned around that night.[2]

I suspect that the father back on the farm doesn't much care whether the son comes home because he has kindly thoughts of the old man or because he's hungry. He just wants his boy home.

V.

That of course is what happens next. The younger son has come to himself and now he comes to his father. He's got his repentance speech all memorized.

But here's the thing, and I know we've talked about this already this year, but it's really important. Here's the thing. The father is not sitting on the porch nursing a grudge, saying to himself: "Well if that boy says the right thing, maybe I'll turn and forgive him."

Before the boy has said a word, just as he rounds the corner, before the father can see how he's looking or hear what he's saying, the father comes running down the road to greet him, throw his arms around him, welcomes him home. And in his heart the father has been welcoming the son from the minute the son turned his back and headed away.

I've said it before, right in this space, and I'll probably say it again. The Gospel of Luke believes, the whole New Testament believes, the Christian church has believed through all the ages that before we could turn to God, God had already turned to us. God longs to welcome us.

And the place where God turns to us; the person in whom God turns to us—that place, that person is Jesus Christ. In him God rushes down the road to throw God's arms around us, to bring us home.

VI.

That's the "forgiven" part, but now comes the "forgiving" part. At other places in his teaching Jesus reminds us that each of us is both forgiven and forgiving . . . "forgive us our sins as we forgive those who sin against us," we pray, at least once a week.

But here Jesus makes the second point by turning to the older brother. And he makes it very clear that, just like the younger brother, the older brother is sustained, surrounded, and embraced by the father's love.

2. James B. Nelson, *Thirst: God and the Alcoholic Experience* (Louisville, KY: Westminster John Knox Press, 2004).

The father is just as concerned to head out to the field to welcome his older son as he is to run down the road to welcome the younger son.

The father says to the younger son, "Welcome home." But to the older son he says: "You're always welcome; you're always home." "Son, you are always with me, and all that I have is yours" (v. 31 NCV).

But now here's the tricky part. Surrounded by his father's love the older son is called to love the younger son. Absolutely sustained by his father's mercy the older son is called to be merciful too.

There's that great exchange that everybody notices when they read this part of the story.

The older brother is complaining: "When this son of yours came back . . . you killed the fatted calf" (v. 30).

The father won't let him get away with that clever distancing: "This brother of yours was dead and has come to life; he was lost and has been found."

"This son of yours," says the brother. "This brother of yours," says the Father.

Beloved, we are all of us, forgiven. From whatever far country has enticed us, God always welcomes us back.

But we do not come back to God alone. For all of us there is that brother we have ignored, that sister we have shunned, that friend in Christ whom we have let drift into enmity.

Welcomed, we are called to welcome. Shown mercy, we are called to be merciful. Forgiven, we are called to forgive.

To Christ be thanks and praise.

Amen.

46

Great Words of the Faith: Creation/Providence

GENESIS 1:20–31
ROMANS 8:18–25

This sermon was one in the series "Great Words of the Faith," preached on October 17, 2010, at The Congregational Church of New Canaan, Connecticut.

I.

As you all know by now, I'm a Baptist. One thing Baptist preachers have in common is that when we preach we preach with the hope that the Holy Spirit will inspire the listeners to make a big decision—a decision to follow Jesus, or a decision to deal more gently with your employees, or on pledge Sunday a decision to give more generously to the church.

We get befuddled when someone suggests that the purpose of our sermon is to give information, to think aloud theologically, to lead a conversation more than to entice a decision.

But here we are, the committee that asked me to preach these sermons asked me to preach on some of the great words of the faith, and there is no way to do that without trying to share some theological reflections, without trying to get a kind of thoughtful conversation going.

Today we are going to think together about two great words of the faith, closely interwoven, "creation" and "providence," and I can't think of any way to do it except just to do it, one suggestion at a time. So here we go.

II.

Suggestion one: for Christian faith, creation is just the beginning. Or to put it another way, for Christian faith the first great act of creation is just that—the first act of a creative process that goes on and on.

There is a striking resemblance between those philosophers who want to argue for "Intelligent Design" and for those philosophers and scientists who lead the ranks of the so-called New Atheists.

Both sides really concentrate on what happened at the beginning of the universe. The Intelligent Design people want to hold that God created the whole universe according to a blueprint established from the very beginning. If you look at the world as it is you have to admit that it had a designer and that the designer was very great indeed. And there you go.

But for Intelligent Design to work the designer might just as well have set the whole thing going in the past and then headed off to greener pastures for the rest of eternity.

The New Atheists want to say that you don't really need to posit a great designer at the beginning of the process. The process just took off by itself and it's been evolving by itself for a very long time until it got as far as us—especially till it got as far as the New Atheists, who apparently have evolved a little farther than the rest of us who still cling desperately to religious faith.

But notice that both groups worry about whether God was or was not back there at the beginning of time. Neither one thinks much about what God might be doing. Both think a lot about what God did.

What if God is not so much an architect as a playwright directing her own play, suggesting to the actors where they might move on the stage and changing the sets from time to time? What if, like many directors, this playwright/director lets the actors improvise, or even changes the script to include an action or a speech that wasn't in the original play at all?

What if God is not so much an architect as composer trying out his unfinished composition with The New Canaan Congregational Church choir, and a bar of the music doesn't sound just right, so the altos try it a little differently and the composer rewrites that bar to make the phrase come out right?

For the Christian faith creation is not just back then; creation is right now. And the traditional word we have for creation right now is Providence. God still at work in the world, like a clever and flexible playwright; like a continually creative composer. A Creator who keeps on creating. What begins in creation continues in providence.

III.

Creation is just the beginning. Then here's a second claim: hinted in the Bible and confirmed by contemporary science. Creation isn't just about us. That's clearest in the very first chapter of Genesis where God makes all kinds of creatures and in each case says: "That's good." God doesn't wait till humankind appears to say of God's creation—"that's good."

And whatever else we've learned from evolutionary science we've learned that the whole creative process isn't just about what God does for human beings, though of course we're especially interested in ourselves. Creation includes millions of species including some that have vanished from the world and some that are yet to appear.

And whatever else we've learned from astronomy we've learned that there is lots and lots and lots of space out there beyond us, and if God is God then all that vast universe of stars is God's turf too, just as much as New Canaan or the Rocky Mountains.

The apostle Paul, with remarkable prescience, knew that the story of humankind is not just the story of humankind. Here's what Paul wrote to the Romans: "the creation waits with eager longing for the revealing of the children of God. . . . We know that the whole creation has been groaning in labor pains until now" (Rom. 8:19, 22).

Creation and providence aren't just about us; they are about what God is doing for the whole creation.

IV.

So creation is just the beginning . . . it goes on and we call it ongoing creation providence. Creation isn't just about us. BUT, and here's the next claim, creation is about us. Creation is in part the gift that God has given us and providence is the way in which the Creator keeps gifting us, guiding us, comforting us, leading us on.

Like my director playwright slipping us new stage directions and sometimes shifting the script to accommodate our visions or our quirks. Like my composer conductor changing a phrase to help the choir sing it more powerfully.

Paul says more about this in that same chapter of that same letter to the Romans: "We know that in everything God works for good with those who love [God]"[1] (v. 28 RSV).

1. The NRSV and the RSV rely on different manuscripts of Romans for their translations. I choose the RSV because I think the manuscripts are equally good and because I find the RSV translation theologically richer.

Notice what the text doesn't say. It doesn't say, everything always works out all right for believers. It says this: "In everything God is working toward the good—with us." Paul makes a very strong claim for providence but it is a kind of cooperative providence.

We cooperate in providence by working toward what we hope God intends. We cooperate in providence by looking for God's hand in the beauty and intricacy of creation.

For all our differences Jonah and I share many enthusiasms, and one of our enthusiasms is for the late novelist and short-story writer John Updike. Updike writes beautifully. It is generally conceded that he writes more wisely and sympathetically about men than about women. But one thing that draws me to him is that almost uniquely among the best novelists of the last thirty years he writes out of complicated but real Christian faith.

And that faith seeps into the last paragraph of the Updike story I suggested that some of you read, called "Pigeon Feathers." The hero of the story, a young boy named David, is much more concerned about ultimate questions than his parents or, alas, his pastor.

His great fear is that at the end of his life God will simply let him go. That he was created not just for death but for annihilation. At the end of the story in a rather odd, paradoxical twist that has more than a touch of the Christian in it, he is assigned by his family to shoot the bothersome pigeons in the barn, and in considering the creation that brought the pigeons into being and the providence that sustains life still, he edges toward faith: he picks up the dead pigeons and looks at the intricacy of their feathers.

> The feathers were more wonderful than dog's hair; for each filament was shaped within the shape of the feather, and the feathers in turn were trimmed to fit a pattern that flowed without error across the bird's body. He lost himself in the geometrical tides as the feathers now broadened and stiffened to make an edge for flight, now softened and constricted to cup warmth around the mute flesh. And across the surface of the infinitely adjusted yet somehow effortless mechanics of the feathers played idle designs of color, no two alike, designs executed, it seemed, in a controlled rapture, with a joy that hung level in the air above and behind him. . . . As he fitted the last two [into their grave] . . . crusty coverings were lifted from him, and with a feminine, slipping sensation along his nerves that seemed to give the air hands, he was robed in this certainty: that the God who had lavished such craft upon these worthless birds would not destroy His whole Creation by refusing to let David live forever.[2]

---

2. John Updike, "Pigeon Feathers," in *Pigeon Feathers and Other Stories* (New York: Alfred Knopf, 1962), 149–50.

V.

So how does it play out, this conviction that God's creation continues in God's providence, God's care for all that God has created and is creating? The conviction that providence itself is innovative, God not just caring for creation but growing creation. The conviction that we are partners with the whole universe in God's great drama, God's great symphony. And the conviction that, however slightly, we help to shape creation. Our improvised movements shift the action on the stage; the note we suggest enriches the harmony.

So what? How does this play out?

One suggestion for today. The environmental crisis. Let's not argue about the science today. Grant me only that we can imagine a less scary future than the one we fear we're apt to get.

What does faith in God's creative providence provide; what does it rule out?

Such faith provides hope and it rules out despair.

Such faith requires action and it rules out apathy.

What we are not allowed to do as Christians is to give up on creation, for in doing so we give up on God. What we do not have to do as Christians is to give up on creation, for we would be giving up on the God who has made us and sustained us, not always as dramatically as we might wish, but clearly steadily.

What we are not allowed to do as Christians is to say that it's all up to us and if we can just figure out the right plan, we can lick this dilemma. Nothing in heaven or on earth is all up to us. We're too little and it's too late.

What we are allowed to do as Christians is to look for those moments and those places where God is moving the whole creation out of its moaning toward the fulfillment of God's promises.

What we are allowed to do is to take our role in the drama we did not begin and will not conclude. What we are allowed to do is to sing as faithfully and tunefully as possible in the chorus that God is still moving toward amazement and delight.

When John Updike was young he wrote about the fear of death and the beauty of the earth and the need for faith. When he got old he wrote about the certainty of death and the beauty of the earth and the need for hope. At the beginning and the end God's creation called him beyond himself, calls us beyond ourselves as well.

The young man in the early story is surely mostly Updike and the old man in the late story is surely mostly Updike, too.

[When I start to wake)]I see in silhouette my wife's torso lift through a diagonal to a sitting position. Her bare feet pad around the bed, and, many mornings, now that I'm retired and nearly eighty, I fall back asleep for another hour. The world is being tended to, I can let go of it, it doesn't need me.

The shaving mirror hangs in front of a window overlooking the sea. The sea is always full, flat as a floor. Or almost: there is a delicate planetary bulge in it, supporting a few shadowy freighters and cruise ships making their motionless way out of Boston Harbor. At night, the horizon springs a rim of lights—more, it seems, every year. Winking airplanes from the corners of the earth descend on a slant, a curved grove in the air, toward the unseen airport in East Boston. My life-prolonging pills cupped in my left hand, I lift the glass, its water sweetened by its brief wait on the marble sink-top. If I can read this strange old guy's mind aright, he's drinking a toast to the visible world.[3]

The visible world.
God's gift.
God's joy.
Amen.

---

3. John Updike, "The Full Glass," in *My Father's Tears and Other Stories* (New York: Alfred Knopf, 2009), 291–92.

47

Great Words of the Faith: Salvation

JOHN 3:11–21
ROMANS 5:6–11

This sermon was the tenth in the series "Great Words of the Faith" preached on May 8, 2011, at The Congregational Church of New Canaan, Connecticut.

I.

Some of the great words of our faith are hard to define. They are slippery, elusive. We are always having to borrow language, images, metaphors to try to speak what doesn't fit very well into our categories.

Maybe this is especially true of today's word, "salvation."

So let me begin by borrowing a story.

In his remarkable novel *To the End of the Land*, the Israeli novelist David Grossman tells the story of two brothers growing up in Israel in the years just gone by.

When the older brother Adam is thirteen years old he begins to exhibit the signs of compulsive behavior. He washes his hands after he touches any object; he goes through elaborate rituals of speech and action before he can move from one room to another. He stops in the midst of what he is doing to count his fingers or blink his eyes for a designated number of times.

His distraught parents read every book they can find and take him to every expert they can afford but nothing much changes.

Then one day Ofer, his nine-year-old brother, takes charge.

"Let me do the eye thing today," he says, "and then you won't have to do it."

Reluctantly Adam gives up his obsessive blinking and gives his brother a turn.

A few days later it's the finger counting.

And a few days later another little compulsion.

And last of all the hand washing; the younger brother washing his hands often enough and hard enough to serve for both of them.

A few years later the boy's mother tells how the story comes out.

> "They played computer games and football, chattered for hours, made up characters, and every once in a while they cooked pasta together." And then their mother says: "And while they did all that—don't ask me exactly how it happened—one of them saved the other."[1]

Listen, beloved, while we were doing all the things we do, one of us saved the rest of us.

He took all our stuff upon himself. Set us free. The official word for that is: salvation. And Paul tells the story this way: "God proves his love for us in that while we were still sinners Christ died for us" (Rom. 5:8).

John puts the story this way: "God loved the world so much that he gave his only son—so that anyone who has faith in the son might not perish but have eternal life" (John 3:16, au. trans.).

II.

I'm a Baptist as you well know, and the rap we get is that while other people meet you and ask about your health or comment on the weather, Baptists ask two questions: "Are you saved?" And if the answer is yes, we march right ahead: "When were you saved?"

So question one: "Are you saved?"

I'm happy to say that the answer is going to be "yes." But the first obvious rejoinder is "saved from what."

And in Paul, but especially in John's Gospel, the claim is very clear: in Jesus Christ we are saved from death.

> "God loved the world so much that he gave his only son—so that anyone who has faith in the son might not perish but have eternal life."

---

1. David Grossman, *To the End of the Land* (New York: Vintage Books, 2011), 464.

Of course that means that in Christ God rescues us from the death that ends our life; that we are promised life beyond our own mortality. And that is what we will talk about in two weeks in the final sermon of this series on Great Words.

But again in John's Gospel the claim is also very clear: through Jesus Christ we are saved from death in the midst of life.

Look at the story with which we began.

Adam, surely the name is not coincidental—Adam, humankind—Adam is living a kind of frantic death in the midst of life. Unable to move on; unable to delight; unable to love others or to love himself; he's stuck.

Quite amazingly his brother takes on his stuck-ness, takes on his frenzy, gesture by gesture, strategy by strategy, until Adam is again enveloped in something very much like calm, rescued into peace.

Sometimes the death we lived in the midst of life seems just the opposite. We are not driven by frenzy but imprisoned in lethargy. Nothing tastes good or looks lovely. We force our laughter to pretend we're really there and we welcome the restless bed after the dull day hoping against the odds that sleep will cure what ails us.

John says that Christ will rescue us from that death, too. Not just in the life to come but now.

For John that "eternal life" that Christ promises is not just life in eternity, it's life right now that is touched by the eternal gifts: faith, hope, love, joy, and the blessing of unfeigned laughter.

Later in John's Gospel, Jesus tells the same story in a somewhat different way: "No one has greater love than this: to lay down his life for his friends" (John 15:13 CSB).

For a time Ofer lays down his life for Adam; gives up all the carefree pleasures of a nine-year-old to concentrate on bailing out his brother. For all time Jesus lays down his life for us, going to the cross to rescue us from the death of distraction and the death of dullness.

Those arms stretched out upon the cross are also stretched out to receive our stuff: the drive that drives us much too hard and the despair that slows us much too hopelessly. There on the cross, by his great love, Christ takes all that to himself.

III.

Which leads us to the second question: "When were you saved?" Now as Baptists we know what answer we are supposed to get. "I was saved when I was sixteen and accepted Jesus Christ as my Lord and Savior," or, "I was saved when I was forty-seven and finally was rescued from the addiction that had driven me all those years."

And both of those are true enough, but perhaps not quite true enough.

Because both for John and for Paul and for the whole long tradition of the great words of our faith, salvation is not so much what we do as what God does for us.

And what God did for us; what God does for us—all that is there upon the cross. That love poured out in pain and love; all our inability to slow down and all our inability to move ahead—taken to himself.

The theologian who taught me that in his writing was Karl Barth, and he'd learned it from John and Paul.

Barth had the right answer to the question we Baptists are bound to ask you: "When were you saved?"

"On Calvary," is the answer. "On the cross."

IV.

But one thing more: "How were you saved?"

And you know the answer already: "through love. God so loved the world that he gave his son." "Nobody has greater love than this, to lay down his life for his friends." That's John. "God proves his love for us in that while we were still sinners Christ died for us."

And here is the claim I think both our texts make and our faith has made through the centuries. It is not that God gives us God's great love and that great love leads to some other wonderful thing called "salvation."

It is rather that God's great love in Jesus Christ is salvation. That love that will not let us go; the love that like a Father welcomes us and forgives us; that love that like a Mother guides us and sustains us—that crucified love that is glad to take upon itself, upon himself, our lethargy and our frenzy. That love is salvation.

When Ofer decided to take on all his brother Adam's fears and pains, it is not just that his love led to salvation, his love was salvation. His loving made it so.

V.

Think of the people who love you the best—your spouse, your partner, your children, your friends. When you celebrate their love you don't celebrate it because it brings about great results for your life. You celebrate that love because it is the great result for our life. You don't say "Beloved, I'm so grateful for everything your love can get me." You say: "Beloved, I'm grateful for your love." (Or, "I'm grateful for everything your love is.")

When John says that God so loved the world and Jesus says that he so loved his friends and Paul says that God shows his love for us on the cross of Christ, it's not that we say: "That love is really useful. That love is going to get us salvation."

What we say is: "that love is salvation. That reaching out, that taking in, that bringing us home . . . that's what salvation means."

VI.

You know the story of Elizabeth Barrett before she became Elizabeth Barrett Browning. Nearly an invalid, nearly captive to her father's well-meaning overprotectiveness, sure that she was forever unlovely and would forever be unloved, until Robert Browning came to call, and then her poem tells of her salvation.

> The face of all the world is changed, I think
> Since first I heard the footsteps of thy soul,
> Move still, oh, still, beside me, as they stole
> Betwixt me and the dreadful outer brink
> Of obvious death, where I who thought to sink,
> Was caught up into love, and taught the whole
> Of life in a new rhythm.[2]

"Caught up into love." "Salvation."
Or another poet of an even deeper love:

> What language shall I borrow
> To thank thee, dearest Friend,
> For this thy dying sorrow,
> Thy pity without end?
> O, make me thine forever,
> And should I fainting be—
> Lord, let me never, never
> Outlive my love to Thee.[3]

To Christ, therefore, be thanks and praise. Amen.

---

2. Elizabeth Barrett Browning, sonnet 7, in *Sonnets from the Portuguese and Other Poems* (New York: Dover Publications, 1992), 26.

3. Attr. Bernard of Clairvaux, "O Sacred Head, Now Wounded," trans. James Alexander, in *The Presbyterian Hymnal* (Louisville, KY: Westminster/John Knox Press, 1990), 98.

48

The Lord Is My Shepherd

PSALM 23

This sermon was preached at Saint Anne's Terrace, a not-for-profit retirement community in the Atlanta area. It is affiliated with Saint Anne's Episcopal Church and is a community where a number of the members of Trinity Presbyterian Church live. This sermon was preached on January 14, 2013.

Grateful to be here and grateful for all that St. Anne's means in the lives of so many.

Let me just say a couple of preliminary words about this meditation.

First of all, I want to walk through the text verse by verse. Just start at the beginning and end at the end. I promise you we'll walk through expeditiously.

Second, I'm going to use the King James Version of the Bible. I was only about eleven years old when the First Baptist Church of Evanston, Illinois, where I worshiped, began using the Revised Standard Version. And then in recent years I have almost always used the New Revised Standard Version.

But today I'm going to use the King James because it is the version I learned even before I was ten years old and the Revised Standard Version came along; and because it is the version we continue to use at special holy occasions.

I.

"The LORD is my shepherd; I shall not want" (Ps. 23:1).

Sometimes when we talk about the Lord we mean the Lord the Creator, the maker of heaven and earth. And sometimes we mean the "Lord Jesus

Christ." (There is no question that when Israel sang this psalm they meant that the Lord, the one we sometimes call "Father"—that Lord was their shepherd. But there is also no question that for two millennia, starting at least with the Gospel of John, Christians have believed that Jesus is the good shepherd, too.)

And we're not left to guess what it means to say that the Lord is our shepherd. The Lord is our shepherd because the Lord makes sure that we have what we want.

Frederick Buechner is a novelist who is also a Presbyterian preacher, and he talks about a shepherd he knows in his hometown of Rupert, Vermont.

> When I think of shepherds I think of one man in particular I know who used to keep sheep here in Rupert a few years back. Some of them he gave names to. . . . If one of them got lost he didn't have a moment's peace till he found it again. If one of them got sick or hurt, he would move Heaven and earth to get it well again. He would feed them out of a bottle when they were new-born lambs if for some reason the mother wasn't around. . . . I've seen him wade through snow up to his knees with a bale of hay in each hand to feed them on bitter cold winter evenings, shaking it out and putting it in the manger.[1]

The Lord is my shepherd, I shall not want.

II.

"He maketh me to lie down in green pastures; he leadeth me beside still waters" (v. 2).

Green pastures are both a resting place for the sheep and a feeding place as well. A place to stay. Enough to eat.

Still waters are waters the sheep can drink from. Enough to quench their thirst.

The Lord our shepherd provides, intends to provide, for everyone a place to stay, enough to eat, enough to drink.

Whenever we see homeless people or hungry people or people who can't find water unpolluted by chemical waste or acid rain we know that we have messed up the Shepherd's pasture and fouled the still waters. When we thank God for what God has done we remember what we are called to do: be good stewards of the green pastures God has given us to tend.

1. Frederick Buechner, *The Clown in the Belfry: Writings on Faith and Fiction* (New York: Harper Collins, 1992), 110, 111.

So we need resting place and food and water, and then perhaps the surprising part: here's what we also want, here's what we also need.

III.

"He restoreth my soul" (v. 3a).

Augustine was the bishop of Hippo in North Africa in the fourth century, and in his memoir called *The Confessions* he prayed a prayer that has moved us ever since.

"You have made us for yourself, O God, and our hearts are restless till they find their rest in you."

Here is the greatest hunger God conquers and the greatest thirst God quenches: God answers our longing for God. God restores our souls by giving us God's own self.

IV.

"He leadeth me in the paths of righteousness for his name's sake" (v. 3b).

"He leads me in the paths of righteousness." The right paths are the paths where we try to do what is right.

For Jews to this day the religious term for instructions that help our conduct be more righteous is the term for "walking." How do we walk? How do we conduct ourselves? We walk in paths of righteousness.

And we don't walk there for our own sake. We walk for "his name's sake." We seek righteousness because we want to honor the righteous shepherd. Our faithfulness gives glory to God's name.

V.

"Yea, though I walk through the valley of the shadow of death, I will fear no evil: for thou art with me; thy rod and thy staff they comfort me" (v. 4).

Notice that it's not the valley of death that scares us. It's the valley of the shadow of death. It's the shadow that death casts before itself, the anxiety of our own mortality. It's the shadow that death casts after itself, the stultifying sense of loss.

In the context it's clear why the shepherd carries a rod and staff; they are there to scare off the enemy. In this psalm the enemy is not death itself; not even the shepherd can save us from our finitude. In this psalm the enemy is fear, and the shepherd uses his rod and staff to drive the fear away.

VI.

"Thou preparest a table before me in the presence of mine enemies" (v. 5a).

We love that picture. Enemies all around us, scoffing away, criticizing or condemning or making fun while we eat happily away.

Except there's more; when we think of God as shepherd we pray for one thing more, we work for one thing more. We pray for the day when our enemies sit down with us at the table.

"Thou preparest a table before me in the presence of mine enemies" . . . and invite them to the table . . . until they are enemies no more.

VII.

"Surely goodness and mercy shall follow me all the days of my life" (v. 6a).

Years ago a humorist wrote an essay on how easy it is for children to mistake familiar words and to hear them just slightly off kilter.

In my own childhood I always thought that the magi came from a distant land called Orientar. "We Three Kings of Orientar."

For the humorist, "Surely goodness and mercy shall follow me all the days of my life" became "Surely Good Mrs. Murphy shall follow me all the days of my life."

But there's something to it. The Psalmist isn't just saying that some kind of disembodied, abstract quality "goodness" or some disembodied spiritual presence "mercy" shall follow me all the days of my life.

The Psalmist means that the Lord the shepherd will follow us all the days of our lives. And as Christians we think of goodness and mercy as embodied, present in Jesus Christ, as close as breathing and as personal as Good Mrs. Murphy.

VI.

"And I will dwell in the house of the LORD forever."

The King James has it best. Not just a long, long time. Not just as long as I live on earth.

But forever; forever. God the blessing shepherd. We the blessed sheep. Forever and ever. Amen.

49

Doing the Word

JAMES 1:17-27

This sermon was preached on August 30, 2015, at The Congregational Church of New Canaan as that congregation was getting ready to welcome its new pastor. The church had just gone through a period of transition from having a long-term pastor and interim and the call to a new senior minister.

I.

We are not sure whether this letter we've been reading was actually written by the apostle James or was written by one of his students, writing in his name.

Here's what we do know, from this letter, from the Book of Acts and from the letters of Paul. We know that the early church was not as harmonious as we sometimes like to think.

In particular there was an ongoing discussion between the early Christians who identified with Paul and the early Christians who identified with James.

James was Jesus' brother, so of course he had special standing with those who had known Jesus during his ministry. And like Jesus, James was a faithful Jew who thought that being faithful included a nearly wholehearted devotion to keeping the law, observing the Torah.

Paul's conversion to Christianity came when he came to believe that the Torah could not bring us closer to God, only God's love in Jesus Christ could do that.

Paul's great claim is that we are saved by faith and not by works.

James spends a good part of this epistle saying that faith without works is dead.

Now Paul didn't think for a minute that having faith means that anything goes, and James didn't think for a minute that being good by itself was enough, but they spent a good deal of their careers arguing about the details of the relationship between God's love and our responsibility.

In the course of fifty years of ministry I have probably preached on Paul about eight hundred times and on James about four times, but today it's James' turn. James is writing to a congregation that may love Paul too much, and he's certainly writing to a congregation that needs to be encouraged in good works. He's talking to them about what it means to be a Christian community, and this is what he says: "Be doers of the word and not merely hearers" (Jas. 1:22).

II.

Now as you wait eagerly for the beginning of Chapin's ministry among you, I want to think for a few minutes about how the church, this church, is doers of the word. I have no doubt that as in the past wonderful words will come from this pulpit; how do we as a congregation do those words?

Two claims really. Sometimes we are doers of the word by doing with words; sometimes we are doers of the word by doing beyond words.

Sometimes we are doers of the word by doing with words.

The Bible from first to last is committed to the power of words. God creates the universe by speaking God's word. The prophets establish justice and raise up servants by proclaiming God's word. Jesus speaks the words that heal and bless. The apostles seek faithfully to let their words show forth Jesus. Week after week the preacher stands in this pulpit and says: "May the words of my mouth be acceptable in God's sight."

Words count. When we were kids the way to fend off insults and abuse, we thought, was to yell at the offender: "Sticks and stones will break my bones but words will never hurt me."

That was of course brave enough but simply wrong. Broken bones heal with time and care, but every pastor, every counselor, every parent, every friend knows that sometimes words do hurt that seems never to heal, pain that is always just below the surface—breaking relationships, fracturing self-esteem.

That's why James says elsewhere in this passage that words of wrath have no place in church. Our anger doesn't grow God's righteousness it just hurts God's people.

Blessedly, you can turn that around. Words of encouragement, words of sympathy, words of love build up our neighbors, build up our church.

In the first church where I served in Minneapolis, I always included in worship a fairly formal pastoral prayer. I had mastered the art of asking for healing in general, justice in the abstract, and comfort for the undefined.

One day a good friend from a neighboring Methodist church came to serve as liturgist. When the time came for the pastoral prayer, he invited members of the congregation to share out loud their joys and concerns for the week and then included them by name in the pastoral prayer.

It was a small church way of doing what you do so effectively with your cards for prayer concerns. And it was personal as my more formal prayers never were. The concrete word made a difference.

Not only did specific people find themselves brought before God, in the time after service and in the coffee hour again and again a parishioner spoke a word that helped another parishioner. "We're praying for you." "How can I help?" "I lost my mother recently, too," and sometimes even, "I know you're looking for a job. Come see me at the office tomorrow."

Words from the pulpit and words from the choir help, encourage, strengthen, but in your prayers and in your conversations dear members of this church it is your gift and your responsibility to let your words do the work: find the friend or the stranger and say the word, write the note, make the call, send the email, or text the text. Do God's mercy with your words.

"Be doers of the word" to one another.

III.

But then James says another thing, as church, be doers beyond the word. It's his old punch line "faith without works is dead" slightly revised: "Let your actions follow your words."

And now he gets quite specific. "Religion that is pure and undefiled before God . . . is this: to care for orphans and widows in their distress" (v. 27).

The concern for widows and orphans in the congregation makes all kinds of sense. For one thing of course we all know the centrality of sympathy when someone suffers a death in the family. But more than that, in those days widows and orphans were left destitute because their economic security depended entirely on the father and husband. Women weren't employed and there was no social safety net. The church was concerned with widows and orphans both because they were in grief and because they were in need.

I have just served in a church very much like this church in many ways. Wandering in one might think that it was a church filled with people who needed nothing.

But I came to know what you know, too. That's simply never true. All of us need loving sympathy and care when we lose someone we love. All of us have needs, need for companionship, need for understanding, and more often than we might think the need to get by; keeping up appearances is not the same thing as being safe, secure, and hopeful.

I gave you a story from the first church I served as pastor, now a story from the last.

It is a story about a people and their pastor, but on other days it was parishioner serving parishioner with the same loving concern, doing the word.

When we, Carol Bartlett and I, got to Oakland, California, in the eighties, we had been married just a few years and our children were young.

Through a quirky side effect of medicine she was taking, Carol got seriously ill and we worried for her life. As you know that turns out fine, so I can move to the point.

For the weeks that she was in the hospital, every night a meal appeared on our doorstep till we were full and the freezer, too. Twice a week I put the laundry at the front door, and twice a week it returned washed and ready. We discovered more honorary grandparents willing to take the boys for a few hours than we would have dreamed.

We were, thank God, neither a widower nor orphans, but people rallied to our need. Church was church indeed. Those dear people were doers of the word.

This week, a new minister comes to this church; an exciting time in your life. But not the main event. The main event is the way you will care for him and his family; the main event is the way you will continue to care for each other in word and in deed, especially in times of need.

You are already an example of that kind of caring, that kind of embodied word. I have preached a story about you from several pulpits, so it seems only fair that I preach it before you now.

In the many years that I preached here I was always especially gratified to see Janet Eberman sitting in about the fourth pew to my left. For a while she was almost a hundred and then she was more than a hundred.

At the door I always asked: "How are you, Janet?" and she always said, "Just fine. How are you Dr. Bartlett?"

What I remember most is that while Janet's mind was sharp till the end, her hearing was not so good. That became clear every Sunday when it came time for the Lord's Prayer. Janet always prayed aloud, but because she didn't hear anyone else, she prayed at her own pace, usually about two beats behind the rest of us.

What I remember most is not just her praying, but the way you prayed with her. The prayer always ended this way.

Everybody but Janet said: "For thine is the Kingdom and the power and the glory forever . . . " and then you all got quiet.

Then—lagging a little behind—Janet said, loud enough for all of us to hear, "For thine is the Kingdom and the power and the glory forever."

And then all of you, Janet and all the rest of you, said, together: "Amen."

Dear church, in the years that lie ahead, continue to be church.

> Wait for one another.
> Listen to one another.
> Lift each other up.

In the name of the Father, and of the Son, and of the Holy Spirit. Amen.

50

The Good Samaritan Yet Again

LUKE 10:25–37

On July 5, 2016, a police officer shot and killed Alton Sterling, a black man who was selling DVDs outside a store in Baton Rouge. Philando Castille was shot and killed in his car by a police officer on July 6, 2016, in St. Paul, Minnesota. And in Dallas, five police officers were shot and killed while monitoring a peaceful rally in downtown Dallas. These were the shootings referred to in this sermon preached at The Congregational Church of New Canaan, Connecticut, on July 10, 2016.

I.

I sat at my desk yesterday wrestling with how to preach on a familiar text at the end of a bad week. A death in Baton Rouge; a death in St. Paul; five deaths in Dallas. What hope could I preach?

The phone rang. It was a summer school student from last year. He is pastor of the Mount Zion Baptist Church in Augusta, Georgia. He was wrestling with how to preach on a familiar text at the end of a bad week.

So there we were, a white minister getting ready to preach to a mostly white, mostly affluent Congregational church in the North and an African American getting ready to preach to a mostly black, mostly blue collar Baptist church in the South.

When I told my family about that, about the two of us wondering how to preach hope at the end of a bad week, they said: "Start with that." They meant start with the fact that as Christians and as Americans Reginald and I wanted to talk with each other. Start with the fact that however different we were from one another, how different our congregations from one another, we started from the same point: from the Gospel, from the good news of Jesus Christ.

II.

Today the gospel of Jesus Christ is found in the Gospel of Luke and in a story that Jesus told. You know how the story goes. A lawyer asks Jesus what he should do to inherit eternal life. Jesus asks him what the Torah, what the law tells him: the lawyer says, "Love God with heart, mind, soul, and strength and your neighbor as yourself." Jesus says: "Do that and you will live."

But the lawyer has a kind of lawyerly question: Okay, I see what the contract says, but I do have one query. "Who is my neighbor?"

Instead of answering him directly Jesus tells him the story of the man waylaid by thieves, of the religious leaders who passed by the on the other side of the road, and of the Samaritan who stopped to help.

And then at the end of all this, our Lord and Savior does an end run around the lawyerly question. The lawyer asks: "Who is my neighbor?" Jesus says: "Go be a neighbor."

Here's what Luke says: Jesus asked the lawyer, "Which of these three . . . proved neighbor to the man?" (Luke 10:36 RSV).

The lawyer answered: "The one who showed mercy on him" (v. 37a).

Jesus said: "Go do the same" (v. 37b CSB).

III.

So what do we notice when Jesus tells us to be neighbors even in difficult times? For this morning: three things.

First, we notice the simplicity of apathy and the complication of compassion.

When I was in junior high school one of the skills we learned was how to diagram an English sentence. There was the subject, there was the verb, and there was the object. "The girl threw the ball." Girl: subject. Threw: verb. The ball: object.

But as we moved from simple sentences to more sophisticated literature, the diagramming got more complicated; more than one subject, more than one verb, subordinate clauses, adverbs, participles.

If we had only to diagram the sentences about the priest and the Levite in this story it would be easy. Luke tosses them off with one simple sentence each: "He passed by on the other side" (v. 31).

But the Samaritan, notice how complicated his life becomes. Diagram the paragraph about his activity, and the diagram takes half a page. He sees; he pities; he pours oil and wine; he applies bandages; he puts the injured man on his own beast; he takes him to an inn; he cares for him for a while; he pays the innkeeper to continue the care; then he arranges for a return visit so that he can pay the innkeeper for any other debts he has incurred.

It is a cliché of our time that when we see an accident on the side of the road, or listen to a tale of woe, we don't want to get involved. It's not because we're not basically nice people, it's just too complicated. We don't want to get waylaid, slowed down, inconvenienced or stretched financially, and we certainly don't want to testify in court about anything, ever. Apathy is so much easier.

It is always so much easier to pass by on the other side of the road. We can do things the easy way, or we can do things the neighborly way, and they're often not the same.

The simplicity of apathy, and the complexity of compassion.

IV.

The second point is a little different, and I got this from Jonah a few years ago when we were both preaching on this parable, and if you heard it from him here, let him know that I did not borrow it without clear attribution.

Let me start with my version of the punch line and then lead up to it again: Here's the punch line. In this country, in this time, we can't be good neighbors unless we are also good citizens.

Listen, Jesus told his story and Luke wrote the story down for small bands of relatively powerless people who lived in an empire over which they had no control. They couldn't much change the way things were, they could just respond in a neighborly way to help the victims.

But we have the vote; we can write letters; we can join committees; we can raise money; we can choose our investment strategies.

If the man had been robbed and beaten on the side of the road in America in the twenty-first century, here are some of the questions we would want to ask:

How is our infrastructure? Was the road from Jerusalem to Jericho basically safe and well-lighted?

Is our law enforcement adequate to the need?

Why were these guys robbing the poor man? Were they just bad guys or were they economically desperate and if so, why?

If this was a second or third offense had the law been too easy on the robbers the first time, or had the prison sentence been too harsh?

If this was an armed robbery, how easy was it for the robbers to get their guns?

Those questions are also questions about how to be a good Christian neighbor. As Christians we can disagree about how we respond to these questions: More government or less? Stricter regulation or looser? Trust the market, or not so much. Vote Democratic or Republican or Libertarian or Green?

What we can't do is say: "We don't care." What we can't do is say: "It doesn't matter."

Which of these proved neighbor to the man? The one who showed mercy on him, said Jesus. "Go and do likewise."

In our country and in our time being a good neighbor means being a good citizen.

V.

And then the third point, maybe especially pertinent for us this week. This parable isn't just a story about being a neighbor, it's a story about being different; it's a story about being the other. The Other.

Friends who have studied how parables worked in Jesus' time, friends who have studied how storytellers told a tale, think they know how Jesus' audience would have heard his story.

> Jesus' audience was made up almost entirely of laypeople; so they listened with interest when Jesus told the story of the officially religious men, the priest and the Levite.
> Jesus' audience was almost all rural people; so they listened with interest when Jesus told the story of the urban priest and the city-dwelling Levite.
> Jesus' audience almost all lived on relatively little, so they listened with interest when Jesus told the story of the relatively wealthy priest and the comparatively comfortable Levite.

So here's how Jesus' audience thought the story would go.

> A man fell among thieves and lay wounded by the side of the road.
> And a priest came along and passed him by (of course, mumbles the audience).
> And a Levite came along and passed him by (just like those Levites; members of the audience nudge each other).

> And then—all of them think they know what will happen next—a poor fellow from the country, a humble layperson will come along and show up those stuffed shirts from Jerusalem.

The people wait eagerly for Jesus as Jesus continues the story: "But one other person was travelling the road" (the audience is ready now) "A Samaritan!"

You've got to be kidding.

A Samaritan: the entirely different; the annoyingly other. In another passage John's gospel makes the social context clear: "Jews have nothing to do with Samaritans" (John 4:9 ERV).

A Samaritan? Fill in the blanks: a Muslim? A black person? A black Muslim? An undocumented immigrant who can't even offer help in good English. A self-righteous fundamentalist, a self-satisfied atheist?

Who is the neighbor? Jesus asks. "The one who shows compassion," says the lawyer. And he might as well have added: the different one, the odd one, the apparently not at all like us one—the Other.

This was a week when we had to deal with otherness, in the midst of a time and a nation when otherness seems to scare us. Jesus never denies that the other is someone else, not just like ourselves, Jesus never lets us forget that these other people—not just like ourselves—are our neighbors, too, are God's children, too.

George Saunders is a highly accomplished short story writer who took time off from writing short stories to write about politics and society in this country in this season.

He writes like a short story writer, not like a parable teller or a preacher, but I think he writes the truth. Please listen:

> From the beginning America has been of two minds about the Other. One mind says, be suspicious of it, dominate it, [avoid it], deport it, exploit it, enslave it. . . . The other mind denies that there can be any such thing as the Other, in the face of the claim that all are created equal.[1]

That's Saunders; here's Jesus.

"Which of these proved a neighbor to the man?"

And the lawyer says: The one who had mercy on him.

And Jesus says: For God's sake, do the same.

Amen.

---

1. George Saunders, "Who Are All These Trump Supporters?" in *The New Yorker*, July 11 and 18, 2016, https://www.newyorker.com/magazine/2016/07/11/george-saunders-goes-to-trump-rallies.

51

Being Saved

This sermon was preached at Bronxville Reformed Church in Bronxville, New York, a church of the Reformed Church of America, on October 9, 2016.

I.

Two weeks ago there was a very brief story in the news. A young man in California had been diagnosed with leprosy. What made the story news was that no one in the United States had had leprosy for a very long time. What made the story brief was that the doctors knew exactly how to cure it.

In Jesus' time leprosy was a very big deal. We're not altogether sure just what sort of skin disease was counted as leprosy but we know that it was very hard to cure, and we know one other fact about leprosy in Jesus' time. Luke's story gives us the evidence:

> As (Jesus) entered a village, ten lepers approached him. Keeping their distance, they called out, saying, "Jesus, Master, have mercy on us!"
> (Luke 17:12–13)

"Keeping their distance." Throughout Luke's Gospel all kinds of people ask Jesus for healing. They come close. They kneel before him. They touch him; he touches them. Not in this story. The lepers keep their distance.

In Jesus' time lepers were isolated, scorned, kept separate—at a distance.

And though none of us have suffered from their disease, many of us have suffered from their sense of isolation.

A new movie came out Friday, *Middle School*. I haven't seen it nor do I intend to see it. But I can guess what it's about: Those most awkward years when you don't feel very good about yourself and the whole world conspires to confirm your suspicions.

Why is that person so popular and I'm so not? Why am I always chosen last? I hate putting this stuff on my face. I smile and smile but she pays no attention.

It's the middle school syndrome. It can hit in middle school of course, or freshman year in college, or the first months in a new job, a new town. It hits hard after a divorce—why couldn't I even keep a marriage together? Or a business failure. Or retirement. One man I knew said sadly: "It's not that I'm no longer wanted; I'm no longer needed."

Or after we feel isolated after another's death. We have a friend who has noticed that since her husband died, all the couples they used to hang around with are very friendly—but not very inviting. She no longer gets invited.

II.

So in our quieter and more appropriate Bronxville decorous way we cry out at least silently: "Jesus, master, have mercy on us." Pay attention.

And here is the good news from our story. Jesus does pay attention: "When he saw them, he said to them, 'Go and show yourselves to the priests.' And as they went, they were made clean" (v. 14).

A quick technical aside: In first century Palestine, if you were a leper you were not only sick you were religiously unclean. It wasn't just that nobody did come close; nobody could come close. On those rare occasions when a leper was actually cured, it was the job of the priest to declare that a leper had been cleansed so that he or she could once again enter into society. That's why Jesus tells the lepers to head to the priest; he knows that they'll be clean by the time they get there.

Of course it takes some considerable courage for the lepers—and for us—to cry out to Jesus. For those of us stuck in the middle school years of the soul that may be the hardest part.

But notice that when the lepers cry out, Jesus does listen; Jesus does attend. And that attention is the beginning of healing.

Some years ago a woman named Bel Kauffman wrote a book about her experience as a middle school teacher in an inner city school. The name of the book was *Up the Down Staircase*.

She writes of her attempts to get a disengaged class actually involved in their own education. One of her devices was to set up a suggestion box at the back of the room so that students could make suggestions for improving the class.

One afternoon after the students had left she opened the box to find the suggestions for the day and found a piece of paper with only this message: "Today is my birthday. I needed someone to know." And it was signed, "Me."

She thought briefly about the poignancy of that isolation and then got to the lesson plan for the next day.

Sometime later in the semester she came up with another teaching device. The students were learning about civics and she set up a mock court and a mock trial where students would play all the parts. She assigned the parts and told the class to prepare for the mock trial the next day. To be judge she chose the quietest person in the class, a young man for whom English was a second language and who spoke only when the teacher insisted.

The next day as the students arrived in came the young man, carrying a black robe he had borrowed from someone and a gavel he must have bought at some store.

As the trial began the robed and gavel toting judge took his responsibility with great care and great flair. Everyone was amazed by his enthusiasm and his acting skill. The teacher praised him profusely and the students were amazed. As the school day ended the temporary judge stopped by the teacher's desk.

"Teacher," he said, "I'm me."[1] I'm me. The anonymous birthday. The unsigned card. The quiet, lonely, immigrant young men, who just like the lepers, had been far off.

Until the teacher attended. Until the teacher noticed. Until the teacher gave him something to do. "Jesus, master, have mercy on me."

Jesus attended; he paid attention. He noticed, he recognized. And he does so still: God in Jesus Christ reaches out to all of us who are far off and recognizes, claims, empowers: Till finally, even in the midst of the middle schools of our souls, we can say quietly, confidently: "I'm me."

III.

Jesus doesn't stop at that. He hears the courage of the lepers who cry out. And he gives them courage to reach out: To go to the priest and to establish

---

1. Bel Kaufman, *Up the Down Staircase* (Englewood Cliffs, NJ: Prentice-Hall, 1965).

communion and community. Their healing comes as they find the strength, as God gives them the strength, to break down their own isolation—to reach out.

At its best church is the place we can reach out, and these people sitting around us are the people who reach out to us.

In the first church I served I began to notice a frequent visitor. He sat in his own corner of the not very big sanctuary. He had been born with some facial disfigurement and the years of plastic surgery since did not disguise the fact that he was somewhat different looking from the people around him.

Somebody in that church had the grace to ask him to attend a young adult social. Something in him found the courage to do so. The visible scars never went away, but the invisible scars got slowly better. From the back pew to a center pew (nobody sat in the front pew in that church either), from sitting alone to sitting with friends.

"Go, show yourselves to the priest."

Bronxville Church, I'm passing through, so I can say this: After this service take a few minutes off from greeting the people you know best in order to greet the one you do not know at all. Next week, sit in another pew next to another person.

Lonely person feeling cut off; move forward a little bit. Don't duck out after the service. This church like every faithful church intends to welcome you; give them a chance.

IV.

But now notice a striking feature of the story. One of the lepers turns back to thank Jesus. Only one. Only the Samaritan.

Only the one who feels most outside of all. Not only a leper, with a scary disease, but a Samaritan. Those awful people from across the border; who are ethnically suspect and theologically heretical.

So if it was hard to be a leper in first century Judea it was really hard to be both a leper and a Samaritan.

The Gospels spend a lot of time urging the early Christians to reach out to the Samaritans; the Good Samaritan in this same gospel who turns out to be the true neighbor; the Samaritan woman at the well in John's Gospel who turns out to be the true believer.

It's not hard to see our own version of Samaritan anxiety these days. I'm just back from leading Bible study at another church where the official subject was the Book of Romans but where lots of the questions were about Muslims.

"How can we welcome a religion that incites violence?" someone asked.

The pastor reminded us that there's a Baptist church in this country whose members go around the country shouting hateful slogans at the funerals of service people to make clear their Christian hatred of same-sex relationships. The pastor who spoke up is a Baptist, so am I. We're not violent and anti-gay. Don't take those people and paint me with the same brush.

Also last week I get a note inviting me to the publication party for a new book by my Yale colleague Lamin Sanneh. Lamin grew up as a Muslim before converting to Christianity and he has written a book I can't wait to read about a long-standing serious movement in Islam—a movement of pacifists. Total nonviolence.

I know you know better, but many of our fellow Christians don't. In first century Judea, they talked about all those Samaritans. We talk about all those Muslims. The Gospel says that all that business about "them" and "us" was a mistake then and it's a mistake now.

One of them, when he saw that he was healed, turned back and prostrated himself at Jesus' feet and thanked him—and he was a Samaritan, a Muslim, an undocumented immigrant—fill in the blanks. One of them, the most outside outsider of all, one of them turned back and knelt down and thanked Jesus.

V.

And then perhaps the most surprising twist of all. Listen to what Jesus says.

> "Were not ten made clean? But the other nine, where are they? Was none of them found to return and give praise to God except this for-eigner?" Then he said to him, "Get up and go your way; your faith has made you well."
>
> (vv. 17–18)

At any rate that's how our translation this morning tells the story, but there's a better translation of the original text. "Get up and go your way, your faith has saved you."

Saved you? Ten people are healed, which is a big deal, but only one is saved, which is a bigger deal. Because here at least in this text being saved means not only being healed, it means being thankful for being healed.

Being saved isn't just receiving Jesus' attention it's being grateful for that attention. Being saved isn't just receiving God's love it is returning that love in gratitude. Being saved includes knowing that you're saved and giving thanks.

There is an old debate in Christianity: who can be saved? Traditional Christianity says only those who publicly follow Jesus Christ can be saved. The clearest proponent of this view was the early church father Tertullian: "Outside the church there is no salvation," he said.

The other point of view is represented by Karl Barth, a theologian I admire so much that Jonah and Elizabeth gave me a picture of a *Time* magazine from the sixties with Karl Barth on the cover. He looked down on me as I prepared this sermon.

Barth takes very seriously what Paul says in the book to the Romans: "as in Adam all die, so in Christ will all be made alive" (1 Cor. 15:22 NIV).

Barth says that in Jesus Christ God reaches out to love all of humankind, believers and non-believers.

Then what advantage do believers have? They know the love of God. They know the Jesus Christ who claims them. They not only are loved, they know they are loved . . . and as Luke would say: they are thankful.

"Your faith has saved you," says Jesus to the Samaritan. "Your gratitude has saved you."

So if you ask do I believe that there is no salvation outside the church, if that means God brings only Christians into eternal fellowship with God's own self, then the answer is, "No, I don't believe that."

But if you mean by that, do I believe that the church is the community of the saved because it is the community of the grateful, then yes, I do believe that.

I believe that in this place and among these people we find the community of the grateful—a community that reaches out to include those who are far off and those who are near; a fellowship worthy of our attendance, our effort, and our resources.

According to this morning's story we are the community of the saved just because we are the community of the grateful.

> As the community of the saved we gather to pray and praise.
> As the community of the saved we bring our tithes and offerings in grati-
> tude for all that we have received.
> As the community of the saved we sing: "Praise God from whom all bless-
> ings flow; Praise God all creatures here below."
> As the community of the saved we gather week after week to sing redemp-
> tion songs:

> Now thank we all our God,
> With heart and hands and voices,
> Who wondrous things hath done,
> In whom this world rejoices;

Who, from our mothers' arms,
Hath blessed us on our way
With countless gifts of love,
And still is ours today.[2]

To Christ be thanks and praise. Amen.

2. Martin Rinkart, "Now Thank We All Our God," *The Presbyterian Hymnal* (Louisville, KY: Westminster/John Knox Press, 1990), 555.

52

Welcome to the Choir

I CORINTHIANS 14:6–19

David first worshiped at Marquand Chapel at Yale Divinity School in 1963 as a first-year student in ministry. This sermon was preached on April 3, 2017, at the chapel for prospective and current students. This sermon was also the last sermon David preached before his death on October 12, 2017.

I.

What should I do then? I will pray with the spirit, but I will pray with the mind also; I will sing praise with the spirit, but I will sing praise with the mind also.

(1 Cor. 14:15)

II.

Sometime about the year fifty-two of the Common Era, the apostle Paul got a letter from some of the Christians in the church he had founded at Corinth.

Among other things they reported on what it might feel like to be a stranger who wandered into the Corinthian church for a worship service.

The service was held in the house of the Stephanas family. Pillows and couches were strewn around the room and people tended to gather more or less in a circle sitting most immediately near worshippers who shared their liturgical enthusiasms.

At one side of the room were the so-called prophets who specialized in Bible study. In one corner were the musicians playing their zithers and joining in or drowning out other forms of worship with praise songs. Sitting fairly prominently toward the center of the circle were the specialists in glossolalia—those who spoke in mysterious languages known only to themselves and the spirit and perhaps the angels. There was no order of worship because there was very little order in worship, but many Corinthians loved the gathering for its sheer enthusiasm and heartwarming spontaneity.

III.

In exactly the year one thousand nine hundred and sixty-three of the Common Era I came as a stranger, or at least as a brand new student, to worship for the first time in Marquand Chapel. The room looked just like a congregational meeting house, which of course was how it was supposed to look.

All the pews sat in orderly rows looking toward the chancel, whose skeletal remains you can see if you look that way. That odd wooden structure to the left of the chancel was an actual pulpit—high and lifted up.

All the congregants faced forward and spoke only when a leader invited us to speak. Mostly we sat and listened while the preacher—often a genuinely distinguished professor—reflected with great care and gentle fervor on a biblical text chosen for the day.

Then we sang a fairly sober nineteenth-century hymn, exchanged polite greetings and headed for coffee hour where we managed at last to enjoy whatever modicum of enthusiasm and spontaneity the day allowed.

IV.

In the complicated dialectic of Christian life you could say that the Corinthians sang with the spirit and needed to be reminded to sing with the mind also, while at YDS we sang with the mind but did not sufficiently attend to the spirit.

As student and teacher, I have spent much of my adult life at this school and I bear testimony that I think this place has come a long way toward delighting in the tension Paul prescribed: those of us who love the life of the mind are often reminded quite simply to rejoice, and those of us who love all kinds of melody are reminded that sometimes the words we speak and sing mean something, too.

A very quick history of what has helped. Not that long after my years as a student, Yale Divinity School married Berkeley Divinity School and astonishingly all of us who had participated in the Lord's Supper discovered the possibilities of something called Eucharist. At one level this was a lovely broadening of our ecumenical vision; at a deeper level now when we Free Church people gathered at the table our somber remembering was sometimes astonishingly turned to joy.

And then came the Institute of Sacred Music. A great change for a school that had been notable mostly as an institute of sacred thought with a nod to the occasional solemn song. Now more and more, spirit and mind came together and the human creativity of music, visual art, poetry, and fiction joined in praise of the creator.

V.

So here is what I still believe are the gifts that God has given this school, for those of you who are visiting and for those of you who have already chosen to give some portion of your life to this place.

Here, to quote Saint Anselm, or as we Baptists say, "Anselm," here faith seeks understanding. However deep, joyful, life changing, and world renewing our trust in God, here we obey Paul's injunction. We are not content to sing with the spirit only; we sing with the mind also. We are not content only to have faith; we think about it.

In my years here as a student I took a course on Paul Tillich, taught by Professor George Lindbeck. Lindbeck was at that time a Protestant observer at Vatican II, and he would fly in from Rome having read Tillich's latest volume on the plane. We talked in class about the way in which wise people like Paul Tillich and the Vatican theologians were helping us speak faith in a new and newly secularized world.

In those same years one of my fellow students accused one of Lindbeck's colleagues: "Professor, the issues are so visceral and you are so cerebral." But what we learned as students in those years is that one can be viscerally cerebral. The intellectual love of God; I will pray with the spirit, but I will pray with the mind also.

VII.

But it is equally true that at Yale Divinity School understanding is invited to seek faith. It is not a requirement of studying religion that one not be committed to religious practice.

Early in my career I taught at the Divinity School of the University of Chicago. One of the most accomplished PhD students who was also a Jesuit said to me one day, "You know at Chicago they always ask what tradition you're from. I want to tell them what tradition I'm in."

Here you're welcome to tell us what tradition you're from, what tradition you're in, or what tradition you're longing for.

Here it is actually all right to stop by at the chapel on the way to the library, to celebrate Eucharist aka Lord's Supper with the community from Berkeley, to attend a concert not only because you love the music but because you are curious, enticed, or even convinced by the words.

Long after George Lindbeck taught us about Tillich and Vatican II and the attempts of really smart people to make faith understandable, he wrote his own book called *The Nature of Doctrine* where he suggests that if you're actually seeking faith maybe your best bet is not just to think about it, but to watch it at work.

If you're curious about worship, attend a worship service. If the hymn puzzles you, sing it. Don't just walk past the chapel at 10:30, drop in.

If Paul had it right, what you find when you worship here will be articulate but not only articulate—maybe also helpful, maybe grace-full, maybe lovely.

VII.

At any rate, dear visitors or citizens, wanderers of course but also maybe pilgrims, here is what I cherish about this school after fifty-four years.

On our good days we sing with the spirit but we sing with the mind also. On our good days faith seeks understanding and understanding at least keeps an eye out for faith.

When George Lindbeck, who turns out to be the protagonist of this homily, when George Lindbeck retired we had a party for him in the common room and asked him to say a few words.

It was Christmastime and Professor Lindbeck had just gotten out of Yale New Haven Hospital where he had been recovering from surgery. His remarks in the common room ended something like this:

"Last week I was listening to NPR and heard the annual Christmas concert of the Saint Olaf College Choir. After the concert the radio host asked one of the Saint Olaf students why she enjoyed singing in the choir. She said: 'Because when I sing in this choir I join in song that began long before I came here and that will continue long after I am gone.'"

"When I do theology," said George, "I join in song that began long before I came here and that will continue long after I am gone."

Welcome to the choir.

Permissions

Scripture Index

CPSIA information can be obtained
at www.ICGtesting.com
Printed in the USA
BVHW080219120220
572107BV00012BA/276